AFRICAN PR

GATHERING SEAWEED

Edited by Jack Mapanje

Heinemann

Heinemann is an imprint of Pearson Education Limited,
a company incorporated in England and Wales, having its
registered office at Edinburgh Gate, Harlow, Essex, CM20 2JE.
Registered company number: 872828

© Introduction, Afterword and selection Jack Mapanje 2002

First published by Heinemann Educational Publishers in 2002

British Library Cataloguing in Publication Data
A catalogue record for this book is available from the British Library.

AFRICAN WRITERS SERIES and CARIBBEAN WRITERS SERIES and
their accompanying logos are trademarks in the United States of America
of Heinemann: A Division of Reed Publishing (USA) Inc.

Phototypeset by SetSystems Ltd, Saffron Walden, Essex
Printed by Multivista Global Ltd

ISBN 978 0 435 91211 6

08 8 7 6 5 4 3 2

ACKNOWLEDGEMENTS

Grateful thanks are due to my publishers Robert Sulley, Becky Clarke, Ruth Hamilton-Jones and Victoria Ramsay for their hard work, encouragement and constant push; Alison McFarlane, Deedah Steels, Michelle Norcliffe and Keith Gailer for their research, typing and xeroxing services respectively; Martin Banham, John Barnard and colleagues in the School of English, University of Leeds, for letting me introduce the Literature of Incarceration module to undergraduates in the school; the students who registered for the module for their enthusiasm, criticism and suggestions that this anthology be compiled; my fellow political prisoners and contributors to the anthology; the Royal Literary Fund Fellowship Scheme and Trinity and All Saints College for offering me time and space; Robert Woof and colleagues at The Wordsworth Trust, Dove Cottage, Grasmere for their charm; and Mercy, Judith, Lunda and Likambale for not minding their being ignored while this anthology was being gathered; its shortcomings are, of course, the editor's own responsibility.

CONTENTS

Arrest, Detention and Prison

Torture

Survival

CONTENTS

The Release

INTRODUCTION

No. *Gathering Seaweed* is not another anthology calculated to negate Africa. I vehemently reject the subtle neocolonial view that the publication of African prison writing fabricates yet another negative image of the continent; arguments like this were death to many creative projects in the last century.

This anthology has no major pretensions. It does not set out to answer the larger question why African governments tend towards despotism even after they have been democratically elected to power. It does not intend to be representative of every country in Africa; the ratio of male to female writers is disproportionately high; the glaring omissions are many. Nor does its appearance at this point in time need justifying. If there is any principal objective for this collection it is that we wish to celebrate the new millennium with some of the last century's excellent rebel writing, fervently trusting that in future fewer African dissidents (political, religious, creative, academic or otherwise) may suffer the horrors of incarceration as did the writers encountered on these pages.

The contributors to this anthology were arrested and imprisoned for long or short periods principally for their views and beliefs which were at variance with those in power at the time: European colonialists, ruthless despots from independent African countries and defenders of the evil political system of apartheid in South Africa. The fragments of prison experiences gathered here have historical relevance; they constitute a defiant recasting of Africa's history through the eyes of some of its finest hostages. This anthology is unique not only as an indictment of the brutality of European imperialism, colonialism and neocolonialism, apartheid and African dictatorship; but it is also an indelible record of the origins, growth and maturity of the struggle for the restitution of human dignity and integrity, justice and peace on the African continent.

Gathering Seaweed assembles stories of incarceration which African politicans today would prefer to bury; perhaps for their convenience; perhaps in their wish to please their neocolonial metropolitan banks; perhaps under the pretext that such horrors must not be mentioned in the name of atonement and reconciliation. *Gathering Seaweed* suggests the pertinent question why the African struggle against European imperialism, colonialism and neocolonialism turned sour; why African leaders seem to have copied only the brutality, corrupt practices and selfish individualism from their colonial masters. The implication is that African leaders are becoming progressively intolerant of constructive criticism from their own people. This anthology should, therefore, be waved as a warning banner to present and future African political leadership, for, through their writings, the dissidents in this volume refuse to be erased from memory and to be made invisible by the autocratic regimes that imprisoned them. Each writer inimitably contributes to the sad tale of intolerance, oppression, imprisonment, torture and the barbaric politics of the countries from which the writings emanate.

In its totality, this anthology registers a culture which the African continent should not be proud of and could well do without, but the memory of the shame and torture endured by these writers must be kept as glowing caution. The struggle for the restoration of human dignity, justice, freedom and peace must continue to burn bright, in the words of Dennis Brutus, 'partly that some world sometime may know' what the writers went through; and partly to admonish future generations of children throughout the globe, about the extent to which humans can inflict suffering on fellow humans without logical explanation.

But let's step back in time. Let's take a portion of modern African history which is fast being forgotten. Let's take the Scramble for Africa. When European heads of state assembled in Berlin in 1884 to share out the African continent into different spheres of their influence – an agenda which historians labelled the Scramble for Africa – they were merely formalizing the political, economic, religious, social and cultural chaos which their missionaries, explorers, economic adventurers and other exploiters had already inflicted on the continent. The new boundaries that made up the African colonies they had created were drawn up for the benefit of Europe and without taking into consideration Africa's natural borders. The European leaders who conceived the scheme did not recognize the multiple identities and cultures of the African peoples they encountered. The African peoples themselves were not consulted about the forms of government they were going to live under. Their chiefs lost the political authority they had to the European administrators who ruled them. Fertile African land was appropriated according to European law, its wealth and culture shamelessly transferred to European capitals.

Clearly, the Berlin Conference leaders did not anticipate African opposition to their division of the continent. They believed that Europe had the political, economic and cultural muscle to contain any African opposition. Throughout the French, Portuguese, British and other European colonies, variants of Special Powers Acts, Emergency Provisions Acts, Prevention of Terrorism Acts, Censorship Acts and others were passed to protect European colonialism and suppress African opposition and rule. African protest did, nonetheless, eventually come. It was the brutal colonial legislation and, among other reasons, how colonial administrators ill-treated even the least politicized of the Africans, which generated protest. The fragment 'Colour Bar' (page 2) demonstrates starkly that even temperate Africans such as Kenneth Kaunda were radicalized against what colonialism stood for largely because colonial administrators discriminated against Africans, treating them as subhuman in their own country of birth. The extracts by Josiah Mwangi Kariuki of Kenya, Kwame Nkrumah of Ghana and the passionate poetry of Agostinho Neto of Angola are testimonies from early African nationalists that, like the Kaunda fragment, demonstrate how colonialism demonized the Africans who fought for independence.

African leaders were often abducted from their homes and their supporters and exiled to the African bush, to far-flung concentration camps or to isolated prisons where they often had to fend for themselves. The colonialists invariably told the people in the villages surrounding such prisons to avoid the 'so-called freedom fighters' as they were 'cannibals'. One African prison memoir after another indicates that an integral part of their struggle for liberation consisted of persuading the people among whom they were exiled that they were normal human beings, not cannibals! The few samples of songs which are recorded from Mau Mau freedom fighters in Kenya and from political combatants in Zimbabwe, who were summarily exiled to the African bush or dumped in isolated prisons and concentration camps, exemplify the kind of politicization that went on among Kenyans and Zimbabweans. Every African colony that fought for independence from Europe, however, teemed with its own defiant political verses, which the Zimbabwean scholar, Alec Pongweni, calls 'The Songs that Won the Liberation War' for Africa.

Watch the irony. It was the African nationalists exiled by colonial administration to the barren African bush or tortured in infamous colonial prisons who became despots after independence, intolerant of multiparty politics, preferring to imprison, exile, even kill their political opponents, writers, journalists, lawyers, musicians, radical thinkers and other rebels, instead of accommodating them within the fabric of their liberated societies. Take Kenya. After the Mau Mau struggle had led the country to independence, it was Jomo Kenyatta himself who began to hunt down the Mau Mau fighters who were dissatisfied with his rule, calling them 'these evil men, vagrants'. Josiah Mwangi Kariuki typifies the ironic situation under scrutiny throughout this anthology. Kariuki was the last of the respectable Mau Mau rebels, having been imprisoned then released by the British colonial government. After independence he was also imprisoned by Kenyatta for his presumed dissenting views, tortured by Kenyatta's Special Branch and murdered in 1975. Ngũgĩ wa Thiong'o was another victim imprisoned by Kenyatta for his writings and his political beliefs; Ngũgĩ was released only after Kenyatta's death and in response to worldwide appeals and protests. The list is long.

In this context, Kenyatta's address on Kenya's independence celebrations included in the *Origins* section of the anthology ('Independence Day – 1963', page 21) is an ironic commentary on the country's leadership. The Kenyan predicament manifested itself in almost every independent African country, where variants of colonial legislation were never substantially revised; instead they were extended to sustain African leaders' programmes of corruption, nepotism, imprisonment, exile, torture and elimination of political dissent. The colonial structure of power whereby political and civic leaders were protected from the truth by their cronies and hit squads extended its tentacles after independence in one African country after another.

Now consider the protracted struggle against apartheid in South Africa. The discovery of gold, diamonds and other precious minerals in South Africa was critical for the 5 per cent white South Africans to dominate the 95 per cent non-white South Africans for so long. The acquisition of the most productive land by whites, their mining of the boundless wealth locked in the land, their exploitation of African labour and their absolute control of non-whites, were effected through legislation which excluded South Africa's majority. The Conciliatory Act of 1924, the Colour Bar Act of 1926, the Native Administration Act of 1927, the Land Act of 1936, the legislation which created the African 'homelands', the travel and pass acts, the acts on Bantu education, coloured education and Indian education – these and their variants excluded non-whites from getting the best form of education, from voting, forming political parties, joining trade unions, participating in strikes – above all, from governing South Africa alongside whites.

Apartheid was total in its elimination and exclusion of white radicals and people of colour: blacks, coloureds and people of Asian origin. It was extreme in its disregard of human life, particularly that of its opponents; its administrators preferred to detain, imprison, exile, eliminate whoever challenged them instead of embracing them within a liberal structure. It was both the racist legislation of apartheid and its segregationist adminis- tration that politicized the South African majority. For apartheid was the South African equivalent of Nazi racism; those who opposed it encountered a ghastly form of incarceration. Radical whites such as Breyten Breytenbach, Jeremy Cronin and others were shattered by the inhumanity of their imprisonment as recorded on the pages of this anthology. Another white anti- apartheid activist Albie Sachs reflects: 'So this is what prison is like. The quiet is complete and I am alone in my cell, the shock of the slammed door still echoing in my head. So this is what it's like' ('Me Singing', page 96).

But as Makhoere, Farisani, Meer and others consistently indicate in this volume, non-white South African prisoners were denied even the basic rights and facilities described by Sachs and others largely because of the colour of their skin. And Robben

Island was the ultimate prison where die-hard opponents of apartheid could expect to be exiled. Summing up the effect of the various prisons in which he had been incarcerated, before entering Robben Island, Mandela says: 'Prison not only robs you of your freedom, it attempts to take away your identity. Everyone wears a uniform, eats the same food, follows the same schedule. It is by definition a purely authoritarian state that tolerates no independence or individuality. As a freedom fighter ... one must fight against the prison's attempt to rob one of these qualities' ('Rivonia', page 194).

Readers leafing through the pages of this anthology should remember that not all the narratives, poems, dialogues, soliloquies, reflections and interviews come from the pens of laureates. For some of the contributors, writing was the only defence they could muster. Such writers forced themselves to tell their story in the only way they knew how; for them this was the first and only time they ever wrote. The niceties of English expression took second place in their search for freedom. Makhoere typifies such writers who appropriate the English language without apology; the narrative about her incarceration, in sharp, often disjointed speech, is essentially an expression of her African idiom in English. In many ways her narrative is reminiscent of Gabriel Okara's in his experimental novel *The Voice*, where the author domesticates the English language in typical African idiom without apology. Other writers describe their horror with such bleak humour that readers cannot help laughing, temporarily suspending belief in the writers' suffering.

But all the writers in this anthology are united in their search for freedom, whose cyclic nature is aptly described by Bisikisi in the words: 'Freedom is wily. Sometimes it retreats, sometimes it goes to ground deep in the hearts of men. And then, lo! it is reborn from its own ashes and rises again, victorious!' ('The Theatre', pages 284–5). The contributors to this anthology did not enjoy the craft of their art; most were not allowed pen and paper; they often used smuggled-in or stolen pens and pencils, toilet paper, discarded soap wrappers and other unimaginable materials in order to correspond with the world outside their prison – in order to make their point. So, however they describe the weeping blisters of their incarceration or the death moans of prisoners in the cell next to theirs, the writers in this anthology have used the best method available to them at the time in order to expunge the horrors they endured.

Whereas writers who describe their incarceration in prose are more direct and more explicit, poets such as Neto, Soyinka, Awoonor and others tend to describe their pain by circumvention and often in a personal, reflective, private accent. In his 'Letters to Martha', Brutus specifically says:

> These are not images to cheer you
> . . . rather I send you bits to fill
> the mosaic of your calm and patient knowledge
> – picking the jagged bits embedded in my mind
> partly to wrench some ease for my own mind.
> And partly that some world sometime may know.

The spirit of stoic resilience embedded in the poetry of Neto, Awoonor, Brutus and others runs through the narratives of such renowned novelists as Ngũgĩ wa Thiong'o, Breytenbach and Sa'adawi; it is also evident in the interviews and reflections of Biko, Ntuli, Ifowodo and others.

This anthology is exciting for other reasons; the texts talk to and complement one another; readers will benefit immensely by treating the various materials intertextually. The 'Testimony' (page 187), from the well-known Egyptian writer Muhammad Afifi Mattar, compares with the experience of Bisikisi from the Democratic Republic of Congo (page 278), which in turn contrasts with the painful depiction of 'Dream of a Wake' (page

168), by the Moroccan Abdellatif Laâbi. When these are compared to the interrogation of the Togo academic, Yves-Emmanuel
Dogbe, as depicted in 'The Prisoner' (page 78), the South, East,
West and North African experiences make a familiar, if frightening, portrayal of the prisoners' torment.

Today, the number of writers, journalists, musicians and
singers who are constantly harassed, incarcerated and 'acciden-
talized' because of the presumed radical message of their writings,
public performances or music, continues to multiply throughout
the African continent. Mzwakhe Mbuli, the famous South African praise poet, still languishes in prison long after the abolition
of apartheid. Journalists such as Ogaga Ifowodo, Kunle Ajibade
and Christine Anyanwu and singers such as Fela Anikulapo-Kuti
may come from Nigeria but their cases manifest themselves
throughout the continent.

The contributors to this publication should be recognized
for having been engaged in worthwhile forms of reconciliation
with themselves and their torturers, in the best language and
form possible, despite the inclement subject matter they describe
and the constraints placed upon them when they wrote. This
anthology presents creative material which stands on its own
terms as serious literature to be read for pleasure, to be cherished
and to be studied in depth for its power, wisdom and relevance.
As readers turn the pages, then, they should remember that
in the conflagration between the political prisoners on the one
hand, and the perpetrators of colonial, apartheid and despotic
administration on the other, it is the writers who come out of
incarceration unscathed.

However physically and mentally disfigured by the despot's
electric tongs, handcuffs, leg-irons and other forms of torture
they might be, the political prisoners represented here are determined not to be silenced. They insist that they will survive long
after their arrest, death, execution – defying their torturers in

their separate recalcitrant voices. Ken Saro-Wiwa and his friends may have been brutally executed in Nigeria, to the shock of the entire world, but their determination to fight for a better Nigeria continues through their writings: Ken Saro-Wiwa's smoking pipe defiantly puffs on regardless.

Jack Mapanje
School of English, University of Leeds, 2002

You Left Me My Lips

You took away all the oceans and all the room.
You gave me my shoe size with bars around it.
Where did it get you? Nowhere.
You left me my lips, and they shape words, even in silence.

Osip Mandelstam of the former USSR, *Voronezh*, 1935
Translated by Clarence Brown and W. S. Merwin

Origins

KENNETH D. KAUNDA: ZAMBIA

Colour Bar

In Mufulira, for the first time, I found myself suffering the indignities of the colour bar. Africans were not permitted to enter the European shops by the front door. If they wanted anything, they had to go to a hole in the wall at the side of the shop to ask for it. I determined to expose this system for what it was, an insult to my race and my people. I told some of the boys in the school that I intended to challenge the colour bar and I chose a certain chemist's shop in town which was notorious for its treatment of Africans. As well as medicines, this shop sold toys and books. While my boys waited outside on the pavement, I went inside and asked politely for a book. I remember it was Arthur Mee's *Talks to Boys* . . .

The girl behind the counter had probably never been addressed before by an African in her own language. She motioned me over to the chemist who stood behind the counter. I repeated my question. Pointing to the door, he said viciously, 'Get out of here.' I said again, 'I am only asking for a book and I can get it nowhere else in town.' He said, 'You can stand there till Christmas and you'll never get the book from me.' I was just thinking that as it was the month of August I would have to wait rather a long time, when two white miners in their overalls walked into the shop. Hearing the proprietor say again, 'Get out,' they took me by the arms and frog-marched me to the door. There they were met by seventeen angry schoolboys who objected strongly to their schoolmaster being treated in this manner and they said so in no uncertain terms. A vigorous

From *Zambia Shall Be Free*, Heinemann Educational Books, 1962.

slanging match followed in which we were called 'black-skinned niggers' and we replied by asking what was so wonderful about a white skin anyway. Being so heavy and outnumbered, the two Europeans made for their car and made a quick getaway.

I immediately went round to the *boma* to make a complaint about the way I had been treated. There was a young district officer there whom I knew well. He took me into his office. He listened with sympathy to my story and began thumping the table in his indignation. He said, 'Look here, Kenneth, if ever you want anything just come along to me and I will give you a note.' 'But,' I said, 'that is not the point, what about all the thousands of others who want to be treated like reasonable human beings in the shops? Have they got to come to you every time for a note?' He promised to write a letter to the chemist and I let the matter drop. A few days later, I decided to go into the shop again to see whether the district officer's words had made any difference. Again I made a simple request but it was a different man behind the counter and he ordered me out of the shop. I said that I would see to it that something would be done. He just laughed scornfully and said, 'You try.' I again went round to the *boma* and this time the district officer accompanied me back to the shop. I distinctly remember him saying to the chemist, 'Do you realize that you have been behaving like this to a man who may before long be sitting in the legislative council?' (It was just at the time when I had been elected to the provincial council.) The proprietor was a little taken aback and asked me into his dispensary to apologize. He said, 'Mr Kaunda, if only you had told me who you were, I am sure I would not have ordered you out of my shop.'

Once again I had to explain that I was not asking for any special consideration for myself, I was simply asking that my people should be treated with reasonable courtesy in their own country. I left Mufulira soon after this incident . . .

I never challenged this issue again until 1957, when I was visiting Kitwe with Harry Nkumbula, President of the African National Congress. This being the white area of Kitwe, there were no African eating houses nearby. We drove to a café, having been told by our driver that this café would sell us what we wanted, provided we did not demand to take our meal there; but he did not tell us that even to do that we had to stand by the door where an African servant could come and ask us what we wanted and could then go in to get us whatever we wanted. We went into the café to the counter and I asked for some sandwiches. In reply a young girl of about seventeen told me that 'boys' were not served at the counter. When I told her that I was not a 'boy' and all I wanted was a dozen sandwiches, she spoke to an elderly white woman who was apparently in charge. On asking me what I wanted, she repeated that 'boys' were not served at that counter. I repeated in my turn that I was not a 'boy'. At this point I was dragged out of the café by my clothes by a European man who had already dragged Harry Nkumbula outside the café. This white man hit Harry and called him a cheap, spoiled nigger. Five other white men joined him in attacking us and we defended ourselves. White men and black men passing by joined in the fight, and an apartheid type of brawl took place. This was my third and last fight.

We were ordered to leave the premises but we refused on the grounds that the white men who had started the fight could get away if we did so. In the end we were given an escort of an African policeman despite the fact that we were the complainants. The white men went to the charge office unescorted.

At the charge office we were asked to make a statement. Harry Nkumbula began by saying that the girl at the counter refused to serve us. Before he could end his sentence, the white superintendent of police who had come to stop the fight said, 'You cannot call a white lady a "girl" or a "woman".' Harry

4

ignored this and went on to say that '. . . after that an elderly woman came . . .' but again before he could finish his sentence, the superintendent said, 'I say, you cheeky nigger, you cannot call a European lady a woman.'

Then this police officer called Harry to a room and closed the door and beat him up. Harry told this officer that he was lucky he was wearing Her Majesty the Queen's uniform, or one or the other of them would have been killed.

When the case came to court, our demand that we should be medically examined by a doctor chosen by us was refused and we therefore chose not to continue with the case.

The following morning, after the incident, a group of mine workers went to the café and said to the proprietor, 'We have heard that our leaders were beaten up here. We have come to have our revenge.' There was a police guard on the café and the leader of the group of men was arrested and fined . . .

Even as I write, in spite of the passing of anti-colour bar legislation by the Northern Rhodesia government, unfortunate incidents can take place. This very month (March 1962) the Vice-President of the Christian Council of Northern Rhodesia, the Rev. M. S. Lucheya, entered a café with his European colleague, the President of the Council, and was refused a cup of tea. Can anyone wonder that we sometimes feel bitter about the European settler who treats us like some kind of subhuman species in the land of our birth?

AGOSTINHO NETO: ANGOLA

farewell at the hour of parting

My Mother
  (all black mothers
  whose sons have gone)
you taught me to wait and hope
as you hoped in difficult hours

But life
killed in me that mystic hope

I do not wait now
I am he who is awaited

It is I my Mother
hope is us
your children
gone for a faith that sustains life

Today
we are naked children in bush villages
school-less children playing with a ball of
    rags
in the sands at noon
we ourselves are
contract workers burning lives in coffee
    plantations

ignorant black men
who must respect the white man
and fear the rich
we are your children
of the black neighbourhoods

beyond the reach of electric light
drunken men falling down
abandoned to the rhythm of the *batuque*[1] of death

your children
hungry
thirsty
ashamed to call you Mother
afraid to cross the streets
afraid of men
We ourselves

Tomorrow we shall sing anthems to freedom
when we commemorate
the day of the abolition of this slavery

We are going in search of light
your children Mother
   (all black mothers
    whose sons have gone)
They go in search of life.

---

[1] *batuque*: dance

OGINGA ODINGA: KENYA

The Rise of Politics

Among the Luo of Central Nyanza, the forecasters had said of the white people 'If you touch them the skin will remain in your hand because they are very soft. But they will come with thunderstorms and they will burn the people.' Umuodo Alogo was the chief elder of my village and he told me he had seen these people, some of whom were as white as snow, some as red as fire, and that they had an instrument that harboured the thunder, and that hit from afar. When these people first came (the story goes), the elders had warned that we should never, never try to fight them because their weapons were better than ours. They would be intent on devouring our land and our wealth but we should be wary of them. If they asked for cooking flour we should give it; we should give whatever they requested, even animals. But we should study their lives and their minds to know exactly what they wanted. We should never fight them. But we knew that when we had studied them our children would probably be able to get rid of them.

Not that we saw many whites. The first white man I saw was the missionary Archdeacon Owen. This was the time of a plague outbreak. The children of our village were taken to be inoculated. We were very frightened, for we thought we might die. We allowed the archdeacon only to touch us, and then ran home as fast as we could. We were lucky we did not catch the plague, for that year it claimed many of our relatives and neighbours. The villagers were told that to stop the plague we should trap the rats, cut off the tails and send them to the chief's

From *Not Yet Uhuru: the autobiography of Oginga Odinga*, Heinemann Educational Books, 1967.

baraza. From there, I learnt later, the rats' tails were bundled in tens and sent to Kisumu headquarters; on the walls of commissioners' offices hung charts of the monthly rat returns. It was in these years that the government started to collect taxes from our people: taxes and the orders to produce rats' tails have always been associated together as the arm of government reaching out to our villages. When the time came to take a register of taxpayers, government clerks were sent to the villages. Our mothers had news of the approach of these awesome strangers and they hid the children in the bush and brought us food there. We children were curious and we crept out to gaze secretly at the encroachers. We watched them take a papyrus reed from the roof of each hut and cut it neatly in two. When the reeds were tied in neat bundles they represented the registration of that *boma*. One bundle was given to the elder for him to take to the chief's *baraza* when he paid in the taxes; the other set of bundles was taken away by the clerks as a tally of the taxpayers of the area, a sort of carbon copy of the registration. The clerks who came with the whites for the tax registration were not people of our tribe; they spoke Swahili and we called them *Okoche*.

We connected whites and government with five main things. There were the inoculations against the plague from which the children ran in fear. There were the tax collections. There was the order to the villagers to work on the roads. There were clothes, *kanzu*, the long robes copied from Arab garb at the coast, given free to the chiefs and elders to wear to encourage others in the tribe to clothe themselves in modern dress. There were the schools, which came later, and to which, in the beginning, only orphans, foster children, poor nieces and nephews and never the favourite sons were sent, for the villagers distrusted the pressure on them to send their children out of the home and away from herding the animals; and the more alert objected to the way the Christian missions taught 'This custom (yours) is bad, and this (ours) is good', for they could see that the children at the missions would grow up to despise Luo ways . . .

In the beginning Britain was more concerned to collect spheres of influence than colonies in East Africa, but the process of the first becoming the second was inevitable. In the scramble for Africa that started in the seventies of the last century, Britain and Germany parcelled out shares of the territories they coveted and handed them over, in the initial stages, to chartered companies. This was to be a cheap and easy way of holding territories against outsiders. For Britain, Uganda was vital: she was the key to the lake system of the interior and the headwaters of the Nile, and was a basis for expansion northwards to the Sudan and Egypt. When the chartered companies wanted to pull out of the East African territories because of the cost of holding them, Britain had to step in to declare a protectorate over Uganda in 1893, and over Kenya (then East Africa) in 1895.

The decisive event in opening up Kenya was the building of the railway. This reached Nairobi in 1899 and Lake Nyanza two years later. It was not long before white settlement was encouraged as the only way to carry the financial burden of maintaining the railway and the administration. At the beginning of 1902 there were half a dozen settlers in the country; by 1903 there were a hundred round Nairobi. That year Lord Delamere, who had been to East Africa on safari, acquired a free grant of 100,000 acres at Njoro, and the same year the prospects of settlement in Kenya were being advertised in South Africa . . .

Hut tax was collected for the first time in 1900, but it was not until some years after the start of the century that the British system of administration began to take hold of Nyanza. Early visitors took over the name Kavirondo which the Arab caravans had once used and gave the same name to all the peoples living in Nyanza, though they comprise totally distinct groups. The same hit-and-miss method was used by the colonial administration in imposing rulers on the people. The first missionaries to enter Nyanza met Mumia, Paramount Chief of the Baluyha (Nabongo), at a time when the whites still did not differentiate between the Luo and the Baluyha, and for a time Mumia was recognized as Paramount Chief of all Nyanza. Men from many villages were conscripted to serve the chiefs, and my father was among those taken to form a bodyguard for Mumia. He was dressed in a stiff uniform and taught to drill and salute. His demonstrations when he was again home among us of how to march in formation, wheel left and right and present arms greatly amused the young boys of our village . . .

Our Luo system of government was by consent and after consultation between the elders. The clan head did not inherit his position but, once he belonged to the right lineage, had to prove his leadership qualities and use them to interpret tribal tradition and weld the agreement of his people. His strength derived from his closeness to the elders and his people. The British changed that. They did not want leaders in whom the people had confidence, but men who could be used for their purposes. When chiefs and headmen came to be selected, men whom the British found in positions of leadership were frequently by-passed, and others installed over them. We had a dramatic experience of how this was done on one occasion in Sakwa Location. One, Jasakwa, had gone for a while to live in Kano where he had learned to speak Swahili. When the time came for administration to be extended to Sakwa, he was sent on ahead to his home to clear the way for the whites. He met the elders of Sakwa and told them, 'New people are coming, the white people. They have dangerous weapons. Don't fight them, but try to make a treaty with them.'

The elders did not all agree with him, but as they talked the party of British was approaching. The chief sent Jasakwa the messenger to greet them with gifts. But he had decided to cast himself in a different role. 'The chief says he cannot meet you,' he told the British. 'He is the leader and it is not, he says, his duty to welcome strangers. I myself bring you these gifts.' This interpreter was proclaimed chief of the location. When the people objected, saying 'We have our chief, the man you have appointed is his messenger and interpreter,' the British would not listen, and there was trouble during which the real chief and some of the elders were sent to prison.

Interpreters were in a key position to ingratiate themselves, and inveigle themselves into positions of authority. It was the chiefs who were first asked to send their sons among the British to be trained as interpreters, but they refused because they feared to lose their sons. So they sent subordinates who, when they returned, had not only a new language and access to the new government, but also a body of askaris with them to enforce their will.

There was not always a consistent way of appointing chiefs. Sometimes individuals were chosen arbitrarily; in other cases there was some attempt at getting the clan to arrive at a popular choice. In many cases the people were given as chiefs individuals whom they would not have chosen themselves. Above all, the candidates for chieftainship had to be acceptable to the district commissioner – and district commissioners often manipulated in the locations to have their favoured candidates imposed. Administration instructions make no bones about the position of a chief. I quote from a district circular: 'A chief is the direct agent of the government in his location; his position is much the same as that of a district commissioner . . . All over Kenya every chief has certain general functions and duties which go with his appointment. Among these are activity to maintain a spirit of loyalty to the British Crown, and to inculcate such spirit . . . to see that all lawful orders are obeyed by the African inhabitants of his location. It is the chief's duty to collect tax in his location . . . he must take a continuous personal interest in the collection of tax.'[1]

Chiefs were no longer the custodians of their peoples' tribal law and custom; they were now civil servants, pensionable, but also subject to instant dismissal by the government. They were the expression of the power of the new government in the village. They could use their position to amass and exercise personal power, something which was previously unheard of among the Luo.

---

[1] Circular of District Commissioner for Meru, November 1941

MAU MAU PATRIOTIC SONGS: KENYA

Why Sell Your Land?

This land belonged to Gikuyu
Ngai created and gave it to his chosen ones,
Gikuyu and Mumbi[1] to live there.

The seer Mugo wa Kibiru said:
'Pink and white butterflies
Will come from the East
And later will vanish.'

And Mugo was given a walking-stick for
    leadership
Like the one which was given to Musa in Misri
To lead the Children of Gikuyu.

Bless him to watch carefully over your children.
The stone which the Builders refused
Is the same stone they later used.

Agikuyu! why throw away your proverbs
When you know them?
You said: 'Unity is strength',
And again, 'The lazy ones don't have cows'.

Our people! why sell your land,
Because of your stomachs?

These prison/bush songs were used as liberation struggle songs. They are not
attributed to a particular songwriter, but have been edited and translated by Maina
wa Kīnyattī.

[1] Gikuyu and Mumbi are the original parents of the Gikuyu people.

Knowing very well that the stomach
Will never be satisfied
While your land is everlasting.

We Oppose Foreign Domination

A lot of discussion and happiness
Ended with my detention.
I shall remember all this after my release.
Wuui,[2] take me home to Gikuyuland,
A beautiful and fertile land,
Belonging to my forefathers.

Our eyes are full of tears,
Our hearts are heavy,
Wuui, take me back home,
A beautiful and fertile land,
Belonging to Mumbi.

Our old defence walls are collapsing,
Though we have put up a hard fight,
You must now fully prepare yourselves.
This is a continuous war.

You traitors to our cause,
You are the real problem.
Why can't you be guided
By hearts' devotion to our noble cause?

---

[2] *Wuui* is a cry of suffering.

When your hero arrived from India,[3]
You were all summoned to Githunguri
For a grand celebration.

At a meeting in Nakuru, Koinange declared:
'We will never accept to be ruled by foreigners,
Better for us all to die.'

After the meeting the cowards
Tried to join the people,
They were laughed at by the children
And were even hated by their colonial masters.

---

[3] Refers to James Beauttah who, in 1947, went to India to attend the All-Asian Conference.

KWAME NKRUMAH: GHANA

The Colonial Student

The lines of the partition of Africa naturally affected the education of the colonized Africans. Students from English-speaking territories went to Britain as a matter of course, just as those from French-speaking territories went to France as a matter of course. In this way, the yearning for formal education, which African students could only satisfy at great cost of effort, will, and sacrifice, was hemmed in within the confines of the colonial system.

Recoiling from this strait-jacketing, a number of us tried to study at centres outside the metropolis of our administering power. That is how America came to appeal to me as a western country which stood refreshingly untainted by territorial colonialism in Africa. To America I therefore went . . . studying and working for a living; teaching and carrying out my own private researches . . .

The ten years which I spent in the United States of America represents a crucial period in the development of my philosophical conscience. It was at the Universities of Lincoln and Pennsylvania that this conscience was first awakened. I was introduced to the great philosophical systems of the past to which the western universities have given their blessing, arranging and classifying them with the delicate care lavished on museum pieces . . .

I was introduced to Plato, Aristotle, Descartes, Kant, Hegel, Schopenhauer, Nietzsche, Marx and other immortals, to whom I should like to refer as the university philosophers. But these

From *Consciencism*, Heinemann Educational Books, 1964.

titans were expounded in such a way that a student from a colony could easily find his breast agitated by conflicting attitudes. These attitudes can have effects which spread out over a whole society, should such a student finally pursue a political life.

A colonial student does not by origin belong to the intellectual history in which the university philosophers are such impressive landmarks. The colonial student can be so seduced by these attempts to give a philosophical account of the universe, that he surrenders his whole personality to them. When he does this, he loses sight of the fundamental social fact that he is a colonial subject. In this way, he omits to draw from his education and from the concern displayed by the great philosophers for human problems, anything which he might relate to the very real problem of colonial domination, which, as it happens, conditions the immediate life of every colonized African.

With single-minded devotion, the colonial student meanders through the intricacies of the philosophical systems. And yet these systems did aim at providing a philosophical account of the world in the circumstances and conditions of their time. For even philosophical systems are facts of history. By the time, however, that they come to be accepted in the universities for exposition, they have lost the vital power which they had at their first statement, they have shed their dynamism and polemic reference. This is a result of the academic treatment which they are given. The academic treatment is the result of an attitude to philosophical systems as though there was nothing to them but statements standing in logical relation to one another.

This defective approach to scholarship was suffered by different categories of colonial student. Many of them had been hand-picked and, so to say, carried certificates of worthiness with them. These were considered fit to become enlightened servants of the colonial administration. The process by which this category of student became fit usually started at an early age, for not infrequently they had lost contact early in life with their traditional background. By reason of their lack of contact with their own roots, they became prone to accept some theory of universalism, provided it was expressed in vague, mellifluous terms.

Armed with their universalism, they carried away from their university courses an attitude entirely at variance with the concrete reality of their people and their struggle. When they came across doctrines of a combative nature, like those of Marxism, they reduced them to arid abstractions, to common-room subtleties. In this way, through the good graces of their colonialist patrons, these students, now competent in the art of forming not a concrete environmental view of social political problems, but an abstract, 'liberal' outlook, began to fulfil the hopes and expectations of their guides and guardians.

A few colonial students gained access to metropolitan universities almost as of right, on account of their social standing. Instead of considering culture as a gift and a pleasure, the intellectual who emerged therefrom now saw it as a personal distinction and privilege. He might have suffered mild persecution at the hands of the colonialists, but hardly ever really in the flesh. From his wobbly pedestal, he indulged in the history and sociology of his country, and thereby managed to preserve some measure of positive involvement with the national processes. It must however be obvious that the degree of national consciousness attained by him was not of such an order as to permit his full grasp of the laws of historical development or of the thorough-going nature of the struggle to be waged, if national independence was to be won.

Finally, there were the vast numbers of ordinary Africans, who, animated by a lively national consciousness, sought knowledge as an instrument of national emancipation and integrity.

This is not to say that these Africans overlooked the purely cultural value of their studies. But in order that their cultural acquisition should be valuable, they needed to be capable of appreciating it as free men.

I was one of this number.

JOMO KENYATTA: KENYA

Independence Day – 1963

It is with great pride and pleasure that I receive these constitutional instruments today as the embodiment of Kenya's freedom. This is the greatest day in Kenya's history, and the happiest day of my life.

Our march to freedom has been long and difficult. There have been times of despair, when only the burning conviction of the rightness of our cause has sustained us. Today, the tragedies and misunderstandings of the past are behind us. Today, we start on the great adventure of building the Kenya nation.

As we start on this great task, it is right that we who are assembled at this historic ceremony here today, and all the people of Kenya, should remember and pay tribute to those people of all races, tribes and colours who – over the years – have made their contribution to Kenya's rich heritage: administrators, farmers, missionaries, traders and others, and above all the people of Kenya themselves. All have laboured to make this fair land of Kenya the thriving country it is today. It behoves each one of us to vow that, in the days ahead, we shall be worthy of our great inheritance . . .

Today is rightly a day of great rejoicing. But it must also be a day of dedication. Freedom is a right, and without it the dignity of man is violated. But freedom by itself is not enough. At home, we have a duty to ensure that all our citizens are delivered from the afflictions of poverty, ignorance and disease, otherwise freedom for many of our people will be neither complete nor

---

From *Suffering Without Bitterness*, East African Publishing House, 1968. This extract is from the speech given by Kenya's new prime minister, on receiving his country's independence, after Kenyatta was released from prison.

meaningful. We shall count as our friends, and welcome as fellow-citizens, every man, woman and child, in Kenya – regardless of race, tribe, colour or creed – who is ready to help us in this great task of advancing the social well-being of all our people.

Freedom also means that we are now a member of the international community, and that we have a duty to work for the peace of the world. Abroad, we shall count as our friends all those who strive for peace.

My friends, we are now an independent nation, and our destiny is henceforward in our own hands. I call on every Kenyan to join me today in this great adventure of nation building. In the spirit of HARAMBEE, let us all work together so to mould our country that it will set an example to the world in progress, toleration . . .

What I have to say now is for the people of this country, but first let me say a word to our brothers in Africa who broke the chains of colonialism before us. I say to them: we are now independent after you. You have already tasted the honey of uhuru,[1] and now that we are with you, I know that this is sweet.

But to all who have independence, I say: this would be meaningless if in our Africa, some of our brothers are still under the yoke of colonialism. We therefore face a great challenge to help those of our brothers who are left behind, still dominated by foreign rule. If we look at South Africa, and if we look at Mozambique and Angola, we find our brothers still being exploited. It is thus our duty to fight, by all means available to us, so that our brothers can achieve their independence.

African unity is very important. If there is no unity in the whole of Africa, we shall still be slaves: we shall have entered

---

[1] Freedom [Ed.]

into a new type of slavery, the slavery of divide-and-rule by more powerful countries which have tasted the sweetness of ruling, and which – whether waking or sleeping – only think of ruling Africa. And when they sleep, a dream comes to them urging them to divide Africa, divide and then rule. It is our duty to stop this, and the only means is unity.

If we achieve unity, the whole world will respect us. We shall be the foundation and the shield of mother Africa. Our Africa has been milked until she is almost dry. Now we want to restore and sustain mother Africa, so we can enjoy the little milk that is left. If we do not do this, we will be finished. I want to emphasize that our salvation must come from unity.

Some people may say that – alas! – Kenyatta now is advocating a colour bar. This is not so; I have no colour feeling at all. What I want is for us to be united, so we can go forward and co-operate with the rest of the world. This is our goal.

And there is another matter: some people are saying – 'Kenyatta, you and your brothers are now independent, so which side will your independence take you to; will you be pro-West or pro-East, on the side of the devils or the angels?' I therefore declare to you now that the aim of my government which starts today is not to be pro-left or pro-right. We shall pursue the task of nation building in friendship with the rest of the world. Nobody will ever be allowed to tell us, to tell me: you must be friendly to so-and-so. We shall remain free, and whoever wants friendship with us must be a real friend.

We shall never agree to friendship through any form of bribery. And I want all those nations who are present today – whether from West or from East – to understand our aim. We want to befriend all, and we want aid from everyone. But we do not want assistance from any person or country who will say: Kenyatta, if you want aid, you must agree to this or that. I believe, my brothers, and I tell you now, that it is better to be poor and remain free, than be technically free but still be kept on a string. A horse cannot choose: reins can be put on him so he can be led around as his owner desires. We will not be prepared to accept any aid that will tie us like a horse by its reins.

Now my words to the people of Kenya: many people may think that, now there is uhuru, now I can see the sun of freedom shining, richness will pour down like manna from heaven. I tell you there will be nothing from heaven. We must all work hard, with our hands, to save ourselves from poverty, ignorance and disease . . .

I thank you as well for electing me to lead you into a new phase in the progress of our country. In the past, we used to blame the Europeans for everything that went wrong. When things went wrong, we used to say the Europeans are bad, they are sucking our blood. When we lacked education, we said the Europeans were only educating their children, and the Asians were only educating their children, so when will ours be educated?

Now the Government is ours. Maybe you will now be blaming Kenyatta, saying: 'Kenyatta, we elected you, but where is this or that?' But you must know that Kenyatta alone cannot give you everything. All things we must do together. You and I must work together to develop our country, to get education for our children, to have doctors, to build roads, to improve or provide all day-to-day essentials. This should be our work, in the spirit that I am going to ask you to echo, to shout aloud, to shatter the foundations of the past with the strength of our new purpose . . . HARAMBEE!

ZIMBABWE LIBERATION WAR SONG

Elder Brother Takanyi

Our mothers are being harassed by the Boers
Who ask them, 'Where are your children?'
Their answer is long-winded,
They never reveal that the children are now
    comrades.

They may reply; 'Our sons are working on farms,
Where they do not need registration certificates.'
This is what we read in the newspapers.
This is what we read in the newspapers.

Mrewa produces tomatoes,
Chiredzi produces sugar.
Centenary is famous for maize.
Gokwe abounds with wild fruit.
We get ocra from Bindura.
Mt Darwin is cotton territory.
Inyanga produces the bulbous root (dhumbe).
There are lots of caterpillars in Bulawayo.

He (the oppressor) is not an impartial ruler.
His justice is one-sided.

If I had wings I would fly,
Back to the masses of Zimbabwe.
Land at Mtoko, Bindura,
Que Que or Umtali and

From *The Songs that Won the Liberation War*, edited and translated by
Alec J. C. Pongweni, The College Press, 1982.

Tell them that we must
Now wrest power from the Oppressor.

But we cannot negotiate now that
We are carrying sub-machine guns.
This will be patently clear, to
Anyone who sees a sub-machine gun.

Caetano was big-headed,
But the comrades hit him hard.
Yet Smith seems to have
Learnt nothing.
The comrades are sorting him out.
Brother Takanyi.

FRELIMO reigns supreme in
Mozambique now.
Mozambique has become synonymous with
    FRELIMO.

You can travel by bus, aeroplane
And no one will harass you.
You can, in Mozambique enjoy
All human rights there.
Yes, brother Takanyi.

NeHanda predicted this war,
This revolutionary war,
Yes, our ancestors foresaw this
Chaminuka also had the premonition;
When he said his bones would
Come back to life.
And this is exactly what has happened.
Yes, brother Takanyi.

As far as he is concerned,
the dog is more precious than a human being.
Something strange to us Blacks.
Then when there is an accident
and the boss is dead.
The police want a statement,
They come to ask me how the boss died,
How am I supposed to know that?
All I can say is that the dog
was with him up front,
Observing how the boss was: changing gears!
This is oppression, an insult to the black man.
We know this from reading Mao's works.
Who states in no uncertain terms
'Political power comes from the barrel of a gun'.
That's why we came here to take up arms.
This is the only way to secure political power.
From the barrel of a gun.
That's the plain truth.
And if all Zimbabweans accept
this fundamental truth
Then we have unity of purpose
Then we can sing our way
To victory.

Do you have any questions, brother Takanyi?
We shall regain Zimbabwe,
Yes, we are bound to liberate Zimbabwe.
There's no doubt about it,
We shall overcome.

EDDISON J. ZVOBGO: ZIMBABWE

Vanished Peace

While the land still lay quiet as at its mother's
    breast,
And the rivers still ran with milk;
While walls still cracked, unable to hold the
    abundance,
And there was food that came out of the caves in
    the ground;
While springs still bubbled with the wild guava
    wine,
Life was sweet to taste.

In those past peaceful days, while the dead still
    returned,
And heaven was as high as the rooftops;
When scorn and robbery were as rare as file
    snakes,
Ugly and rude children, as miscarriages, still an
    omen;
While snakes still gave themselves up for belts and
    beadstrings,
The land was at peace.

There was no quarrelling at the doorways,
The breasts of maidens were still as true as thorns,
No need for simulation or support.
Young men still hunted lions
With arrows, sharp and blunt, and kerries
To win their tokens of love.

Translated from the Shona by George Fortune and Aaron C. Hodza.

The lice still swarmed, washing an annual event
  with the rains,
Weaklings and cripples you would hardly see in
  the land,
Dried vegetables and fried nuts
And bean stew were the commonest relish.
At home sleep was undisturbed,
Peace on every side.

The spirits of founding fathers and ancestors still
  came forth;
Adultery was still an offence,
And sorcerers still exterminated like vermin.
Thieves could still be caught by charms,
Rainmakers could still bring rain and tame the
  lightning,
Goblins and owls could still be sent to forage,
There was peace and there was gladness.

FELIX MNTHALI: MALAWI

Neocolonialism

Above all, define standards
prescribe values
set limits; impose boundaries

and even if you have no satellites
in space
and no weapons of any value
you will rule the world

Whatever tune you sing
they will dance
whatever bilge you spill
they will lick
and you may well pick
and choose
their rare minerals
and their rich forests

They will come to you
in fear and trembling
for the game will be played
according to your rules
and therefore the game will be played
only when you can win

Above all,
prescribe values
and define standards
and then sit back
to allow the third world
to fall into your lap.

STEVE BIKO: SOUTH AFRICA

Our Strategy for Liberation

Stephen Biko: A number of our organizations are operating at different levels. The history of it starts off after 1963–4. If you remember, there were many arrests in this country which stemmed from underground activities by PAC (Pan Africanist Congress) and ANC (African National Congress); this led to some kind of political emasculation of the black population especially, with the result that there was no participation by blacks in the articulation of their own aspirations. The whole opposition to what the government was doing to blacks came in fact from white organizations, mainly student groups like NUSAS (National Union of South African Students), the Liberal Party, the Progressive Party. Blacks who were articulating any sense were far fewer by comparison to the olden days, and they were dispersed amongst these particular organizations.

When I came to varsity [Durban University], which was some time in 1966, in my own analysis and that of my friends there was some kind of anomaly in this situation, where whites were in fact the main participants in our oppression and at the same time the main participants in the opposition to that oppression. It implied therefore that at no stage in this country were blacks throwing in their lot in the shift of political opinion. The arena was totally controlled by whites in what we called 'totality' of white power at that time.

So we argued that any changes which are to come can only come as a result of a programme worked out by black people – and for black people to be able to work out a programme they

Interview given to a European journalist in 1977. From *I Write What I Like*, Heinemann Educational Books, 1979.

needed to defeat the one main element in politics which was working against them: a psychological feeling of inferiority which was deliberately cultivated by the system. So equally, too, the whites in order to be able to listen to blacks needed to defeat the one problem which they had, which was one of 'superiority'.

Now the only way to bring about this of course was to look anew at the black man in terms of what it is in him that is lending him to denigration so easily. First of all, we said as black students we could not participate in multi-racial organizations which were by far white organizations because of the overwhelming number of white students at universities in this country.

Second, these organizations were concentrating mainly on problems which were affecting the white student community.

Third, of course, when it came to political questions they were far more articulate than the average black student because of their superior training and because of their numbers – they could outvote us on any one issue. Which meant that NUSAS as an organization gave political opinions which were largely affected by the whiteness of that particular organization.

So in 1968 we started forming what is now called SASO – the South African Students Organization – which was firmly based on Black Consciousness, the essence of which was for the black man to elevate his own position by positively looking at those value systems that make him distinctively a man in society.

Like what?

First of all, we were of the view that this particular country is almost like an island of Europe in Africa. If you go through the whole of Africa you do find aspects of African life which are culturally elevated throughout the continent. But in this country – somehow any visitor who comes here tends to be made to believe almost that he is in Europe. He never sees blacks except in a subservient role. This is all because of the cultural dominance of the particular group which is now in power.

To what extent have you been successful?

We have been successful to the extent that we have diminished the element of fear in the minds of black people. In the period of '63–'66 black people were terribly scared of involvement in politics. The universities were putting out no useful leadership to the black people because everybody found it more comfortable to lose himself in a particular profession, to make money. But since those days, black students have seen their role as being primarily to prepare themselves for leadership roles in the various facets of the black community. Through our political articulation of the aspirations of black people, many black people have come to appreciate the need to stand up and be counted against the system. There is far more political talk now, far more political debate and far more condemnation of the system from average black people than there has ever been since possibly 1960 and before.

I'm referring here to the whole oppressive education system that the students are talking about. After complaining about it, the government wants to further entrench what the students are protesting about by bringing in police and saracens [armoured cars] and dogs – almost soldiers, so to speak.

Now the response of the students then was in terms of their pride. They were not prepared to be calmed down even at the point of a gun. And hence, what happened, happened. Some people were killed. These riots just continued and continued. Because at no stage were the young students – nor for that matter at some stage their parents – prepared to be scared. Everybody saw this as a deliberate act of oppressive measures to try and calm down the black masses, and everybody was determined equally to say to the police, to say to the government: we shall not be scared by your police, by your dogs and by your soldiers. Now this is the kind of lack of fear one is talking about which I see is a very important determinant in political action.

Since last June something like 400 young blacks were killed.

499 actually.

Do you think this will not be a deterrent?

No. I think it has been a very useful weapon in merging the young and old. Before then there was a difference in the outlooks of the old generation and the younger generation. The younger generation was moving too fast for the old generation. The old generation was torn between bantustan politics on the one side – old allegiances which were not progressive alliances, to groups like ANC, PAC, without any result in action – and there were those simply too scared to move.

Do you condemn bantustan leadership?

Yes, of course. We condemn bantustan leaders, even the best of them like Gatsha Buthelezi.

Just say a few words on that.

Our attitude here is that you cannot in pursuing the aspirations of black people achieve them from a platform which is meant for the oppression of black people. We see all these so-called bantustan platforms as being deliberate creations by the Nationalist government to contain the political aspirations of the black people and to give them pseudo-political platforms to direct their attention to.

Now men like Gatsha Buthelezi, Matanzima, Mangope and so on are all participants in the white man's game of holding the aspirations of the black people. We do not feel it is possible in any way to turn such a platform to useful work. We believe the first principal step by any black political leader is to destroy such a platform. Destroy it without giving it any form of respectability. Once you step in it, once you participate in it, whether you are in the governing party or the opposition, you are in fact giving sanctity to it, you are giving respectability to it.

So in a sense people like Buthelezi, like Matanzima, like Mangope, are participants in a white man's game and they are participants at the expense of the black man. They are leading black people to a divided struggle – to speak as Zulus, to speak as Xhosas, to speak as Pedis – which is a completely new feature in the political life of black people in this country. We speak as one combined whole, directing ourselves to a common enemy, and we reject anyone who wishes to destroy that unity.

We are of the view that we should operate as one united whole toward attainment of an egalitarian society for the whole of Azania. Therefore entrenchment of tribalistic, racialistic or any form of sectional outlook is abhorred by us. We hate it and we seek to destroy it. It is for this reason therefore that we cannot see any form of coalition with any of the bantustan leaders, even the so-called best of them like Gatsha Buthelezi, because they destroy themselves by virtue of the kind of arguments that one has put up.

The government of course has said that all this unrest really is due to communist agitation. Are you a communist?

We are by no means communist. Neither do I believe for a moment that the unrest is due to communist agitation. I do know for a fact that there has been participation, it would appear anyway from signs, by a lot of people in the unrest. But the primary reason behind the unrest is simple lack of patience by the young folk with a government which is refusing to change, refusing the change in the educational sphere, which is where they [the students] are directing themselves, and also refusing to change in a broader political situation.

Now when these youngsters started with their protests they were talking about [exclusive use of] Afrikaans [in black schools], they were talking about Bantu education, and they meant that. But the government responded in a high-handed fashion, assuming as they always have done that they were in a situation of total power. But here for once they met a student group which was not prepared to be thrown around all the time. They decided to flex their muscles, and of course, the whole country responded . . .

There are lessons to be gleaned from this whole unrest situation of last year. In the first instance, I think blacks have flexed their muscles a bit – and they now know the degree of dedication they can find among their own members when they are called to action. And they now know the kind of responses they will get from the various segments of the population – the youth, the older ones and so on.

The second lesson is of course the response from the government and the white population at large. The government responded in one way, and the white population also in another way. One doesn't want to get into details here but reading these newspapers you get some kind of idea of the extent of fear that was prevalent in white society at a particular time, especially just after the first onslaught in Soweto, where there was a real fear throughout the community, throughout the country. Nobody knew just where something would happen next.

So how will these lessons express themselves in the future?

I am of the view that any recurrence of disturbance of that nature can only result in more careful planning and better calculation, thereby achieving the desired results to a greater extent than this spontaneous situation we had last year, for instance.

Do you believe that by these means you will bring about a real change of this society?

I see this as only one form of expression of discontent inside. I am of the view that the whole change process is going to be a protracted one in this country. It depends entirely on the degree to which the Nationalist government is prepared to hold on to power. My own analysis is that they are wanting to hold on to power and fight with their backs to the wall.

Now, conflict could only be avoidable if they were prepared to avoid it. Those who are at the seeking end, that is those who want justice, who want an egalitarian society, can only pursue their aspirations according to the resistance offered by the opposition. If the opposition is prepared to fight with their backs to the wall, conflict can't be avoidable.

Now we as BPC – I am a member of the Black Consciousness movement, I was a member of BPC before I was banned, and now I've been, I'm told, appointed honorary president of BPC – now the line BPC adopts is to explore as much as possible non-violent means within the country, and that is why we exist.

But there are people – and there are many people – who have despaired of the efficacy of non-violence as a method. They are of the view that the present Nationalist Government can only be unseated by people operating a military wing.

I don't know if this is the final answer. I think in the end there is going to be a totality of the effect of a number of change agencies operating in South Africa. I personally would like to see fewer groups. I would like to see groups like ANC, PAC and the Black Consciousness movement deciding to form one libera-tion group. It is only, I think, when black people are so dedicated and so united in their cause that we can effect the greatest results. And whether this is going to be through the form of conflict or not will be dictated by the future. I don't believe for a moment that we are going to willingly drop our belief in the non-violent stance – as of now. But I can't predict what will happen in the future, inasmuch as I can't predict what the enemy is going to do in the future.

Can you guess at all at the number of years the change might take?

That is a very difficult exercise. I don't want to get involved in that kind of exercise. Some people say five years, others say ten years. I think that we are not at the stage yet where it is possible to fix a precise timetable.

You speak of an egalitarian society. Do you mean a socialist one?

Yes, I think there is no running away from the fact that now in South Africa there is such an ill distribution of wealth that any form of political freedom which does not touch on the proper distribution of wealth will be meaningless. The whites have locked up within a small minority of themselves the greater proportion of the country's wealth. If we have a mere change of face of those in governing positions what is likely to happen is that black people will continue to be poor, and you will see a few blacks filtering through into the so-called bourgeoisie. Our society will be run almost as of yesterday. So for meaningful change to appear there needs to be an attempt at reorganizing the whole economic pattern and economic policies within this particular country.

BPC believe in a judicious blending of private enterprise which is highly diminished and state participation in industry and commerce, especially in industries like mining – gold, diamonds, asbestos and so on – like forestry, and of course complete ownership of land. Now in that kind of judicious blending of the two systems we hope to arrive at a more equitable distribution of wealth.

Do you see a country in which black and white can live amicably on equal terms together?

That is correct. We see a completely non-racial society. We don't believe, for instance, in the so-called guarantees for minority rights, because guaranteeing minority rights implies the recognition of portions of the community on a race basis. We believe that in our country there shall be no minority, there shall be no majority, just the people. And those people will have the same status before the law and they will have the same political rights before the law. So in a sense it will be a completely non-racial egalitarian society.

But will the vast number of blacks after all their experiences be able to live their life without giving vent to feelings of revenge, of . . .

We believe it is the duty of the vanguard political movement which brings change to educate people's outlook. In the same way that blacks have never lived in a socialist economic system they've got to learn to live in one. And in the same way that they've always lived in a racially divided society, they've got to learn to live in a non-racial society. They've got many things to learn.

All these must be brought to them and explained to the people by the vanguard movement which is leading the revolution. So that I've got no doubt in my mind that people – and I know people in terms of my own background, where I stay – are not necessarily revengeful, nor are they sadistic in outlook. The black man has got no ill intentions for the white man. The black man is only incensed at the white man to the extent that he wants to entrench himself in a position of power to exploit the black man. But beyond that, nothing more.

We don't need any artificial majorities, any artificial laws to entrench ourselves in power because we believe once we come into power our sheer numbers will maintain us there. We do not have the same fear that the minority white government has been having all along, which has led to his many laws designed to keep him there.

As you know the main argument of the government is always that the black man just isn't on a civilization level at present to pull his full weight politically. Do you think of a one-man, one-vote franchise?

Yes, we do think so. Entirely. Entirely one-man, one-vote, no qualification whatsoever except the normal ones you find throughout the world.

Don't you think that the black man in fact is perfectly well able . . .

The black man is well able – and the white man knows it. The irony of that kind of situation is that when the white government negotiates so-called independence for the so-called Transkei, they don't speak in terms of a qualified franchise. In the Transkei, every Transkeian votes. You get white nationalist politicians arguing that this is a system that is going to work for the Transkei. But somehow, when it comes to the broader country, the blacks may not vote because they do not understand the sophisticated economic patterns out here. They understand nothing. They need to operate at a different level. Now this is all nonsense. It is meant to entrench the white man in the position in which he finds himself today. We will do away with it altogether. There will be a completely non-racial franchise. Black and white will vote as individuals in our society.

This is all fascinating. As an outsider, as a visitor, I can only say that my feeling is that this is bound to be a very long and probably very bloody road.

There is that possibility. There is that possibility. But as I said earlier on, it will be dictated purely by the response of the Nationalist party. If they have been able to see that in Rhodesia Smith must negotiate with the leaders of the black people of Rhodesia . . .

I think conflict is unavoidable given the predictable response from the present system. And this conflict can be pretty generalized and extensive and protracted. My worst fears are that working on the present analysis, conflict can only be on a generalized basis between black and white.

We don't have sufficient groups who can form coalitions with blacks – that is groups of whites – at the present moment. The more such groups which come up, the better to minimize that conflict.

Mr Biko, thank you.

JEREMY CRONIN: SOUTH AFRICA

Faraway City, There . . .

Faraway city, there
with salt in its stones,
under its windswept doek,
There in our Cape Town where
they're smashing down homes
of the hungry, labouring people
– will you wait for me, my love?

In that most beautiful,
desolate city of my heart
where if staying on were passive
life wouldn't be what it is.

Not least for those rebuilding
yet again their demolished homes
with bits of plastic, port jackson saplings,
anything to hand – unshakably

Defiant, frightened, broken,
and unbreakable are the people of our city.

– Will you wait for me, my love?

MONCEF MARZOUKI: TUNISIA

Winning Freedom

If you wish to be a writer in a Muslim Arab country, you should be aware of the numerous pitfalls of the profession. The writer is faced not only with the enormous scale of illiteracy and the daily struggle with survival (which makes reading a real luxury for the majority of people) but also with the limitations of the publishing market, increasingly circumscribed by governments that, over the course of the last fifteen centuries, have grown ever more mean and quarrelsome. These are the technical obstacles which may stand in the way of publishing any given book. But there are other obstacles which pose a real threat to the future of the writer himself.

Arab authors today are necessarily conscious of the tragic fate which has befallen so many writers throughout the long history of Arab culture. Over ten centuries ago, Ibn El Mogafaa, Abdulhamd El Kateb, El Hallaj were murdered on the orders of the authorities. The great Averroés was persecuted and then exiled from Cordova to Marrakesh in 1198. Numerous other names could be mentioned and tragic stories told in the history of our search for freedom. If we turn to the twentieth century, the climate is only a little more tolerant. In the 1960s, the writer Sadek Jalal El Azim wasn't exactly crucified, but he was hauled before the courts, harshly treated and condemned for having lampooned religious sensitivities.

This is the stifling context in which the present struggles in Tunisia must be understood, as part of a struggle which has

From *Index on Censorship*, 1/89.

gone on for centuries. It is precisely because they are indicative of a wider problem, one that transcends the particular time, place and figures involved, that they deserve to be reported.

The setting, then, is as follows: an apparently interminable *'fin de régime'* represented by a bastard form of transitional government: the 'monarchist republic' or republic in embryo (the monarchy was abolished after independence in 1956, but had left its imprint everywhere); Bourguiba's personal power in ruins, with too much power vested in the coteries surrounding him; grave political instability resulting from the flare-up of Islamic feeling and the tidal wave of demands for democracy; and all this happening against the background of an economic crisis which came to a head on 3 January 1984, when a sharp increase in the price of bread triggered off a popular uprising.

In such situations, writers necessarily bear witness to the events around them and are forced to take a stance. The independent press was the first to enter the fray. On one side of the battle were newspapers such as *Errai, El Mostakbal, Etterik el Jedid, Realités, El Mawkaf, Le Maghrev* and *Le Phare*; on the other, an extremely repressive press law. It was scarcely surprising that none of the newspapers mentioned was able to publish for more than six months at a stretch. Seized, banned or heavily fined, some (such as *Errai* and *Le Phare*) went under during the period of upheaval; others succeeded in rounding the Cape and survived the end of Bourguiba's reign. Between 1979 and 1987, however, numerous journalists were hauled before the courts: among them were Hassib Ben Ammar, Moncef Ben M'Rad, Mohamed Mali and Ismail Boulahia. The usual charges were made: spreading false news, slandering the state, its institutions and the head of state himself.

Their real crime, of course, was that they had called for democracy, denounced abuses by the state, the use of torture, and so on.

The role of the independent press in the political evolution of the country is incontestable. It was the press which won the battle of words and ideas; everything which followed can be attributed to this victory.

On 7 November 1987, Tunisia underwent a change not only of president but of style and orientation. The key words and phrases that had come to dominate the press – democracy, human rights – quickly became the slogans of the new regime. Previously banned books were once again allowed, impending law suits dropped, Ben Othmane's sentence was quashed at an appeal court, and the author, too, was spared from catching cold and developing rheumatism in Tunis central prison.

As for the journalists and writers who paved the way for change, the heat of the battle has now subsided. To be sure, journalists have continued here and there to lash out at survivals of 'Bourguibisme', but their fury has died down. No need, as they say, to shoot at an ambulance.

The real question is whether all this will prove to be a flash in the pan, or whether what we have witnessed is the beginning of a new relationship between the press, literature and the authorities.

For writers, however, there are still two important barriers to be overcome. First, self-censorship has become second nature to many of our 'literati'. This self-imposed limitation has paralysed the pens particularly of journalists. Criticisms are often made so coyly, with such kowtowing to the authorities, that they are all but worthless. It will be some time before broadcasters feel free to speak their minds.

The second major obstacle is posed by social mores. As it happens, the subjects that are still taboo are all the ones it would be most interesting to discuss: God, sex, male domination. Obviously, a literature from which all these subjects have been expurgated is rather like a diet without meat, fresh fruit or cakes. This may explain why so much Arab writing seems insipid, indigestible, un-nourishing.

What has been going on in Tunisia represents only part of an on-going struggle between liberty and censorship. To be sure, liberty has won a great victory in Tunisia, but the state's censors haven't put away their scissors yet, and there are plenty more battles ahead. Here, as everywhere else, freedom – the most precious of all goods – will not be given for free, but must be won.

KEN SARO-WIWA: NIGERIA

Ogoni! Ogoni!

Ogoni is the land
The people, Ogoni
The agony of trees dying
In ancestral farmlands
Streams polluted weeping
Filth into murky rivers
It is the poisoned air
Coursing the luckless lungs
Of dying children
Ogoni is the dream
Breaking the looping chain
Around the drooping neck
    of a shell-shocked land.

Arrest, Detention
and Prison

KWAME NKRUMAH: GHANA

Cell Number Eleven

Whilst I didn't exactly expect to be made to feel at home in James Fort, it was somewhat of a shock to me to discover that, as a political prisoner, I was treated as a criminal. Sometimes I used to speculate as to what my lot would have been as a hardened gaol-bird. It was difficult to imagine that there could be worse treatment if the minimum of health and sanity of the inmate were to be preserved.

For eleven men we were supplied with a bucket in one corner of the already over-crowded cell to serve as a latrine. After a few weeks most of us managed to overcome the fearful indignity of using this so very public convenience. If only we had been permitted the flimsiest of straw mats to partition the thing off, it would at least have been an attempt to preserve a sense of decency but it seemed that, like animals in a cage, we had to act our part without complaint. We used to take it in turns to clean this receptacle each day and we did what we could to make the best of a bad job. But it was most unpleasant, especially as the wretched food that we had was invariably upsetting our stomachs. It was all most embarrassing and most degrading.

The food was both scanty and poor. For breakfast we were given a cup of maize porridge without sugar. For the midday meal and for the last meal of the day at four p.m. we were given either boiled cassava, *kenke* (corn meal) or *gari* (a cassava farine) with red pepper. On Sundays and Wednesdays we had a watery soup with the minutest piece of meat thrown in. This was purely a gesture, for it was as hard as a bullet. Sometimes

From *Autobiography of Kwame Nkrumah*, Thomas Nelson & Sons, 1957.

we would get a piece of smoked fish with pepper. Rice was a luxury and only given to those who were unwell and for whom it was prescribed by the prison doctor.

When we first arrived, my colleagues were so disgusted with the food that some of them went on a hunger strike. I was against this for I saw that it would get us nowhere; on the contrary, it was necessary to eat all we could in an effort to keep our strength up. There was much work to do when we were eventually released and it was going to be no good to anybody if we had to be invalided out. After much persuasion on my part, the strikers gave in.

I used to fast for one or two days a week because this had been a former habit of mine. But apart from the spiritual value derived from this, during those prison days it also helped my stomach to right itself again. I had never cared much for food in any case, so I was perhaps more fortunate than my fellow prisoners.

We were let out of our cell from seven in the morning until eleven o'clock for exercise and to work, either at weaving fish-nets or at cleaning cane ready for basket-making. Then we were locked up again until one o'clock and we were finally locked up for the night at four p.m. after our evening meal. All our meals were eaten in our cell, which probably added to the unpleasant-ness of the food.

It was of course forbidden for me to have pencil and paper or to read any newspapers and my greatest anxiety at that time was how the Party was faring during my absence. It was permitted to write one letter per month to one's parents or near relatives, but as a warder was always standing over your shoulder and the letter had to be censored by the prison auth-orities, there was little apart from a flourishing account of one's health that would have got through.

Fortunately, just before I was locked up I was able to have a few valuable minutes with Gbedemah who, having served his prison sentence for 'publishing false news', was preparing to leave. In those few minutes I committed to his charge the full responsibility of running the *Evening News* and the Party.

'I'll do my utmost to keep in touch with you somehow,' I whispered to him, 'though goodness knows how!'

There was, I realized, only one way I could keep in touch with the Party outside those whitewashed walls – by writing. My whole life then centred around the problem of how to get hold of a pencil and a supply of paper. Before long I managed to pick up a mere stump of a pencil which I kept safely hidden inside the band of my trouser tops. The paper looked like being a major problem until I suddenly saw the answer staring me in the face. Each day, we were given a few sheets of toilet paper. I got the bright idea of appropriating these, as many as I could get. I don't know what the other prisoners must have thought was wrong with me when I made known to them my urgent need of additional toilet paper, but they were quite willing to exchange what they could spare for bits of food and anything else I could offer them. This precious store of paper was kept carefully under my straw sleeping mat.

As soon as it was dark and we were thought to be asleep, like the many cockroaches that roamed freely about the cell I, too, started to work. Writing in that cell was no easy matter for the light was from an electric street lamp that penetrated through the bars at the top of the wall of the cell and cast its reflection on a part of the floor and a section of the opposite wall. I used to lie in this patch of light and write for as long as I could until cramp made it unendurable, then I would change to a standing position and use the spot of light on the wall. On one occasion I remember covering fifty sheets of this toilet paper with my scribble. The written sheets were then folded minutely and wrapped in another piece of toilet paper, and this eventually found its way to Gbedemah outside. How they got there is quite another matter, but by the same means that my toilet paper scribbles found their way out of gaol, so Gbedemah was able to send me from time to time a full report of what was going on outside.

It was no easy task for Gbedemah to keep the Party united, and it was especially difficult when so many of the members were vying with one another for leadership. By reading out my messages from prison, however, Gbedemah managed to keep my name alive in the minds of the people and encouraged them to carry on their struggle under his guidance until the day that I would be once more able to lead them. Once or twice a week I could hear evidence of the success of this, for crowds used to assemble outside the prison and sing party songs and hymns. One that I particularly remember was 'Kwame Nkrumah's body lies a-mouldering in the cell' to the tune of 'John Brown's Body'. It boosted up my morale a great deal to hear these voices and to know that I had not been deserted and forgotten.

I decided to grow a beard after discovering that we were expected to share one razor blade and one shaving stick among us. Although I was rapidly learning that the sooner I lost my self-respect the sooner I would settle down in my uncomfortable and unsavoury surroundings, I could never get used to the idea of a communal razor blade and shaving soap. I preferred letting my whiskers grow to running the risk of skin infection.

I used to look forward most eagerly to Sundays as we were excused our usual labours on that day and, after washing my prison clothes, I used to search for a quiet corner in the prison yard where I could sit and reflect. One Sunday morning I gathered my fellow Party prisoners together and we organized a committee, of which I was the chairman, in order to work out the plans which the Party outside were to follow. At the same time we elected two sub-committees, one composed of the ex-servicemen and the other with Kojo Botsio as its chair-man. We met regularly thereafter and discussed our common problems. This was unknown to the warders.

On Sundays also we were allowed to attend whatever service was being conducted in the prison, the most popular of which was that of the Apostolic Faith. During this particular service there was much clapping of hands and movement. Every pris-oner, old and young, Christian and atheist, was glad to join in this service; in fact we looked forward to it, for we managed to get not only fresh air but also exercise and relaxation from boredom. Some of the prisoners got so carried away during the service that they shed tears like children as they reflected and confessed their past misdeeds, begging for remission of their sins. In fact some of them who confessed their sins were so repentant that when they were released they vowed they would never commit a crime again. But, in spite of these good inten-tions, I used to notice that in a matter of weeks the same men were back again for the same crimes.

After about a month or two the hardship and monotony of prison life began to get the better of some of us and we started quarrelling and blaming one another for what had happened. Some of them couldn't understand why we should be forced to suffer and quite a fracas ensued. Many times I had to act as mediator and often had to beg and plead with my companions to keep peace and order within the confines of our small prison cell. This feeling of general unrest and discomfort brought out feelings of bitterness, selfishness and revenge. I remember how on one occasion I had managed to get hold of a copy of the *Evening News*. As soon as we had been locked in our cell, one of our number became so embittered when he saw me reading this precious paper that he reported the whole thing to one of the warders. A search was made of our entire cell and the newspaper was run to ground and confiscated. I was so relieved that my stump of pencil had not been found and that the sheets of toilet paper were unsuspected of playing a duplicate role, that I gladly accepted my punishment of short rations. The normal rations were barely adequate to keep body and soul together and any reduction in this amount was certainly no joke, but I stuck it out.

Apart from Sunday service there were two things that supplied a little relief to the boredom. One was an occasional concert that the prisoners used to get up which, in spite of the crudeness of the performance, was, compared with the dark walls of the cell, grand entertainment. The other pastime that we enjoyed was gambling. There were three items of value in the prison; toilet paper, nut kernels and soap. These things were so precious and so much in demand that they always represented the stakes in our gambling games, for money was quite useless to us. I became a keen gambler as far as the toilet paper was concerned, because I could never get enough of this to write all I had to say. The nut kernel was generally used by the prisoners to oil their bodies because, on account of the rotten diet and the poor quality of the soap, the skin became scaled and cracked. By chewing the nut kernel and then smearing your body with it, it was possible to get enough oil to lubricate the most affected parts of your skin at least.

The most demoralizing moments that I experienced in prison were when a prisoner was committed to be hanged. These unfortunate men were brought in in chains and were kept in solitary confinement away from the ordinary prisoners. We all knew when the day of execution arrived for we were made to get up earlier than usual and taken from our cell to an upstairs room where we were locked in before six o'clock. Some people used to try and peep through the window to see if they could catch a glimpse of what was going on, but it was quite impossible. By about ten o'clock we were let out and the only sign of the grim event was that there was sometimes an occasional bloodstain on the ground near where we went to have our ablutions, for the gallows was situated in the vicinity of the washroom. To see a man brought in one day and disappear completely a few days later was something that really affected the other prisoners. There must have been on an average one execution a month during the time I was imprisoned and most of these men were hanged for killing their wives or for killing men who they had believed were having illicit relations with their wives.

I used to reflect after these awful moments and I wondered whether prison punishments really did achieve their purpose in reforming the criminal and whether capital punishment was a solution to murder cases. Criminals, after all, are human beings. No man is born a criminal; society makes him so, and the only way to change things is to change the social conditions; it is only from the social standpoint that crime and punishment can be effectively approached. I have always been against the death penalty, even before I came so close to understanding what this meant during my prison life. I believe that it is a relic of barbarism and savagery and that it is inconsistent with decent morals and the teaching of Christian ethics. The aim of punishment should be that of understanding and correction.

I looked back on my own boyhood. I was brought up in a particularly primitive society but during the whole of my eighteen years or so of boyhood life in Nzima, I can only remember there being one murder case, and that was a case in which a sexual maniac was involved. The taboos of primitive society generally curb crime. The impact of western culture on the African mind brought in its train as much bad as good. Offences like forgery, bribery and corruption, for instance, were practically unknown in our early society.

My experience of fourteen months in prison convinced me,

moreover, that in a very short time prisoners lose all their individualism and personality; they become a set type in an unhappy world of their own. They lose confidence in themselves and are so unequipped to meet the outside world that it is little wonder that they hanker for the misery and boredom of their prison cell, a protective shelter for their lost and shattered souls.

JOSIAH MWANGI KARIUKI: KENYA

Kowop Camp

Kowop was a small tented camp in the valley between three rocky hills. It was 25 miles north of Baragoi and about 60 from Lake Rudolf. Near Ngiro Hill there is good grass on which the nomadic tribes of the Samburu and the Turkana seasonally pasture their herds and flocks. Sometimes from the desolate and stormy landscape a group of their living huts (*manyatta*) would emerge like upside-down birds' nests, so flat and shallow that no one could stand up in them. Although Kowop was in Samburu District, many Turkana also came there and the two tribes existed side by side amicably enough. The climate was dry and hot and very different from Kikuyuland or the Rift Valley. There was no water anywhere except in a borehole from which it came with a taste of sulphur. Skin washed in this water with soap looked afterwards as if it had been smeared with lime, and many of the detainees got severe diarrhoea after drinking. I stayed in this camp until 20 August 1954 when it was closed down.

In the beginning there were only 36 of us there. We were very proud of our status as detained persons as opposed to convicted prisoners. This meant that we did not have to work except on our own chores; we could wear our own clothes; we could keep our money and we were allowed to wander freely about the compound in the evening. There was only one barbed wire fence around the perimeter, and this was so loose that goats could easily hop in and out if the wire was held open for them. No one seemed to be in the least worried that we should escape.

From *Mau Mau Detainee*, Oxford University Press, 1963.

Later we learnt the reason why. The Turkana said that they had been told by the District Commissioner that we Kikuyu were very disgusting people whose custom it was to eat the breasts of our women and even the embryos of children in the womb. Any Turkana or Samburu who brought him the head of an escaped detainee would be rewarded with *posho*, sugar and tea. When the Gold Coast was fighting for its Independence, Muturi and some other farmers used to tell their labourers that Ghanaians were cannibals and ate their own children. We became frightened in those days that Ngorogothi (people from the Gold Coast) would come to eat us. It seems that all Africans fighting for independence ate their children in the eyes of the Europeans in Kenya.[1] The people in Samburu District are always hungry in their harsh and inhospitable country and when they heard this many of them decided to stay around in the three dry hills waiting for us to escape.

A small committee had already been established among the first group of detainees under the leadership of Gad Kamau Gathumbi, a Kiambu man who had a shop in Nakuru, and Samuel Kiburi, a former police officer from Embu District. (Gad is now a trader at Limuru and a strong KANU leader in the area.) A few rules had been made by the committee and anyone who broke one of them was automatically fined a ram (*ndurume*) which he had to buy from the Turkana and which was then eaten by all the other detainees. Fighting in the compound was forbidden as was using insulting words to another detainee. Orders issued by the committee for cleaning the camp must be obeyed and anyone asked to help carry food from the store must comply. Finally, no one was allowed to interfere with Wanjiku,

---

[1] This is a reference to Kenneth Kaunda's *Zambia Shall Be Free*, where he says, 'Villagers had been told that these Zambia men were cannibals. They especially liked children since these provided tender meat.'

who was the only female detainee in the camp. She was in a difficult position, especially as many of those desiring her falsely promised they would marry her when they were released. The committee were remarkably successful in protecting her although a man called Thuo who went too far had to pay a ram. We arranged ourselves to partition off a separate place for her in the biggest tent so that she should not have to sleep in the same place as the men.

The rations were excellent. We received six ounces of rice, one pound of maize meal, half a pound of vegetables, half a pound of beans, ten ounces of potatoes and two ounces of sugar a day and every week two and a half pounds of meat and three and a half ounces of tea. The medical treatment was poor. A half-trained Turkana dresser was attached to the camp. He knew how to prescribe some simple medicines like mist. Kaolin, mist. culminative, and mist. soda sal., but that was all. Fortunately among the detainees there was a fully qualified hospital assistant called Timothy Mwangi from Fort Hall and under his instructions we arranged to buy for our own use in the compound supplies of any medicines needed from Baragoi. Timothy was taken back into the Medical Department after his release and has been working as a hospital assistant in his own district.

Kowop was the most pleasant of all the camps in which I was detained. Those of us who still had money found we lacked nothing, including the essential cigarettes and snuff. One of the police constables attached to the camp, a Luo called Joram, had been a great friend of mine in Nakuru. He was most upset at my detention and losing my business, and arranged for two newspapers, the *East African Standard* and *Baraza*, to be sent to the camp for me under his name. One of my jobs was to translate these into Kikuyu for the other detainees. Although the government could not compel us to work, we were kept busy by the committee. Apart from running a course in English for Gad and a few of the others, I was also appointed the writer of official letters of complaint.

When I first reached Kowop the officer in charge was a European from the Kenya Police Reserve who was lame and so was given the Kikuyu nickname of 'Gathua'. He was a good and quiet man who spent most of his time in his house or his office. He did not like visiting us in the compounds. He never punished anyone nor did he quarrel with any of us. He was later shot by another European at Thomson's Falls in a drunken brawl and we were all very sad to hear this. Gathua had a Kenya-born European assistant who was not a good man and used to sleep with the Tukana women.

One day we refused to eat some meat which had gone bad and this European assistant was frightened there might be a disturbance. He therefore informed the Thomson's Falls police and the next morning an assistant superintendent came out to see us. He was a hard man and spoke very toughly. He said that if we went on refusing to eat the meat we would be facing very bad trouble as sure as his name was Derby. He was frightened of nobody and nothing and he had been fighting and killing the 'Mau Mau' for a long time. We were only a little thing. He then called out Gad Kamau Gathumbi and told him to shave his beard. If Gad refused or caused any more trouble he would take him out of the camp and shoot him. He said that we grew beards because each of us was pretending to be another Kenyatta. Well, Kenyatta and his beard were now facing a very great trouble in a jail somewhere else.

He may have been only threatening but some of the detainees who had known him in Thomson's Falls thought he might well shoot Gad. However, we remained absolutely silent and did not give him any answer as we thought his speech extremely stupid. The Camp Committee had ruled that Gad was our spokesman on these occasions and if he remained silent everyone else should. After Derby's departure Gathua came back and spoke to us. He said that were Derby to return to the camp and see us still with our beards, he would be in great trouble. He appealed to us to shave them off. As the last thing anyone wanted was to get Gathua into trouble we agreed to do so. We grew beards because they help to make someone appear a good politician and they enlarge one's personality before the public. At Kowop we all tried to grow beards and it was a sad day when they were taken off, especially for the old men. Secretly I was highly amused, especially as for some reason or another mine had refused to grow.

One day the committee decided that we should try to open amicable relations with the Turkana and the Samburu. Twice a week a lorry used to go out to collect firewood. So, filling our pockets with *posho*, tea and sugar, we gave them away to any Turkana we met. Slowly they began to trust us more and became friendly. They soon told us why they had been so reluctant to talk with us. The committee passed a regulation forbidding anyone to sleep with the Turkana women and girls and when their men heard about this they began to respect us. It was difficult to talk politics with them and it was best done in parables. We tried to show them that when the Africans ruled Kenya the backward tribes would get much more help than the British were giving them now.

I had one particular Turkana friend called Ashakala, who was a rich and clever man and had once been in the army. His Swahili was excellent. He had a wife and three grown-up daughters and I became virtually a member of the family. Whenever the lorry went out there was something on it for them from me, either a cloth or some rice or sugar. Eventually I decided that our relationship was so special that they should be given the names of my mother and sisters in accordance with the Kikuyu custom. So Ashakala's wife became Wanjiku and the three daughters Nyakio, Njoki and Wangui. They were overcome with happiness and pleasure and said that the new names seemed as a blessing to them. I took some photographs of them, which were confiscated at Manyani. On Christmas Day 1953 we organized some traditional Kikuyu dances in the camp and many Turkana came to see and enjoy them.

In December 1953 and January 1954 another 190 detainees were brought in relays to Kowop from Nyeri and Embu and 22 small green tents came to accommodate them. Halfway through the move Gathua and his assistant were transferred elsewhere and two new officers came. The senior man was, I think, called Sampson (E). He had been a member of the Metropolitan Police in London and was a humble and friendly man, wholly lacking in malice. As he did not know Swahili I used to interpret for him. His assistant was another Kenya-born European. He was a large man called Newbury and seemed slightly simple. His apparent lack of brains led to his getting the nickname *Marebe* (Empty Tins).

By the middle of January all the new detainees had arrived and one day, when Sampson was away, Newbury told us that it was the government's intention that they should dig the latrines which we had refused to dig because we were not convicted prisoners. We had now re-formed our committee to include representatives from the new intake and it consisted of Gad Gathumbi, Tiras Muchiri (from Kibutio, a village in South Tetu, Nyeri, and now a teacher and politician), Peterson Kariuki (who had been Chief of Location 14 in Fort Hall and is now a businessman), John Mwangi Gachuhi (formerly an African District Council clerk from Fort Hall, now a clerk with a business firm in Nairobi), John Kamonjo, Samuel Kiburi, and six other elders. This committee was unanimous that no one should agree to dig the latrines. I think Newbury had decided on this action off his own bat as Sampson would never have consented. We have a saying in Kikuyu, *Ndiri njego ndiringanaga na muthi mwega*, which is to say, 'A good pestle never has a good mortar', and certainly we never seemed to have two good officers at the same time.

Newbury had shovels, pickaxes and crowbars brought and ordered the new detainees to start work. Justus Kangethe Gachui, an old man who had been a teacher at Kagumo Secondary School, acted as the spokesman and said they were not going to work. Newbury kept them outside sitting in the burning sun all day until the return in the evening of Sampson, who was very angry with his assistant and ordered Justus and his group back into the camp, telling us that there was no law to compel them to work. He then employed some Turkana to dig the pits for wages. This was not the only time that we wondered at the difference between Europeans born in Kenya and those born in Europe: we began to think that some Kenya European parents must train their children to hate all Africans.

Sampson encouraged us to go hunting to supplement the meat ration and the lorry left for these expeditions loaded to capacity with policemen, Kikuyus and Turkanas. It was good sport and once we brought back the carcasses of two wildebeeste. The Turkana could run very fast and used to act as guides. On one occasion we went to Ashakala's house and joined in an unrestrained beer party, policemen, detainees and Turkana all together, and when we got back to the camp many of the group were drunk and behaved badly. As a result I proposed to the committee that they should proscribe beer-drinking. This was accepted by the elders and became a regulation . . .

Some other Kikuyu women had joined Wanjiku at Kowop and they now had their own tent. The committee tightened the regulations but found that many devices were being used to evade them, including nocturnal assignments in the bathroom. We therefore sent a deputation to the Commandant and explained to him that the present arrangements were not good and suggesting that he should have a separate place constructed for them outside the wire. This improved the situation although some men continued trying unsuccessfully to find ways and means of meeting them until one day all the women were transferred from Kowop to Kamiti Prison in Kiambu District near Nairobi, where we heard that Nyamathira, their leader, later died . . .

SAM MPASU: MALAWI

The Interrogation

When the large, metal door of Zomba Central Prison closed
with a bang behind me, I came face to face with the prison
warders. They seemed too busy to attend to me so I sat down
on a form. It seemed to me that good manners were out of
place.

'Sit down on the floor!' one of them shouted at me very
angrily. 'A prisoner does not sit on a chair!' he added.

It did not make sense to me that I should sit down on the
floor while there were unoccupied chairs in the office. Nevertheless, although dressed in a suit, I sat down on the floor. I was
simmering with rage at my humiliation and helplessness.

At last one of them took out a blank, red folder and started
to take down my personal details of name, village, date of birth,
next of kin and so forth. Then I was ordered to empty all my
pockets, take off my wrist-watch and wedding ring. I surrendered all to him. Then he demanded my tie, belt, shoes and
socks as well. He shoved all of these into a cloth bag which he
tossed into the corner of the office. He was through with me.

I was taken out of the administration block into the courtyard. We immediately turned right. The next block served as a
clinic on top but underneath were three cells. The prison warder
opened the middle cell and pushed me in. He closed the door
and bolted it from outside. It was a bare, empty cell. A few
minutes later, the door opened again. The guard tossed an old
threadbare blanket at me. I caught it with my hands before it
could fall on the floor. He looked at me with contempt as if I

From *Political Prisoner 3/75*, African Publishing Group, 1995.

was not worth speaking to. As far as he was concerned, I was probably less than human or an animal.

He walked away without saying a word. His colleague, who carried a gun, closed the door and then stood guard outside. He used a peep-hole to check on me regularly. I wondered if they would spare the life of that warder if by any chance I escaped. It seemed to me that they, too, were prisoners of a sort. They had to do what they were doing even if they hated it.

The thought of escape was utterly unrealistic. The walls were very thick. The door itself was thick and made of hardwood. There was a tiny window at the top but it was full of thick, steel bars. Besides, the window itself was so high that one would need a ladder to reach it. And it was on the same side where the guard stood. The ceiling was the concrete floor of the upper storey. There was no lighting. Digging the floor was impossible with bare hands. It was concrete.

My threadbare blanket was more than a blanket. It was a bed, a mattress, a bedsheet and a blanket, all rolled into one. It was the only thing between me and the bare concrete floor. I was so bewildered that I could not believe or understand what was happening to me. Luckily, the weather in January was fairly warm, but I dreaded what it was like in June when the temperatures dropped.

I spread the blanket on the bare floor. I lay down. I folded my jacket to use it as a pillow. I blinked wide awake for a good part of the night wondering what was happening to me. I was very worried about my wife and her delicate condition. I had not eaten anything the whole day yet they had locked me up for the night without giving me a glass of water or a morsel of food.

It was a long, long night. Morning broke in the end. I heard the sound of keys in the padlock and then the bolt being pulled back. The door was opened to check if I was still in. For some strange reason they kept the door open this time. Later on they allowed me to step outside if I wanted to, but not much farther than the doorstep. The armed guard was trying to be friendly as soon as he ensured that none of his colleagues was looking at him. I sat on the doorstep.

'Is it possible for me to go the toilet, wherever it is?' I asked him.

'Let's go. I will escort you,' he replied. 'But you must not speak with anyone.'

With his gun on the shoulder he came behind me. He stood by as I faced the urinal. The thought of walking barefoot in that busy toilet, which was hardly clean, filled me with fear about contracting all sorts of diseases.

On returning to my cell we found an old prisoner with a wizened, weather-beaten face and a head which was entirely covered with grey hair, waiting for me. He had brought me an old, badly dented, aluminium plate, half full of porridge. He looked at me with understanding. He shook his head in dismay.

'Eat!' he said. 'Prison food is nothing like home food, but that is the only way to stay alive here.'

'Where is the spoon and the sugar?' I asked him in all sincerity.

'Sugar and spoon, in prison?' he asked me, in total disbelief over my naivety.

He laughed a little. He then demonstrated how I could eat the porridge. Eating on a table while sitting on a chair was a luxury that was not available. I sat on the floor.

I lifted the plate on my lips with both hands. I sucked the porridge into my mouth a little at a time. He watched me excitedly as if he was watching a child who was beginning to walk. He displayed a big smile after I had finished.

'Do not be disheartened, this is what men must sometimes go through in life,' he told me encouragingly.

'Why am I not allowed to speak to you or to anyone?' I asked.

'That is nonsense. Do not bother about them,' he said nonchalantly. 'They are trying to intimidate you.'

I was really glad to have someone to talk to. At least someone who was not afraid of the arbitrary rules. Apparently, they had appointed him to look after me as a way of preventing me from meeting the other prisoners. He brought me food from the kitchen every day and took back the plate. They did not want me to move away from my cell.

'What are you in prison for?' I asked him.

'Theft,' he said quite happily, as if theft was something to be proud of.

'How long have you been here and when are you getting released?' I asked him again.

He laughed a bellyful.

'You see,' he said, 'they built this prison in 1938 and that was the first time I came in. I built it. I have been here ever since.'

This was 1975. I could not believe that the man had been in this horrible place for 37 years.

'Are you here for murder perhaps?' I asked him.

'No, no. The only crime I know is theft,' he replied honestly.

'You see, when they first locked me up, I was young. After my sentence I went home but I felt out of place. I had no family and no friends. They all felt ashamed of me. They kept away from me. So I stole again in order to come back. This is my home now. I will die here. Whenever my sentence is over, I reserve my place in the cell. I get back the same day. All I do is pick somebody's pocket at the bus station in full view of a policeman. Sometimes I just snatch a banana from a baby's hand and if it cries then that is it; I run a little to allow the people to catch me. When they take me to the police station, I know I am back in prison. The only regret I have is that such small thefts do not get me many years of imprisonment,' he said with a straight face.

I could not believe what this old man was saying. One day in that place was too long for me. Yet he wanted to spend the rest of his life there.

'When they let you out, why don't you get a job?' I asked him.

'And look after myself?' he asked me as an answer. Then he laughed. 'I tried that one but got bored with waiting for my payday. I stole my employer's wrist-watch in order to come back here.'

'Don't you feel like having a wife and children? Having a family you can really be proud of?' I asked him.

'What can I give to a family?' he replied.

I got the impression that life had no real meaning to the man. His permanent stay in prison was all that life meant to him.

He disappeared at two o'clock in the afternoon and brought me a plate of badly cooked *nsima* and a metal mug half full of badly cooked pigeon peas. That was both my lunch and dinner. The food was very unpalatable, but he encouraged me to eat it in order to preserve my life. At four o'clock in the afternoon I was ordered back into my cell. The door was bolted from outside and locked.

When they opened my cell again in the morning I was surprised to see a white man sitting on the doorstep of the next cell. He, too, was completely bewildered. I gathered a little bit of courage to defy the orders. I greeted the white man in the presence of the prison guard. We got talking. The guard ignored us. The only thing the white man could not stomach was the terrible food. He refused to touch it. He told them that he was prepared to die from starvation. They buckled down and brought him half a loaf of bread and a small can of sardines. His problem was how to eat that bounty without the aid of a table knife, a fork or a spoon. But he soon overcame that by using his unwashed fingers.

Apparently his crime was that he made some remarks about the political situation in the country when one of his employees was picked up by the Special Branch. Without checking out the veracity of the allegation, he was pulled out of his car and rushed to Zomba prison in a police car. That was his arrest, trial, conviction and sentence. That morning he was making a great deal of fuss about the need to see his ambassador urgently. He was a South African and general manager of a company in Blantyre. In the afternoon his ambassador, accompanied by his wife, arrived to see him. Later in the evening the police came to take him out. I learnt that he was deported out of the country on 24 hours notice.

On Friday morning, I was on my way to the common toilet when a sick man called my name out from the balcony of the upper storey which served as a clinic.

'Hey Sam, it's me, Richard. Richard Sembereka!'

The name did not fit the appearance of the man. I was horrified with what I saw. I had known Richard Sembereka for many years. The last time I had seen him he was the Minister of Labour, a plump and well-dressed man. That was several years before but here was a pathetic-looking skeleton of a man, completely disfigured and destroyed by his long imprisonment. My eyes welled up with tears as I desperately tried to take in the entire picture. The unanswered question I asked myself in my mind was, if this cruel and beastly government could do that to its own cabinet minister, then how much more would it do to me, a humble civil servant.

According to the story which circulated at the time Mr Richard Sembereka disappeared, he had been driving in his ministerial black Mercedes Benz car from Zomba to Blantyre, with the pennant flying on the bonnet, when the police stopped the car at a road-block. Without much ceremony the police pulled him out of the ministerial car and shoved him into a waiting police vehicle. He was then driven straight to Zomba prison for his long, indefinite imprisonment without charge or trial. Five or so years on, he had been reduced to this pathetic skeleton in front of my eyes. I think he saw the distress in my eyes and read my mind.

'Steel yourself up,' he said, 'it is a very tough world!'

I waved my hand feebly at him, but the prison guard pushed me on. We continued to the public toilet.

On return from the toilet, I was called out to the administration block. Charles Ngwata had come for me. I was led out of the prison to a waiting small van. I was told to go into the back of that van. He closed the door from outside and turned to join the driver in the cab. There were no seats in the van. I sat on the floor.

On arrival at Zomba Police Headquarters, I was led to the Special Branch offices which were in a two-storey block on its own. We climbed the stairs to the upper storey where the office of Focus Gwede was. He was not in. I was made to wait in an adjoining office. What I immediately noticed was the atmosphere of fear and trepidation which pervaded the whole place. The policemen could not even mention the name of Focus Gwede but referred to him reverently as 'Bwana'. He was obviously something of a small god around there. On the grass lawn outside sat small groups of men, women and children, waiting fearfully for this small god to give them permits to visit their relatives in Zomba and Mikuyu prisons.

Focus Gwede was Deputy Head of the Special Branch at the time but he behaved very much as if he owned the place entirely. His close association with Albert Muwalo, who was both the Secretary General and Administrative Secretary of the Malawi Congress Party, ensured that he wielded a lot of power. Mr

Muwalo was virtually Home Affairs Minister, although none of that was reflected in his job title. Pretty soon, the Head of the Special Branch, Mr Kumpukwe, was appointed into the diplomatic service and posted to Britain. Focus Gwede then formally took over as Head of the Special Branch.

A poor messenger was getting out of Gwede's office where he had gone to leave files. He was spotted by none other than Gwede himself. Gwede came up the stairs seething and trembling with rage. He went straight for the messenger. Gwede repeatedly and threateningly jabbed his right-hand forefinger on the messenger's chest.

'You do not enter my office when I am not there! Do you understand?' shouted Gwede repeatedly in his rage.

'Yes, sir! No, sir! I am sorry, sir! I will not do it again, sir!' whined the poor messenger subserviently.

He was expecting the whole world to explode in his face any moment.

I watched the whole incident with disgust. I do not know if the incident was stage-managed by Gwede for effect on me and the others. If it was, then it certainly lowered my opinion of Gwede in my mind. I had known Gwede before for some years. I had never known him or even imagined him to be such a mean-spirited terror. If a messenger in full police uniform could not enter Gwede's office, then why on earth was the office left open and why didn't Gwede clean his own office?

Anyway, Gwede cooled down. The poor messenger gratefully walked away, thankful that his explanations and apologies had been accepted. The fact that he had been humiliated in public counted for nothing. I could not understand why he did not stand up for his own human dignity and tell Gwede to piss off. Maybe the job meant much to him or maybe he could have been locked up summarily as well.

It was my turn. Gwede sat me on a chair in his office, opposite

his. Between us was his large wooden desk. The desk was totally
bare except for an old tape recorder and a horse-whip. Charles
Ngwata sat on another chair but on Gwede's side.

'Yes, my friend! Why are you here?' Gwede asked me.

'You called for me,' I replied.

He then pulled out the drawer of the desk and laid a sheaf of
blank paper on the desk. He pulled out another drawer, pulled
out a revolver for me to see and then put it back. From his
jacket he pulled out a BIC pen and got himself ready to write.

'Who appointed you to go into the diplomatic service?' he
bellowed at me.

'You should know!' I said to him.

'I am asking you!' he retorted angrily.

'Listen,' I said, 'I never applied for the job. Nobody applies
for that kind of job. I was just told that the President had
appointed me to go into the diplomatic service. How the hell
would I know who had recommended my name?'

Gwede tore up whatever he had been writing and tossed the
pieces of paper into a waste-paper basket by his side.

'All right, let us start again,' he said getting another blank
sheet of paper ready.

'Who did you meet while you were in the diplomatic service?'
he asked.

I really thought it was an asinine question.

'You meet and see thousands of people every day. And you
ask me who I met in a period of over two years?' I replied.

'OK, did you meet any of the rebels?' he asked me.

'Look,' I said, 'even if I met any of them now, I could not
recognize them. I saw both Mr Kanyama Chiume and Mr Henry
Chipembere, here on Malawi soil, when I was a young boy in
secondary school and they were cabinet ministers.'

'We know that. If you had met any of them we would have
known immediately,' replied Gwede boastfully.

'So, why did you ask me?' I said angrily as I stood up.

I leaned on his desk with my left hand and attempted to reach out for his shirt-collar with my right hand. Gun or no gun, I was going to punch his face. He drew back out of my reach.

'All right, let us start again,' he said when he realized that my temper was not as long as he thought it was. 'Sit down. Do you want a cup of coffee?' he asked.

'I do not want your coffee!' I replied as I sat down.

He tore up the piece of paper he had been scribbling on and threw the bits into the waste-paper basket again.

'You came back from the diplomatic service over a year ago. Why were you still using a diplomatic passport? We found a diplomatic passport in your house!' he started again.

'Every time I go out of the country or come in, I pass through the Immigration. Are you suggesting that the immigration officers of Malawi do not recognize a Malawi diplomatic passport?' I asked him.

'Answer the question!' he demanded.

'For your information, I went to the Immigration Office immediately after my return from the diplomatic service. I gave them my diplomatic passport and asked for my ordinary passport, but they refused. They said that I should hang on to my diplomatic passport because they are wasting a lot of money. They exchange an ordinary passport for a diplomatic passport and a few months later the same person is appointed into the diplomatic service again. Ask them! Ring them now!' I said to him.

Gwede tore up the sheet he had been writing on and threw the pieces into the waste-paper basket.

'All right, let us begin again,' he said. 'You wrote a book about the President. You said that he has no friends.'

'Have you read the book?' I asked him.

'Answer me!' he demanded.

'*Nobody's Friend* is the title of the small novel I wrote. It has absolutely nothing to do with Dr Banda or anyone else. It is a book about ordinary people. It is fiction. You should have read it,' I told him.

'But there is a passage about a president being assassinated in that book,' he said triumphantly.

'That is rubbish!' I said. 'Have you read *Hamlet*, *Macbeth* or *King Lear*, all by William Shakespeare? There are passages in all those books about kings being assassinated. Have you banned those books because they mention the assassination of kings? Have you banned the Holy Bible because it mentions that Jesus was killed?'

'Let us begin again,' Gwede said as he tore up the sheet of paper he had been writing on. He threw the pieces into the waste-paper basket. This time he did not bother to write again.

'Listen to me, my friend! You are finished, finished, finished! I am the last word on detention in Malawi. No one else is above me. As you sit there I have three options for you. Firstly, I can release you now. Yes, you can go home to your wife and back to your job. Secondly, I can take you to court for trial where you will get many years of imprisonment. Lastly, I can send you to Mikuyu Maximum Security Prison, without trial, where you will count the hair on your head. You will never come out. I have decided to send you to Mikuyu where others like you are rotting,' he said chillingly. 'As long as I sit on this chair, you will never come out. You will rot there!'

He said all this emphatically as he banged the top of his desk with his right-hand fist. I looked at him very defiantly.

'Gwede,' I said, 'last year, you were not sitting on that chair. Next year, you do not know if you will still be sitting on that chair. Only the Almighty God knows. If God has made it for me to live the rest of my life and die in Mikuyu Prison, so be it. It is not you who has done it. You are just an instrument used by God. But I assure you that if God has not made it for me to die in Mikuyu, I shall come out alive and well. And much earlier than you think.'

What I said unnerved him a bit. He had played his last card. He had failed to reduce me to a cowering, tearful coward, crying for mercy at his feet. The degree of my defiance shook his self-confidence thoroughly.

'You go for lunch. We shall meet again this afternoon,' he said to me as he terminated the interrogation.

Charles Ngwata took me outside. Gwede closed the door of his office. A police constable gave me a plate of rice and red beans. What was strange was that they gave me a spoon as well. That was on Friday, 25 January 1975. My interrogation had taken Gwede's entire morning.

YVES-EMMANUEL DOGBE: TOGO

The Prisoner

The Renault 12 sped through the gate to the military camp. I was led like a calf to the slaughter across the terrace to the General's quarters. There already waiting were the few ministers, hastily assembled on the General's orders, who were to pass judgement on me in an *ad hoc* High Court of the Supreme Command.

A few soldiers were posted outside . . . Some watched me pass with that disdainful air of contained aggression reserved by the military for those considered 'trouble-makers'; but, I thought, I could also detect signs of pity in the controlled expression of the others which gave me some degree of comfort. It crossed my mind that these, at least, might hit me with a little less force and a little more consideration when the time came . . .

The Chief of Security took me in to the General. I found myself standing in front of the assembled ministers, all seated in comfortable armchairs: Education, Culture, Foreign Affairs, Health (this man was also head of the Gendarmerie) – all were there, together with the deputy Army Commander-in-Chief. This was the 'High Court' which was to decide my fate.

'Monsieur le Président,' I addressed the General as soon as I was brought in front of him. He said nothing, but gave me an odd look which revealed nothing of what he might be thinking. At that moment, the Minister of Culture stood up.

'Monsieur le Président de la Republique, this' – indicating me – 'is Professor Senam, and this' – showing the paper he was holding – 'is the document for which he is responsible.'

From *Index on Censorship*, 3/80.

'Did you write this?' enquired the General, looking me straight in the eyes.

'Yes, Monsieur le Président.'

'Make him read it out to us,' ordered the Minister of Culture, who himself held out the stapled typescript pages for me to read. My hands were trembling. I knew I was in deep trouble, but I told myself I had to go through with it to the bitter end, since they would tear me to pieces anyway. I took several deep breaths and began to read, half amused and half terrified . . .

'Demagogue!' shouted the General before I had got very far. The anger in his voice brought me out in a cold sweat. 'Demagogue! You'll go to prison for this, just you wait and see. You're nothing but an imperialist agent! There'll be a public confession for this!'

'There's more to come, Monsieur le Président,' piped up the Minister of Culture.

'Go on,' said the General.

And I began again, painfully.

But at the thought of his words – 'You'll go to prison for this' – I found myself unable to continue. If I was accused of being an 'agent of imperialism' by the General, that was worse: it might mean death. Weren't the party activists always crying 'death to imperialist agents'?

The General was disdainful: 'Take it away from him!'

The Minister of Culture took back the text in his outstretched hand, and began to read out the offending passages, working the General's surly anger up into a paroxysm of rage so as to complete my downfall.

> . . . The leading exponents of the idea of a Return to
> Authenticity are neither intellectuals nor poets, but
> political men drawn from a military background. We hear
> a great deal about 'safeguarding black civilization' and

'restoring our African cultural heritage' without any very clear idea of what these phrases 'culture' and 'civilization' mean.

'What!' the Deputy Chief of Staff exploded, when he heard that the politicians were neither poets nor intellectuals but military men. 'What's that he said?' He leapt at me and slapped me sharply round the face. 'We've seen enough intellectuals in this country. Where were you when they went around spreading disorder? That's why the Army had to step in to put things right!' he yelled. More slaps. I told myself not to play it tough. Once the Colonel ran out of steam, he would call in the young soldiers, who were just waiting for a chance to finish me off. I played safe and collapsed on the floor, as if reeling under the repeated blows.

The Chief of Security and his deputy, who had been waiting in a corner of the room, leapt forward and picked me up, negligently as if I were a bundle, and set me back on my feet.

'Don't hit him,' said the General.

But the Colonel gave me another couple of slaps for good measure before returning to his place. All the ministers' eyes were on me, as if glad that the military had found such an ideal scapegoat. Then each tried to outbid the next in heaping scorn on me, in the hope of impressing on the General how far they agreed with his judgement, at the same time trying to save their own skins. Yet all I had done was voice the unspoken sentiments of scores of intellectuals and civilian politicans throughout the country.

'It's unbelievable that you should have written anything like this,' rasped the Information Minister.

'Who told him to write it?' the General asked the Minister of Culture.

'No one. The professor was on the Steering Committee for

the Lagos Festival, and each member was supposed to write something on the theme "Black Civilization and Education". The two others opted out; only the professor went ahead and wrote his paper . . .'

'. . . because he knew just what he wanted to put in it,' insinuated the General.

'I admit I did see a draft text,' the Minister of Culture went on, 'and passed it – because at the time it didn't contain any of the incredible comments we've just heard in the present text.'

The Minister's remarks were riddled with inaccuracies which I might have picked up point by point in my defence, but something told me to hold back and not to point an accusing finger at anyone present if I wanted to save my skin. Besides, it wasn't worth trying to explain a scholarly discourse to these people, who were quite incapable of understanding it. Instead, I should try to play on their weaknesses, influence their feelings, and above all their inflated sense of their own importance.

'What made you write that?' asked the General.

'Let him speak and he will tell us,' said the second Colonel, who was Minister of Health and Director of the Gendarmerie.

'The text wasn't intended for anyone in this country,' I said, 'including its leaders, for whom I have a great deal of personal esteem and admiration. It was meant for black communities around the world who would be represented at Lagos. And it's a scholarly piece of work, based on the most recent research into African cultures. The essential arguments have already been published in my doctoral thesis.'

'What recent research are you talking about?' asked the Information Minister. I cited a number of specialist articles which had criticized the outdated attachment in some quarters to a certain idea of 'African culture', which had been disinterred from a supposedly glorious past.

'I don't believe you,' he shouted back in my face.

'You might have put it another way,' remarked the Foreign Affairs Minister, quite a cultivated man who gave me the impression that he was saying it because he had to say something I looked at him almost with gratitude and could find nothing to reply.

The General appeared impressed by what seemed to him a high level of intellectual debate. I am sure that if one of those ministers had had the courage to minimize the charges of subversion levelled against me, given the beating I had already received, I would have been set free.

'Come and sit here,' he said, indicating a vacant armchair next to my recent boss, the Minister of Education. 'Let's put all our cards on the table. Tell us the truth! Who told you to write something like that?'

I went over and sat back in the soft chair, already feeling somewhat reassured by his gesture, for if I was in for severe punishment it was hardly likely he would have asked me to sit down with them.

The General got up and went to fetch a plate of kebabs from a side table, and as he passed close to me, the Deputy Chief of Staff got up and stood behind me, as if he thought I was going to leap up and attack the General. He clapped his two hands with all his strength on each side of my head, making my ears ring. The noise in my head continued for several minutes, but luckily his blows were not quite simultaneous. Otherwise I might have been deaf for the rest of my days – or those days the General chose to leave me to enjoy.

'Don't hit him!' the General once again ordered the Colonel. Then turning to me: 'Was it your wife who told you to write like that? She's white, isn't she?'

'Yes, Monsieur le Président.'

'It must be his wife who dictated it,' added the Deputy Chief of Staff triumphantly.

The Minister of Culture had read out a passage in which I commented on the policy of rejecting 'imported names': that it was inconceivable that anyone should prevent you from using a name or giving it to your children because you liked it or because it represented something for you. I am every bit as much an African if I call myself Felix or Koffi, and neither the one nor the other will turn me into a saint if I am not. It is not new names which will make us worthwhile members of society, but the moral and intellectual effort of each citizen . . .

So the General asked me: 'What is your wife's name?'

'Anne.'

'And why isn't she called Adzo or Afi like our sisters?'

I was naïve enough to reply: 'Because she doesn't come from here.'

'Then why do you want our sisters, who don't come from her country, to have one of their names?' he countered, triumphing in his own logic.

'That's not what I was trying to say,' I said, hoping to get back to the subject.

The General and all his ministers pounced on this.

'Not what you wanted to say? But it's what you wrote!'

'All I meant was that I consider it a secondary consideration given all the problems facing Africa today.'

A few moments' silence.

'Speak,' I heard the order behind me.

'Monsieur le Président,' I said, 'I drafted this text without a second thought. In all my writing, all my books, I've always said exactly what I thought. I've a great deal of admiration for you – I'm just like your little brother. And I respect the members of your government.' I turned to the Minister of Education, in a visible attempt to seek the protection of my former patron, in whose house I had frequently been a welcome guest. But he didn't rise to the occasion.

'Monsieur le Président de la Republique,' he said, 'Professor Senam is a difficult customer. When he returned from France, I appointed him a professor at the University, but he found it hard to get on with his colleagues and I was obliged to transfer him to the Lycée at Tokoin, where he is now a supervisor. Isn't that right?'

'No, Minister. I'm a teacher at the Lycée now,' I replied, without attempting to correct the other false information he had just given in order to protect his career. The General was known to be impulsive.

'This document simply serves to confirm his colleagues' complaints about his bad character.'

After this irremediable condemnation by the Minister of Education, a heavy silence fell on the assembled ministers. They finished eating their kebabs and placed the skewers back on their plates – they had not stuck them into my flesh as I had at one point feared (such was the force of the horror stories I had heard about these sessions).

Their anger seemed to have dissipated. They didn't speak to each other and hardly dared to exchange glances. I watched the General, who appeared to be wondering what he was going to do with me.

I was the one who broke the silence. Looking back, I don't know how I dared. And perhaps it was a mistake . . .

'Monsieur le Président, I humbly beg your pardon.'

The ministers seemed to want to mock me. They would far rather I had played my protest role to the limit, even risking my life if that could have changed any part of the military discipline to which they were enslaved. They would rather see me killed, if that could spark off a popular uprising which might finish off the General and return power to civilian hands. They were disappointed I wasn't going to see it through to the end.

'Well then, we're going to put you in prison,' said the General after a moment. 'We're going to make enquiries. And if we're mistaken, then God will forgive us.'

Judgement was thus passed. I was to be kept in prison, though I didn't know for how long and was careful not to ask.

MAU MAU PATRIOTIC SONGS: KENYA

A Letter from Prison

When I was at home I had many friends,
But when I went to prison they all abandoned me.
That is why those who are not committed to the
  cause
Cannot be trusted at all.

We agreed that I would find them waiting for me,
What happened to make them deceive me?
They will realize that jail is not death
And I will surely return home.

My prison term will be over, dear mother,
I implore Ngai to return me home safely,
To see each other with our own eyes
So you can truly believe that I'm still alive,
And I shall die when Ngai wills!

When I am led to the quarry by the warders
Pick-axe on the shoulder,
Karai[1] on the head
The warders often pray that their jobs
Last for many more years to come,
But me, I pray: 'Return me home soon!'

The half-cooked *posho* we eat, dear mother,
Is wrapped in a dirty rag like a dead body,
But we dared not refuse it,

Translated by Maina wa Kīnyattī.
  [1] A metal basin used by prisoners to carry concrete.

Ngai is great,
We will surely return home.

If you glanced inside
Through the prison gates, dear mother,
You cannot find a European or an Asian –
Only us the children of the soil being tortured.

Our Leader, Dedan Kimathi

When our Kimathi ascended
Into the mountains alone
He asked for strength and courage
To decisively defeat the colonialists.

He said that we should tread
The paths that he had trodden,
That we should follow his revolutionary footsteps
And drink from his cup.

If you drink from the cup of courage,
That cup I have drunk from myself,
It is a cup of pain and of suffering,
A cup of tears and of death.

We are tortured because we are Black;
We are not white people
And we are not of their kind.
But with Ngai in us
We shall defeat the colonialists.

Do not be afraid of imprisonment
Nor should you lose heart for being detained.
Even when they confiscate our property

And kill us
Do not ever despair:
Because of our faith and commitment
We shall defeat the enemy.

You must take his courage and endurance
To courageously face tribulations or death,
Knowing that you will belong
To the Black people's state of Kenya.

KWAME SAFO-ADU: GHANA

It Is Darkest Before Dawn

Nsawam Medium Security Prison
15 January 1972

My dear A—

I am now the distinguished guest of the infamous Nsawam
Medium Security Prison of Ghana. I am here with a host of
Ghanaians, ex-cabinet ministers, members of Parliament, Progress Party functionaries and supporters – all of us to be kept
here, ostensibly for our protection, for an indefinite period at
the sole pleasure of the Armed Forces of Ghana. I only pray
they are not molesting and harassing you and those of you who
are outside. For myself, I feel somehow proud, insanely proud,
this particular evening for being here in Nsawam of all places,
for I know grey-haired J. B. Danquah, one of the greatest
African fighters for True Freedom, was also detained here and
died here.

I am writing this letter in a small cell I share with five other
detainees. As I rest on my back scribbling (for there is no table
in this bug-infested bunk), I can see, through the curling yellow
smoke of the smuggled Tusker cigarette, blurred passing pictures
of our yesterdays which have just vanished past. Our small
'colonial' residence on Cantonments Hill in Accra now seems
like an enchanted little kingdom, a fairy world.

Time passes so very slowly here. I cannot believe I have been
here for only three days. One minute ticks slowly into the next;
and the morning glides into the afternoon like a lazy snake

From *Quo Vadis Africa? Letters from Ghana Prison*, Vantage Press, 1972.

which coils up motionless, seemingly asleep until the chill of the evening rouses it into serpentine awareness. One can only sleep and dream in prison. And what a fantasy of dreams: Dreams of a wasted past and a seemingly murky future. Dreams of what one should have done and did not, dreams of what one would do if one had another chance. One thing, however, stands clear in this bewildering maze – how utterly futile and irrelevant are the great majority of military coups and countercoups in Africa's search for stability and democracy. Ghana is one of the worst victims of this form of instability: she has been caught in a vicious circle of convulsions of coups and countercoups, five so far in five years! Two successful, three abortive. And is Acheampong the last of the military adventurers? Why all this instability, one may ask?

The reason is quite simple. The harsh realities of post-independence have led to a general disenchantment in Ghana. Our achievements have not matched our aspirations and we are all too desperate and too ready to blame the other person for our poor performance. What is not easy for even the most sober-minded of us to accept is the unpleasant fact that we seem unable to fulfil in our generation those great expectations of Independence and so bridge in our lifetime the abysmal gap between backwardness and enlightenment, between poverty and prosperity.

You and I had hoped that, with Independence, Africa might have been able to do better than Europe after the collapse of Imperial Rome; for Africa has at least the advantage that she can learn from the experience of others. We are not proving any wiser notwithstanding the lessons of history. A post-decolonization period of instability and lawlessness seems to be a law of history.

Frantz Fanon in his classic, *The Wretched of the Earth*, shows how extensive and deep is the economic, cultural and psychological degradation caused by imperialism or colonialism on subject peoples. The degradation is fundamental, pervasive and malignant, and the healing process if not properly handled, I am afraid, will spread over several generations. The spontaneous and automatic political, social, cultural and moral recovery we had hoped for after gaining Independence from our colonial 'masters' seems an idle dream. The birth of the Great New Africa we dream of and hope for is going to be prolonged, difficult, perhaps bloody, labour even under the best conditions. Of course, we are incorrigible optimists, you and I; but I now realize that we should never lose sight of the formidable dangers ahead if we are to maintain our sanity and continue the heroic struggle. The old Africa will surely pass away. It will give way to the irresistible will-to-conquer in the fight for true freedom. A new Africa, new beyond whatever any of us may conceive, will surely be born out of our present travails. That is why none of us should ever give up the fight and let our hopes scatter to the winds.

Right now, however, Independence is fast becoming a very bad joke. Our youthful ambitions all seem now beyond realization. As I look into the future from the vantage point of my detention cell, my disillusioned gaze sees the immediate future of Africa as wave upon wave of upheavals and disorder, of outbursts of violence, of even some savagery. It is not easy to peer through the maze of the immediate future to the New Africa of our dreams – and the dreams of Kwegyir Aggrey, Mensah Sarbah, Casely-Hayford, J. B. Danquah – full of men and women, noble beyond compare, brave beyond words, men and women whom we had naively assumed Independence would somehow create, as if by some miracle, one great transfiguration of our continent. Meanwhile, almost all over Africa the more ruthless, the louder-mouthed, among us appear to be carrying the day. The majority just stand and watch silent and dazed.

Quo vadis, Africa? Now that Independence is here with us,

where do we go from here? Obviously we need a guide, a signpost, an idea. Yes, an idea like Boris Pasternak's, inspired yet concrete, an idea as clear to a child or an ignorant fool as lightning or a roll of thunder. An idea that will show a clear path along which Africa can safely journey into a better future. African Unity? And after Unity what? Unity for what? Or is African Unity an end in itself?

It will be easy to endure this present period of increasing nightmare, increasing instability and increasing poverty of ideas if we knew where we wanted to go.

There are over 2,000 prisoners crowded into this prison and the majority of them are youths under 25, all young men in the prime of life! And the majority of them are here for political reasons. There is, of course, a lot of talk in Addis Ababa and New York of the New Emergent Africa making great strides for freedom. Where in Africa is this new-found freedom? Africa's bright and boundless future is being straitjacketed and wrapped within the narrow confines of rigid ideologies, as in Tanzania and Guinea; and in the interest of corrupt tyranny as in Zaire and our own Ghana. In the process, unnecessary and senseless suffering is being inflicted upon thousands of ordinary, innocent and well-meaning Africans. And all that is supposed to be done in the supreme interest of the people.

The ordinary peoples of Africa are well known to you and me. Don't they live the drabbest of lives eking out a harsh existence from a very harsh environment, even in Independent Africa? In the supreme interest of the people indeed! As I lie now in my cell here, detained here by an army, most of whom are, like me, the sons of these same ordinary Africans in the bushes of Ghana, I wonder very much whether the soldier, my conqueror, and I, his captive, fully realize what we owe to these people, our people; whether these violent upheavals and jungle politics are what they need or want.

It is very late now. My wrist-watch was, of course, confiscated at the prison reception and so it is difficult to know what hour it is. I am writing this letter by the light of the pencil torchlight you smuggled to me. All is silent except for the distant songs and the haunting, throbbing sounds of the drums of Nsawam Village. Africa will always drum, sing and dance, for a wedding or for a funeral, for life, and for death. Perhaps this is how we have managed to survive.

When I consider what Africa has passed through – four centuries of slavery and about a century or so of colonialism – I become tolerant and even *thankful* for the new order, this Independent Africa. But how can I in all honesty be proud of 'modern' Africa on her own showing and record so far? For on her showing and record, modern Africa has more to her debit than the credit side. Her leaders, in many places, are fast proving as callous and as brutal and, perhaps, as rapacious as the colonial regimes or the slave merchants. Is this callous brutality teething problems, or boisterous 'signs of constructive energy and feverish creativity'? If it is the latter, what are we supposed to be creating? Another Europe, another America, another Soviet Union or an entirely New World? Have we seriously given the problem a thought at all?

I am not for one moment forgetting that with the great changes that are sweeping Africa, some innocent ones will suffer and perhaps even perish. Suffering and even death can be ennobling to a people if it is for a great cause. The suffering and killings that are taking place in *Independent* Africa are, I am afraid, quite senseless: Africa, like Hitlerite Europe, has become a cannibal gobbling up its own flesh and blood.

'Out of Africa always comes something new', some Ancient Roman historian is supposed to have said. What new thought, new institution is modern Africa offering the world? All through my youth I had dreamt and hoped that somehow, in our generation, the glorious beginning of the New Africa will dawn and that Africa, 'the question mark among the Continents', will at last yield us her secret. Africa must have a mission and a destiny and, in due course, she will assume her proper role despite this poor beginning and this false start. The greatest comfort is this: that at least we have weighed anchor and are adrift! But whither?

AGOSTINHO NETO: ANGOLA

two years away

Greetings – you say in yesterday's letter
when shall we see each other
soon or later
tell me love?

In the silence
are the talks we did not have
the kisses not exchanged
and the words we do not say
in censored letters

Against the dilemma of today
of being submissive or persecuted
are our days of sacrifice
and audacity
for the right
to live thinking to live acting
freely humanly

Between dreams and desire
    when shall we see each other
    late or early
    tell me love!
more justly even grows
the longing to be
with our peoples
today always and ever more
free free free

PIDE Prison in Oporto, February 1957

ALBIE SACHS: SOUTH AFRICA

Me Singing

So this is what prison is like. The quiet is complete and I am alone in my cell, the shock of the slammed door still echoing in my head. So this is what it's like. The floor is hard, fresh creamy paint shines on the walls and the windows are high – higher than my eyes can reach even if, as now, I stand on tiptoe. In the corner, partly partitioned off, is a toilet moulded in concrete with two wooden strips for the seat. The water in the pan is clean. A metal loop juts through a hole in the wall. That must be the chain. I put my finger through the loop and pull. It is the chain, which like a snake's tongue sticks out from the wall before sliding back into the hole. Water is disgorged and the room echoes with the surf of the refilling toilet. I pull the loop again. It flushes instantly: an excellent lavatory: my only source of music. I flush it once more. A wonderful mechanical contrivance. I reach yet again for the loop . . . no, don't be silly, I tell my arm, and I turn round to survey the rest of my domain. The walls are quite clean and antiseptic. On the floor is a mat woven of dried grass, yellow and long, with a pile of dirty grey blankets at one end. I lie full length on the mat. It is not too hard and a little longer than I. I sit up and decide to count the blankets. Should I stand while I count or should I sit on the mat? Standing and bending is tiring and I'm very tired. If the cat sat on the mat why shouldn't I? It's awkward sitting on the floor. There are six blankets. That's quite a lot really.

The cell is completely bare; no bed, no mattress, no bunk, no chair, no table. Hell, that's terrible. Not even a bunk. I gaze

From *The Jail Diary of Albie Sachs*, The Harvill Press Ltd, 1966.

round and round. The world, even this tiny alien world, looks peculiar from the floor. There is something else wrong with this room. It is not just the angle from which I see it that makes it look so strange. I have it now; it's not a room at all, it's an empty concrete cube with me, a human being, inside. Gravity keeps me to the floor, otherwise I would float around like a spaceman. That's what is wrong. There is no world outside. There is no outside that I am aware of. *I cannot see out of my cell.* The windows are too high. The walls are the outer limit of my environment. I jump up rapidly and then tell myself wryly, there's no hurry, no hurry. Ninety days is a long time. And then another ninety days, and another, and another . . . no hurry. I slowly work out the dimensions of my new abode. Heel, toe – my shoe is exactly a foot long – heel, toe, heel, toe. First this way, twelve feet, then that way, ten and half feet. I'm walking around quickly now, feeling the walls, sliding my palms across the shiny surface, pressing and prodding for weak spots. I stretch up to the metal grid over the window and tug. Then, bending down, I scratch with my finger at the floor, first in one corner, then another. I walk to the toilet, and fancy my body gliding down its bowl and out. I must get out. I'll dig a tunnel. I'll hit the guards over the head and grab the keys. My friends will come and blast a hole in the wall. They'll catch the police by surprise, and I'll duck in the opposite corner so the blast won't hit me, and then I'll leap through the hole . . .

Don't be silly you know you can't escape, I tell myself. Better unpack your stuff and start making yourself at home. I become conscious of a rational brain operating, speaking silently inside my skull. I unzip the small canvas bag containing my belongings, which I unpack and spread out on the floor: sand-shoes, a towel, pyjamas, a bag of toiletry, a change of clothing, and a jersey: my belongings, almost my companions. I take off my suit and hang the jacket and trousers on large metal nuts protruding from the frame of the window grid. The trouser legs dangle like two men suspended from the same noose, but the cell looks less arid now. I hang the towel from another nut. It is a beach towel, its bright checks as colourful and stimulating as a scene through a window, something on which my eyes can rest during their frantic journey round the walls. I take off my white shirt and place it over the trousers. My coming-in shirt, it will be my going-out shirt, whenever that might be, and to wherever that might be. Now, let's see, if I pile up the blankets like this then I don't have to sit right on the floor. That's better. The room looks a little more cheerful now. I wish they hadn't taken away my watch – I wonder what the time is? There's no sunlight in the place at all, though it's not too dark.

Why did it seem so quiet at first? A train rattles past and I hear the faint din of heavy motor traffic some distance away. It is a voiceless world though. The police have disappeared through a series of gates which, like so many valves, open and close and lead to the charge office in the front portion of the building. Above the noise of the traffic I hear a different sound coming from a long way off – the chimes of a church clock striking. It is the three-quarter hour. Oh wonderful, if I listen carefully I can keep track of the time. They can stick my bloody watch. Stripped of access to timepieces, shut off from the sun and deprived of the work periods of a normal life, I will listen for the chimes ringing out over the rooftops, just as the medieval citizenry kept an ear open for their giant communal town clocks.

I walk round the cell again, thrilled by the great new sound; stopping at the toilet, I pull the snake's tongue out of the wall and feel excitement as the water bubbles into the bowl before surging out down its depths.

I clap my hands to see if there is any echo. There can't be anything wrong with clapping my hands, they can't punish me for that. After a short wait I purse my lips and blow air through them in a faint tentative whistle. Nothing happens. No one comes to tell me to be quiet. I whistle louder and louder still, and I stride up to the massive, handleless steel door, and whistle at it furiously, sharp, stentorian notes from Beethoven's Fifth. This is music, the 'V for Victory' theme from the war. You policemen out there, I'm not scared if you hear me, you don't even know what I'm whistling. Now I'm sitting down again, staring once more at the walls, trying to integrate the parts of the cell, to see it as a whole. What a dismal place, how cruel of men to shut other men up in such a tomb, not even a bed, or a bunk. If they treat me, a white man and an advocate, like this, how terrible it must be for the Africans. The walls are so smooth and monotonous, there is nothing on which to focus. God, how lousy it is. I feel so peculiar. I thought I would be able to take it better than I am doing. I never realized it would be this bad. I must stick it out. I wonder who else is locked up in these cells. Hell, surely I'm not going to break down.

I have an idea. I am going to break the smoothness of the walls. I will imprint something of myself and at the same time secure my memory on that sterile surface. The toilet bag contains the necessary instrument. They've kept my razor but left me a tube of shaving cream. The tube's back edge is sharp and firm, and it scratches well into the paintwork. I choose a spot on the wall near the door, so that when they come in they won't be able to see it. Slowly I mark out a map: a sketch of the police station in which I am lodged, based on intensive visual observation on my part as I was moved from one section to another. Most important is to mark the entrance, the main road, the position of the centre of the town, and the mountain. Now working inwards I scratch the charge office, the passage, the gates, the yard, and finally my cell. This should help me locate myself; I will be somewhere not just in a concrete cube; and who knows, it may turn out to be useful for me to have a sketch of the building in which I am shut. It is Tuesday, 1st October. I scratch the figure 1, stroke 10, stroke 1963. The marks are faint but clear enough for me to find again, although a visitor would not notice them. Then a special stroke for the first day. I will keep track of the days. Oh why didn't the previous inhabitants scratch something on the walls and impart something of themselves to this desert spot. In another corner I scratch my initials. They won't be able to prove that it was I who drew the map, for my initials are far away. Any successors of mine in the cell will know I've been there, for whoever lives in a cell soon trains his eyes to pick up any traces of previous occupancy. I'm not the first to have been in the cell and many will follow me. The chain of political prisoners extends far back in time and will go on well into the future.

I am back on the mat. I feel very sleepy, but decide not to close my eyes for fear that to sleep now in the afternoon will make it more difficult for me to sleep tonight. I long for tonight, for darkness and for sleep. Just as one gets instant coffee and instant vegetables, so sleep is instant time; a whole night compressed into a closing of eyes and an opening of eyes. Night will also be a marker, denoting the passage of time. After tonight I will have been in solitary confinement for a whole day. I wonder though, how well I will sleep. I never sleep well the first night in a strange place, even in the best of circumstances. It will be dreadful if I can't sleep. Anyhow, no use worrying about that now. The thing to do is to stay awake so that I'll be utterly exhausted when night comes. Let's see, what can I do next?

I stand up and clear my throat. I cough a few times a little more boldly. Then I hear my voice, humming at first and slowly sounding out snatches of song. This is my voice; I am singing. It's true that things are harder than I thought they would be. I didn't imagine that isolation could be so complete and so punishing. Yet if there is anyone out there also a prisoner, listen this is me singing, I've come to join you, and I'm going to be here a long, long time, because I'm not going to break down, whatever happens. I'm not going to give in. I must see it through.

DENNIS BRUTUS: SOUTH AFRICA

On the Island[1]

1

Cement-grey floors and walls
cement-grey days
cement-grey time
and a grey susurration
as of seas breaking
winds blowing
and rains drizzling

A barred existence
so that one did not need to look
at doors or windows
to know that they were sundered by bars
and one locked in a grey gelid stream
of unmoving time.

2

When the rain came
it came in a quick moving squall
moving across the island
murmuring from afar
then drumming on the roof
then marching fading away.

And sometimes one mistook
the weary tramp of feet
as the men came shuffling from the quarry

---

[1] Written in 1964 when Dennis Brutus was a political prisoner on Robben Island. [Ed.]

white-dust-filmed and shambling
for the rain
that came and drummed and marched away.

3
It was not quite envy
nor impatience
nor irritation
but a mixture of feelings
one felt
for the aloof deep-green dreaming firs
that poised in the island air
withdrawn, composed and still.

4
On Saturday afternoons we were embalmed in
     time
like specimen moths pressed under glass;
we were immobile in the sunlit afternoon
waiting;
Visiting time:
until suddenly like a book snapped shut
all possibilities vanished as zero hour passed
and we knew another week would have to pass.

JOSÉ CRAVEIRINHA: MOZAMBIQUE

Black Protest

I am coal!
And you uproot me brutally from the earth
And make me your mine
Boss!

I am coal!
And you set me on fire, boss
To serve you eternally as a source of energy
But not eternally
Boss!

I am coal!
And yes, it is my nature to become heat
And burn your world of exploitation
Burn until I become cinders of malediction
Burn with live heat like tar, my Brother
Until I am no longer your mine
Boss!

I am coal!
It is my nature to become heat
And burn everything with the fire from my
    combustion.

Yes!
I will be your coal
Boss!

Translated from the Portuguese by Don Burness.

AHMED FOUAD NEGM: EGYPT

Prisoner's File

Name:	Sabr.[1]
Charge:	That I am Egyptian
Age:	The most modern age; (though grey hair in braids flows from my head down to my waist).
Profession:	Heir, of my ancestors and of time, to the creation of civilization and life-force and peace.
Skin:	Wheat-coloured.
Figure:	As slim as a lance.
Hair:	Rougher than dried clover.
Colour of eyes:	Jet black.
Nose:	Aquiline like a horse's.
Mouth:	Firmly in place (when I attempted to budge it, some mischief happened).
Place of birth:	In any dark room under the sky, on the soil of Egypt. From any house in the middle of palm trees, where the Nile flows – as long as it is not a palace.

Translated from the Arabic by Janet Stevens and Moussa Saker.

[1] Sabr is a common Arabic name which means 'patience'.

AHMED FOUAD NEGM

Verdict:

For seven thousand years
I have been a prisoner asleep,
grinding stones with my molars,
out of frustration,
spending the nights in grief.

*The question of
release*:

Someone asked me:
'Why is your imprisonment so long?'
'Because I am a peaceful and humorous man.
I did not break the law,
because I am afraid of it;
the law holds a sword in its hands.
anytime you want –
ask the informers about me
and you will hear and understand
my story from A to Z.
My name is Sabr,
Ayyub,[2] patient with catastrophes,
like a donkey,
I carry my share of the burden
and wait.
I drown in rivers of sweat
all day long.
At night I gather my troubles
and upon them I lie,
do you know why?'

---

[2] Ayyub is a personality in Arab folk literature known for his unending patience.

WOLE SOYINKA: NIGERIA

The Man Died

The groans of anguish began just after supper time. They came from the direction of that wall which faces the entrance to my cell. The wall has two flood-holes in it, both covered by iron grilles. The mesh is large enough to permit a cat to pass through. From bits of fur which are left clinging to it, I know always when he has used the passage in the night. Then he darts across the intervening space so bare and full of danger, vanishes behind the hut, looking for scrap. A gutter runs through my domain just behind the hut. It links the yard of lunatics across the crypt to the compound for women. The gutter is the subterranean link of all the catacombs of Hades.

Now there is a smell of death in the air. I cannot mistake it. So I must think only of living things, shut out the stench in my nose, the supplication of skeletal hands on my impotence.

We had a birth here some weeks ago. I heard a baby's cries and wondered how this could be. A baby in this hell? And it was evening, nearly the same time as the present intrusive groans began. It could hardly be a wife visiting her prisoner husband with a new-born child.

Is it not strange? I had heard the women's voices before but thought that they were children's. Several months passed before I knew that my crypt was placed between the yard of lunatics and that of women! Their voices are so thin, as if piped through a crevice in a distant cavern. They play childish games in the evenings – from the sound and the giggle they must be the kind of games children play. And those tunes which I had imagined

From *The Man Died*, Rex Collings, 1972.

came from without the prison? On a very quiet evening I even made out some words:

> Brother Johnny
> Brother Johnny
> Do you sleep?
> Do you sleep?
> Wedding bells are ringing
> Wedding bells are ringing
> Ding dong ding

They sang in that listless, unmeaningful tone in which our schoolchildren sing foreign songs – *The Bluebells of Scotland*, *Ash Grove*, *The Lass with Her Delicate Air* – which are forced upon the curriculum by unimaginative missionaries. The words are delivered flat even when such songs are accompanied by games. The words hold no meaning for them, the territory and sentiments are strange, and so this anaemic rendering is all that the misguided music mistress can obtain from them. It must be remembered quality which made me imagine for so long that the voices which I heard at song and play came from children playing in the outer world under the mango trees. That world lies beyond Amber Wall; the sun rises just behind it.

A road runs along Amber Wall, not a busy one by the sounds. Or perhaps it is simply that it runs so far from the wall that the sound of vehicles seems muted. A certain amount of distortion does take place especially in direction. What is certain is that there is a wide swathe between the wall and the road and this space is occupied by a grove of mangoes whose tops are visible. I watch the buds appear, the efflorescence and the first green teardrops on the branches. Fat swarms of bluebottles follow human marauders at the first sign of ripening as all objects in the broad catalogue of missiles hurtle towards the fruits. They land often in the Crypt and I hear the guard swear and throw some back. I do not mind. Even the danger of being brained by a chance missile in the mango season becomes a spice of ecstatic possibility that livens up the tedium. A painful crack on the head is a token of life, of vitality. No, I do not think I would have minded at all.

I look up one morning – my early morning stroll just after opening hour – and there, right on the topmost branch, a territory hardly capable, I had always thought, of supporting more than the weight of the fruits, perched a little boy reaching for the topmost mangoes. His head was higher than the crown of the trees itself; he swayed gently with the motion of the branch. I was certain that there was just that last bunch of mangoes on the tree. Often the crown of the tree would move, violently shaken by one or more marauders on the lower branches but no one had dared climb this far before. His hand was on the goal when he looked down and encountered my gaze. He paused We stared at each other. I smiled but his response was one of complete bewilderment. Then he took his gaze away and looked over to the other side. I saw his alert mind racing and questioning for he was now looking over into the teeming compound next to mine. The sun rose slowly behind him, too brilliant for me to sustain my gaze. I continued my stroll round the hut. When I came back he was back to staring into the Crypt. When I came round again he was gone, and the mangoes with him.

When I heard treble voices later that evening, I imagined him among others of his age, playing games in the moonlight. For the first time it conjured up, try as I would to repress them, childhood memories, a parsonage filled with children. I made a final effort and I shut down that scene, violently. In its place came the smell of flowers, a sunrise, the trill of a guitar, the wistful pagan ending of Cocteau's *Orphée Nègre*, the dance of spring by the two children, heirs to the evocative magic of sunrise, of seed awakening in the soil beneath their tread of innocence . . .

For unto us a child is born . . . It was the cry of a newborn, that child's. It contained the distressing urgency that made up all its new world, a single-minded thrust of all the intensity of its tiny body. I heard a mother's crooning and I was certain. Another female voice, querulous and petulant joined in and the scene became almost human – the voice of the common mother in all our women offering anxious advice, taking the side of the child. But the voices remained muffled, the women unreal. They were not beings of the sun, not like the throbbing mangoes up against the sunrise. Ghosts, sheer weightless ghosts drifting in caverns of mists. Within their nether world the child is a full-throated freak, a changeling. I reflect now, somewhat sadly that the birth has come in the wrong season – it ought to be Spring. Still, if it is a girl we can ignore the timing and name her Persephone.

Still no solace at the Wailing Wall and close to midnight. I shut my mind to the other sounds that began some two hours ago, sounds that were soon bullied into silence. The other inmates, companions to the groaning man had set up a cry for help. I heard hysterical voices screaming Warder! WARDER!!! It went unheeded for nearly 30 minutes. Then it was augmented by banging – doors, windows, buckets. At least 30 voices were now screaming for help. And steadily below it all, in an unchanging tone and pace as if his pain had sublimated itself into this last automated sound, the groan persisted. I heard the sound of running boots, several. Heard the clang of iron as gates were swung open, heard the threats, the shouts. Heard the determined response of demands. Accusation. Heard these shouted down. One long tread of authority approaching the bed of the ailing man. I heard him bend down and make an examination that told him nothing. Heard the steps return. A babble of excited voices meant that he was leaving without saying what would be done. If anything would be done. I think I made out the repeated word – doctor. He shouted it down flatly, angrily. The doors clanged to, the locks snapped their finality, the boots walked away. The murmurs of retreating guards were the protests of wronged men, of men whose leisure had been needlessly broken.

The groans do not cease nor do they diminish. The bloodless inhuman steadiness of this sound of human suffering is the most unnerving aspect of it all. It does not come from volition but from the weak inertia of a muted pulse. As if the man has merely left his mouth open and the sound emerges with his breathing out.

It is close to dawn when the sound stops. Abruptly. No weakening ever, neither faltering nor a rallying intensity. I know it is over.

My body is straining for the lightest sounds. One man has got up, he is gone near the silence to enquire. Others sit up in their beds, a few join the first by the bed. A minute later I hear the murmuring of prayers. The prayers continue until the doors are open. A warder steps in, pauses, shouts for his superior.

Soon it is that hour when 'all the dead awake'. As the key turns in my lock I ask the warder what became of the suffering man.

'The man died,' he said.

KOFI AWOONOR: GHANA

The Second Circle

    Cell No. 2

They say those about to drown
always see their entire life
flash before them.
It did not happen to me
So I will not drown.

    Fear,
      for friends, comrades,
but never for yourself
because your death cannot
matter very much to you,
    Can it now?

So much does a little bird know
about the world.
    So much.

in the still hour of the night
I dream of fliers and conjurers
I met a little flyer
in the fields.
Where are you heading, I asked
Don't you know?
    Home.

INGOAPELE MADINGOANE:[1]
SOUTH AFRICA

black trial/seven

i have crossed rivers and
trudged the barren plains
from the hangman's noose
i have stumbled tripped and
fallen hard on my back
hauled myself up and tried
once again to face the world
i've never been knocked out
but my soul is still scarred
from the pains sustained
and my fingers still bleed
from the cuts received
while trying to get a good
grip of my evasive roots
and mine alone

i heard them sing
i heard them sing
oh yes i did

on my homeward way
africa abound
towards sunrise
it was hard
the road was steep
it was heavy

---

[1] Poet laureate of Soweto by the people's will. [Ed.]

113

but i heard the beat
and i heard them sing
i heard it blown
the golden horn
i heard the echo
stirring my soul
i heard them cry
tears wetting dry earth
from eyes that have seen
the bitterness of life
i heard those voices
yes i heard them sing
i felt the pain
when my eyes beheld
how man can turn
his fellow men
into beasts of burden
i saw them struggle
i saw them kicked
and saw them die
i heard voices mourn
i heard them sing
when we buried them
i saw them pray
and by god they did
and the tears kept on raining
as they kept on screaming
to man the inflictor to show them mercy
i hit my chest
and a cry escaped my lips
god let it come to an end

FATIMA MEER: SOUTH AFRICA

Saturday, October 30, 1976

The lieutenant came on her inspection tour at something past nine. Seeing us in our nightdresses, she said we would never be ready for church service. Then she asked what swearword she had used the other day.

'Not a damn!' Vesta said.

'I very rarely swear,' the lieutenant said. 'You can take it from me. I must have been very cross!'

'And I was very hurt,' said Joyce, 'for it was my remark that provoked you.'

The lieutenant was genial about it. Joyce then asked permission for me to attend the Catholic mass.

'No, they don't like it.'

'Who doesn't like it?'

'The Church.'

'I think, Lieutenant, you are out of touch with the Church! The Catholics welcome everyone. I am a Catholic so I should know,' Joyce said.

The lieutenant did not argue with her. She gave me permission to attend the Catholic service.

We were taken to a large cell in the European section next to the surgery, opening onto a very pretty lawn bordered with a profusion of fuchsias.

We got a peep into European standards. The 'cell' was a very large room with four beds and large windows with orange drapes. There was a washbasin with hot and cold water and next to it, partitioned by a half wall, a waterborne toilet. The

From *Prison Diary: One hundred and thirteen days*, Kwela Books, 2001.

seat was attractively covered and on a shelf behind it stood two toilet rolls, one blue, the other white. The beds had pretty bedcovers and lockers next to them. There was a large steel cupboard in the room.

I couldn't get over it. The room was as pleasant as any four-bed ward at the private Indian hospital in Durban! The contrast between our facilities and those of the whites was outrageous. The door to the cell was not steel-plated, but had a handle which turned from the inside. We can't open our cell doors from the inside even when the doors are not locked – we are dependent on the wardress to open them from the outside.

The service was conducted by a Catholic nun. She said that Christ had died for a political crime. Vesta said she had expected to have mass. She had missed mass for nine Sundays now. The nun was pleased to hear that mass mattered to Vesta. She said there was no sin in Vesta having missed mass. God understood her position. The nun was critical of the priests who refused to come to prison to conduct mass. She said that some priests did not appreciate the meaning of mass. It is the real presence of God. It is thus greater than everything.

'Perhaps they think the venue is not right, but this room is good enough.'

She then asked if I knew of Mother Theresa. I said I didn't, and she proceeded to introduce me to the Calcutta Saint.

On our return to our cells, we passed the convicted prisoners in the main circular hall, sitting massed together on the floor in their bright blue overalls and red doeks, singing their hymns. Ayesha Bux was seated among them, perfectly integrated. Their eyes followed us until we disappeared from their view. I had a surging desire to go up and talk to them. I felt I had so much to say to them.

In the passage, awaiting-trial prisoners lounged in their own clothes. One sat very indecorously on the floor, with no bloomers. The matron escorting us reprimanded her. 'That's not the way a woman sits,' she said. The prisoner jumped up and apologized, 'Sorry, my Nonna,' but there was mischief in her eyes. A blue-uniformed prisoner, catching my eye, gave me the Black Power salute and I returned it.

FELIX MNTHALI: MALAWI

Solid State Physics

Yes, you stood solidly behind me
because I was the sun
and you were moons and stars
giving back to man on earth
the pale reflection of my rays

You could well defy
the heat and dust of October
stand firm against the frost of June
and the downpour of February

But I am no longer firm now,
no longer at the centre of creation
the dust of September
will stick into your eyes
and the rains of February
will melt your bones:
the *Chiperoni*[1] will shake you
to your bare foundations

You may stand behind
but I no longer precede you
you may stand solidly
but you stand not
on the firm earth, rather,
you are precariously perched
on the feelings of migrating birds

---

[1] Very cold wind from the east (Mozambique). [Ed.]

You were
    but are no longer
solidly behind me.

EDISON MPINA: MALAWI

On 6 December

I hear Mafisi[1] below giggle like virgins;
On the west bank I watch
rebellious floods uprooting banana shoots

with the messy methods of an ill-intentioned
    dentist;
On the west bank, sugar canes
have already lost the war

Canoes have surrendered; weary crocodiles
are staring through new frames, unwonted
    spectacles.
The river banks have become a battlefield

In my Mafisi village, the ascending smells
of roasting goatmeat have reached blocked noses.
    This
is the month of sacrificial offerings to lull
ancestral spirits back to assignment

---

[1] Hyenas. [Ed.]

KEN SARO-WIWA: NIGERIA

To Mandy Garner

A year is gone since I was rudely roused from my bed and clamped into detention. Sixty-five days in chains, many weeks of starvation, months of mental torture and, recently, the rides in a steaming, airless Black Maria to appear before a Kangaroo Court, dubbed a Special Military Tribunal where the proceedings leave no doubt at all that the judgement has been written in advance. And a sentence of death against which there is no appeal is a certainty.

Fearful odds? Hardly. The men who ordain and supervise this show of shame, this tragic charade are frightened by the Word, the power of ideas, the power of the pen; by the demands of social justice and the rights of man. Nor do they have a sense of history. They are so scared of the power of the Word, that they do not read. And that is their funeral.

When, after years of writing, I decided to take the Word to the streets to mobilize the Ogoni people, and empower them to protest the devastation of their environment by Shell, and their denigration and dehumanization by Nigeria's military dictators, I had no doubt where it could end. This knowledge has given me strength, courage and cheer and given me psychological advantage over my tormentors.

Only yesterday, the Spirit of Ogoni magicked into my cell a lovely poem by Jack Mapanje, the veteran of Kamuzu Banda's jails. Four years without charge. I had met Jack in Potsdam in person in 1992 and wondered how he had survived it all. Writing from Leeds University, his poem urged me to wear the

This fax was sent by Ken Saro-Wiwa from prison in 1995 to International PEN, London, an association of writers committed to freedom of expression.

121

armour of humour. The note at the end was also signed by Chengerai Hove, the award-winning Zimbabwean novelist. How wonderful to know how many fine men, the best brains, care for one's distress?

And yes, there has been humour along the way. At noon, on the 16th of March, 1995, my arch enemies, Shell, and the Nigerian Government met at the Northumberland offices of the Nigerian High Commission. They had some interesting consensus. Shell had not been paid for four months. The High Commissioner promised they would be paid. The High Commissioner, nettled by the endeavours of Anita and Gordon Roddick[1] on behalf of Ken Saro-Wiwa and the Ogoni people, devised 'ulterior motives' (such as a *coup d'état* against the latest Nigerian military dictator, you know) and wondered how Shell could help with 'counter measures'. Shell assured the unhappy men that they were up to the antics of the 'propagandists', and were scoring successes. Shell was making its own film which would balance the films commissioned on the Ogoni by Channel 4. Shell had even succeeded in convincing some campaigners of the rightness of its cause. The High Commissioner, pleased by that development, urged that the Shell film be screened before the Channel 4 film being produced by Catma Films. He promised to assist Shell 'overcome any bureaucratic problems they may encounter in producing the films'. Shell reminded the High Commissioner how one Mr Boele had pretended to travel to Nigeria as a tourist but used the opportunity to conduct his research and interviews with various groups and individuals. The lesson, beware of human rights activists masquerading as tourists. Do not grant them visas. But please, the Nigerian

---

[1] Anita Roddick, founder of the Body Shop in the United Kingdom, and her husband Gordon, campaigners for 'profits with principles' worldwide. [Ed.]

Government must pay Shell because 'lack of payment often land(s) [sic] to unemployment and unrest'. Meeting ended.

Thus the Conspirators. Nothing about ending the genocide of the Ogoni, the trumped-up charges of murder against Ogoni leaders, the widespread misery caused to the Ogoni by the conspiratorial efforts of Shell and successive Nigerian military dictators. Just money and how to deflect concerned public opinion.

Ultimately, however, the fault lies at the door of the British Government. It is the British Government which supplies arms on CREDIT to the military dictators of Nigeria knowing fully well that all such arms will only be used against innocent, unarmed citizens. It is the British Government which makes noises about democracy in Nigeria and Africa but supports military dictators to the hilt. It is the British Government which supports the rape and devastation of the environment by a valued taxpaying, labour-employing organization like Shell. I lay my travails, the destruction of the Ogoni and other peoples in the Niger delta at the door of the British Government. Ultimately, the decision is for the British people, the electorate, to stop this grand deceit, this double standard which has lengthened the African nightmare and denigrates humanity.

Whether I live or die is immaterial. It is enough to know that there are people who commit time, money and energy to right this one evil among so many others predominating worldwide. If they do not succeed today, they will succeed tomorrow. We must keep on striving to make the world a better place; for all of mankind. Each one contributing his bit, in his or her own way.

I salute you all.

Summing-up: Defence Statement

My lord [the judge], we all stand before history. I am a man of peace, of ideas. Appalled by the denigrating poverty of my people who live on a richly-endowed land, distressed by their political marginalization and economic strangulation, angered by the devastation of their land, their ultimate heritage, anxious to preserve their right to life and to a decent living, and determined to usher to this country as a whole a fair and just democratic system which protects everyone and every ethnic group and gives us all a valid claim to human civilization, I have devoted all my intellectual and material resources, my very life, to a cause in which I have total belief and from which I cannot be blackmailed or intimidated. I have no doubt at all about the ultimate success of my cause, no matter the trials and tribulations which I and those who believe with me may encounter on our journey. Nor imprisonment nor death can stop our ultimate victory.

I repeat that we all stand before history. I and my colleagues are not the only ones on trial. Shell is here on trial and it is as well that it is represented by counsel said to be holding a watching brief. The company has, indeed, ducked this particular trial, but its day will surely come and the lessons learned here may prove useful to it for there is no doubt in my mind that the ecological war the company has waged in the delta will be called to question sooner than later and the crimes of that war be duly punished. The crime of the company's dirty wars against the Ogoni people will also be punished.

On trial also is the Nigerian nation, its present rulers and all

From *Writers Behind Bars*, International PEN, Vol. 46, 1/96.

those who assist them. Any nation which can do to the weak and disadvantaged what the Nigerian nation has done to the Ogoni, loses a claim to independence and to freedom from outside influence. I am not one of those who shy away from protesting injustice and oppression, arguing that they are expected of a military regime. The military do not act alone. They are supported by a gaggle of politicians, lawyers, judges, academics and businessmen, all of them hiding under the claim that they are only doing their duty, men and women too afraid to wash their pants of their urine. We all stand on trial, my lord, for by our actions we have denigrated our country and jeopardized the future of our children. As we subscribe to the subnormal and accept double standards, as we lie and cheat openly, as we protect injustice and oppression, we empty our classrooms, degrade our hospitals, fill our stomachs with hunger and elect to make ourselves the slaves of those who subscribe to high standards, pursue the truth, and honour justice, freedom and hard work.

I predict that the scene here will be played and replayed by generations yet unborn. Some have already cast themselves in the role of villains, some are tragic victims, some still have a chance to redeem themselves. The choice is for each individual.

I predict that a dénouement of the riddle of the Niger delta will soon come. The agenda is being set at this trial. Whether the peaceful ways I have favoured will prevail depends on what the oppressor decides, what signals it sends out to the waiting public.

In my innocence of the false charges I face here, in my utter conviction, I call upon the Ogoni people, the peoples of the Niger delta, and the oppressed ethnic minorities of Nigeria to stand up now and fight fearlessly and peacefully for their rights. History is on their side, God is on their side. For the Holy Quran says in Sura 42, verse 41: 'All those who fight when

oppressed incur no guilt, but Allah shall punish the oppressor.'
Come the day.

The True Prison

It is not the leaking roof
Nor the singing mosquitoes
In the damp, wretched cell
It is not the clank of the key
As the warder locks you in
It is not the measly rations
Unfit for man or beast
Nor yet the emptiness of day
Dipping into the blankess of night
It is not
It is not
It is not.
It is the lies that have been drummed
Into your ears for one generation
It is the security agent running amok
Executing callous calamitous orders
In exchange for a wretched meal a day
The magistrate writing into her book
Punishment she knows is undeserved
The moral decrepitude
Mental ineptitude
The meat of dictators
Cowardice masking as obedience
Lurking in our denigrated souls
It is fear damping trousers
We dare not wash of our urine
It is this

It is this
It is this
Dear friend, turns our free world
Into a dreary prison

Detention Haircut

I had a haircut today
After a long delay
My prison hair had grown so long
I thought it was full of lice
It looked thoroughly unkempt
A barber my jailers refused
So I did it just my way.

And oh, when I was done
You'd think I'd been visited
By a carpenter rude and crude
Or that an army of mice
Had raided my lovely head.

I could not stand the mirror
It told a tale of horror
But what most I feared
Was my aged mum would dream
I'd had this grisly haircut
As once before she had
And came upbraiding me
'Cause I looked like a convict
A disgrace to her proud womb.

OGAGA IFOWODO: NIGERIA

A Room of My Own

'Separate these two men,' Orangutang ordered Smiley, and returned to his office. I tried to find out from Akeem what happened between him and Orangutang but Smiley, not wishing to bring a fresh humiliation on himself, gave no chance for that. He gestured to me to come out of the cell. I asked him where he was taking me. He said simply, 'Don't worry, you're not going far.'

Leaving Yellow to lock Akeem back in, he took me upstairs. I still connected him with the grimy, flooded toilet, which was the first door along a corridor just after the landing. What was it going to be this time? A flooded room? A roach-and-rat-infested cell? A cubicle without light or air?

We passed the toilet. Its door was shut so I couldn't tell if it had been restored to any usable condition. Smiley selected a key from a bunch and opened the second door on the right of the corridor, same side as the toilet. This was my new cell until further notice. I was not to come out during the daytime or at all, except to go to the toilet. I was to lock myself in. He was going to let me have a key because he trusted I would do as he had said. If I didn't, then he would be forced to lock me in and take the key from me. I noticed that apart from the lock that came with the door, another popularly known as 'jam-lock' – it locked as the door shut – had been installed. He shut the door and locked it from the outside.

I took two steps from the threshold and paused to survey my new lodgings. It was a disused office. Tables, some with chairs

From *Homecoming*, Ogaga Ifowodo's forthcoming prison memoirs.

and some with their drawers on top of them, were piled against the walls. A dirty brown rug stretched from wall to wall. In the absence of any kind of bedding, I was glad for the underlay now worn thin. But the rug, as the rest of the room, was dusty. I stamped on it and a cloud rose in the air, settling in a fine powder on my foot. The room was unbearably stuffy. There were two windows. Through a small gap between the two tables, I worked my way close enough to try to open the one nearer to me and expel some of the bad air trapped inside. I felt something scurry across my face. I jerked a hand over my face and caught a spider's thread. As I returned to the window, I saw the spider scampering away, making a fresh web between two legs of a chair sitting upside down on one of the tables. The latch on the half of the window I tried to open was very stiff. I struggled with it and managed to push it open halfway. The other half would not give an inch. A thin stream of fresh air wafted in. I manoeuvred my way to the second window but there I had no luck. None of the latches could be prised off the hooks.

It was a dim prospect, even dimmer than in the cell downstairs. There, I had something I could call a bed; here there was nothing of the kind. There, some form of cross-ventilation was possible through windows on two adjacent walls; here I could barely force a crack. I stood still in the centre of the room wondering how I was going to survive with my allergies now playing up. And just then, a fit of sneezing and blowing shook me so violently I had to sit down. Luckily, I had taken the half roll of toilet paper I had in the cell downstairs with me. After what seemed like an eternity, the sneezing subsided, to resume intermittently with varying ferocity throughout the rest of the day. Accompanied by a runny nose. I wondered what vast ocean of phlegm lay buried in my chest and so untiringly fed the flow.

How was I going to pass the time in this dreary room?

Without Akeem or any other person to talk to, or to just fill the air with unspoken conversation, the silence was oppressive. All the offices in this part of the building seemed empty. I imagined similarly cramped and dusty rooms along the corridor. Now and then, I heard a voice on the staircase, then footsteps along the corridor. They petered off into the far end and until they returned, I heard nothing more. How long was I going to be condemned to stay in this gloomy room?

It was clear I had to find a way to beguile the time. And to know that I had considered time in the cell below – a nice and cosy place by comparison to this – so slow and oppressive I had begun a poem titled 'Unmarked Hours Beat their Hands Against the Wall'! I had stopped at the fifth couplet when I couldn't find the right word to sustain the rhyme scheme and continue the sense of the thoughts in the previous lines. Jokingly, I said to myself, here, unmarked hours will *break* their head on the wall! With 'hands', I had the metaphor of the hands of a clock which, stopped from moving in this manner of speaking, produced the stillness of time in a cell. And so the beating of their frustration against the wall as might the prisoner in a cell. But with the 'head' I now playfully substituted for hands, I hesitated to think literally!

A key turned in the lock. Yellow entered with my supper. I asked him if he could get me a mattress. He thought it unlikely but promised to look anyway. If he didn't find anything tonight, then I would have to make do until he returned to work in two days' time; he would be off the next day. In that case, could he get me a broom? There was no problem with that. I asked him to bring my water bottle from the cell downstairs. I had another request. That he take Akeem and I out to bathe at the same time as he had when we were kept together. He said he could only do so if he was sure Oga was not likely to show up on an inspection visit. Or if Supervisor – he made it sound like a name

– would also not be around. But he said he would see what he could do and left.

We had finally settled on a routine of taking our bath late in the night, just before we slept. That way, we cooled our body temperature enough to be able to sleep in the heat, especially after we had closed the windows in the hope of reducing the mosquito menace. As we had to bathe in the open, night was plainly the best time too.

Yellow came to tell me it was time to bathe, bringing a broom with him. I swept the part of the room I had chosen for my bed. The dust that rose in the air set off a short frenzy of sneezing. Yellow had, without my asking him, brought the spray mosquito repellent. Even in the daytime, I had been given good notice of what to expect in the night. I knew I would be the booty of a starved army of mosquitoes that couldn't wait for the looting to start. So although my asthma advised strongly against flitting the room, the terror of the rampaging bloodsuckers awaiting a feast carried the day. I pressed the nozzle and would have emptied it had Yellow not interrupted my spraying. He had come to urge me to come now if I intended to bathe tonight. I had held my breath while spraying and dashing out of the room, exhaled mightily.

Akeem had deliberately taken his time so we could have time to talk. He had brought out my toilet bag too. He didn't know why Orangutang suddenly decided on separating us. He was asked just about the same questions he had been asked ever since our arrest. Why was he away for so long abroad? Who paid for his trip? What was his true mission, besides the writing he claimed? Where is the book he wrote then? Who did he hold meetings with and what was the ultimate purpose of those meetings? Why did he choose to enter the country by road? Why did the two of us travel together if the real purpose of our journeys was not the same? Why was he carrying subversive documents on Ken Saro-Wiwa? Why had he joined the campaign to tarnish the image of Nigeria abroad? And so on, *ad nauseam*. He had also been made to write yet another statement. And he had no idea that we would be separated. Maybe they felt our staying together was in some way impeding their interrogation. Or maybe, it was sheer psychological warfare.

What we feared most was a transfer out of Lagos. That was bound to make an already dreadful situation truly inconceivable. But again, a kind of optimistic resignation seemed our best ally since that fate could not be avoided by anything we could do. Yellow was soon hurrying us inside. We tried to cajole him into giving us more time outside. He said he had to bring two other detainees out to bathe. We knew these detainees would have to be Janson and Femi, both of whom we were still dying to see. We wheedled some more and he relented.

When Janson and Femi came out, it was difficult keeping our voices down. We hugged and backslapped. We quickly updated each other. Femi had been arrested some two days after us at the same Seme border. He too had spent a night there before being brought here. Femi had to be quite a hirsute fellow for in just two weeks he was already sporting a formidable beard. Given two more weeks or, let's say, a month, it seemed sure to rival any true rabbi's! A lanky fellow, he looked lean and unwell. He was having a most horrible time with mosquitoes in the airless room they kept him, alone. His white underwear T-shirt was so soiled with his own blood it was hard to believe he was still standing on his feet. Even his grey boxer shorts were visibly bloody. Like us, he had had to remain in his scanty apparel ever since he was brought in. Ours, like his, were so filthy by now they constituted in themselves a serious health hazard. Yet, the only option open to us was to strip naked. And even then, our very skin should in no time become as filthy. What would we do then?

Janson had been arrested at the studio of the Nigerian Television Authority where he was anchoring his Saturday morning sport talk programme. His captor was a woman Yellow and everyone else among the lower echelons of the staff, as we were soon to find out, spoke of with considerable awe. She reportedly had backing from Abuja and seemed to wield more power than the boss of the headquarters annex. Referred to as 'madam', she was, consequently, more frequently mentioned than any of the other two very senior staff. She seemed to be a hard taskmistress too, given snatches of grumbles against her that we heard every once in a while.

It turned out my speculations on why they would arrest Janson were not too far off the mark. They wanted him to give the vital information needed to arrest the remaining founding editors of the magazine he edited. That would lead to a more effective siege to shut down completely the magazine's production. For as it is, despite a more or less permanent siege, all its titles were still hitting the street. Yet, although they had now got one of the big fish, Femi, they still held on to Janson. Apparently, they operated with the time-tested philosophy of the fellow in Kafka's story: guilt is never to be doubted. Unlike the fellow, however, they still asked questions after arrest, not perturbed by the unpleasant task of untangling the lies and more lies that Kafka's jailer knew would be the answers to any questions he might ask. Yet, there was another meeting ground. For they, too, held dearly the creed of not letting your man go once you had got him. 'As it is, I've got my man and I won't let him go,' the philosopher-jailer said. Well, they had got two men – no, three for we have to remember Kole Ajilade – why let any of them go?

Janson didn't betray give-away signs of a cruel time as Femi did. A man of robust physique, all that showed he had been away from home for over a week was a pencil line goatee and a moustache just beginning to grow wild. He said he had struck a good rapport with Yellow and had managed to get along in a relatively better way than he could see we had. But he was, more than anything else, bored to death. It had got so bad he gave Yellow some money to buy him a novel. And Yellow had bought a miserable romance paperback from the nearest bend-down bookshop – or BDB as they are popularly known – where anything from trash to treasure could be found. With the dearth of locally published books and the foreign ones unaffordable owing to the criminal exchange rate of the naira to the major foreign currencies, BDBs had come to be the saving grace of those that still read. Like all such saccharine pulp fiction of thin and simplistic plots, he had raced through the book in under two hours, predicting rightly the rest of the story as soon as he had met all the characters by the third chapter. Did we have any book to relieve his boredom with?

I told him what I had was not a novel and I doubted if it would serve his need. He agreed with me after I gave him the title. Akeem alone had the book he needed, but he was taking his time so as to stretch out his entertainment and stave off the dismal day when he should at last have nothing to read. Akeem would later confess that he had finished reading *Angela's Ashes* and begun to re-read it while I waited for him! I asked for Janson's romance and he promised to send it to me through Yellow.

To enable us to see each other and talk, Yellow had gone to alert his colleague on sentry duty at the gate. A signal came and we were hurried inside. About an hour after, Yellow came with the book. *Gentle Pirate*. It was the very type, complete with the cover photograph of a tall, muscular, handsome man carrying a svelte young woman in his arms. Needless to inform you, the beauty, hands clasped desperately around his neck, long blonde hair like liquid gold dripping to the floor, was gazing adoringly into the eyes of her Prince Charming now bearing her away to ever-ever Loveland there to live happily ever after. There was nothing for it. That was all I had and I was going to deliberate over my reading of it from cover, to blurb, to the copyright and printing history page, down to the final full stop. And if I still lacked something else to read when I was through, start all over again!

I went inside my cell to spend the first night alone since our arrest. The smell of poisonous insecticide was still too overpowering. I was in a dilemma what to do to ease out the smell. I was sure if I spent the next five minutes in the room in that state, I would faint. I thought of opening the half-window. But that would defeat the entire purpose. On the thinking that there were bound to be fewer mosquitoes in the corridor, inside the building than outside, I opened the door, first fully, and then after a few minutes, kept it ajar. Although the smell began to reduce, it was still too strong, and I could hear a faint wheeze begining to pipe out of my lungs. My chest was getting tight and heavy. Then I sneezed. And followed it quickly with another sneeze. And another. Three sneezes in rapid succession broke my resistance. Between mosquitoes and an asthma attack, the bloody insects seemed the kinder devil. I opened the window and stuck my nose out. Unmindful of the mosquitoes that swarmed my face, I gulped as much air as I could to relieve my lungs. Until two flew into my mouth, greedily open!

After about half an hour at the window, I put *Gentle Pirate* under my head and, hoping he would be a gentle pillow, closed my eyes. And commenced slapping myself all over in the vain hope of warding off the insects that massed on me as they began their long-awaited feast. I beat myself in vain. They feasted till dawn. My jersey sleeping clothes were of ox-blood colour. But for that, I thought it would be a difficult contest indeed if anyone had to pick the more bloodied apparel between Femi's and mine.

TORTURE

AGOSTINHO NETO: ANGOLA

create

Create create
create in mind create in muscle create in nerve
create in man create in the masses
create
create with dry eyes

create create
over the profanation of the forest
over the brazen fortress of the whip
create over the perfume of sawn trunks
create
create with dry eyes

create create
bursts of laughter over the derision of the
    palmatória
courage in the tips of the planter's boots
strength in the splintering of battered-in doors
firmness in the red blood of insecurity
create
create with dry eyes

Create create
stars over the warrior's sledge-hammer
peace over children's weeping
peace over sweat over the tears of contract labour
peace over hatred
create
create peace with dry eyes

Create create
create freedom in the slave stars
manacles of love on the paganized paths of love
festive sounds over swinging bodies on simulated
gallows

Create
create love with dry eyes.

LEILA DJABALI: ALGERIA

For My Torturer, Lieutenant D . . .

You slapped me –
   no one had ever slapped me –
electric shock
and then your fist
and your filthy language
I bled too much to be able to blush
All night long
a locomotive in my belly
rainbows before my eyes
It was as if I were eating my mouth
drowning my eyes
I had hands all over me
and felt like smiling.

Then one morning a different soldier came
You were as alike as two drops of blood.
Your wife, Lieutenant –
Did she stir the sugar in your coffee?
Did your mother dare to tell you looked well?
Did you run your fingers through your kids' hair?

Translated from the French by Anita Barrows.

OBAFEMI AWOLOWO: NIGERIA

The Transfer

The next morning, at about three o'clock, I heard the clanging of the keys; my cell was opened; and there was Mr Boyd together with Mr Ogundahunsi and two others. I was asked to get dressed and be ready to move. The rule was that when a CP travelled out, he did so in his own attire. But I adamantly refused to wear my own dress. Consequently, I put on my prison uniform, and was ready. But before we left, I gave my private attire to Mr Ogundahunsi for delivery to my private secretary, Mr Biodun Falade.

I requested for certain facilities. After the hearing of the appeal, I had sent away all books and papers relating thereto. I was allowed to retain a number of books dealing with non-law subjects. I wanted this facility to continue. I also wanted my personal doctor, as distinct from the prison doctor, to visit me once a month at government expense. These requests were agreed to; and I had no earthly reason to continue my refusal which, in any case, had proved futile.

On the journey to the airport, I was accompanied by Mr Boyd and one other officer in the same car. Another car followed with three occupants.

At the airport, a mild drama occurred. After I had boarded the plane with two escorts, the engines of the plane, a Fokker 27, failed to start. They tried, and tried, and tried, and tried, for about fifteen minutes without success. Everybody, except me, was visibly worried. The door was opened and I heard someone shout, 'This is surely a sabotage!'

My own guess was that the two airport workers who had

From *My March Through Prison*, Macmillan, 1985.

seen me board the plane and were not too sure whether it was I or not, but wanted to be sure, had decided to delay the plane's take-off until daybreak.

After a flurry of activities and after, I suspected, an appeal had been made to the two workers who apparently had been specially assigned to this unusually early and unscheduled flight, the engines started. It was now about five o'clock, and we took off.

At Calabar Mr M. A. Ifijeh the superintendent, and Mr Ewohunmi his assistant, met me at the airport in their ceremonial uniforms. They stood to attention and gave a salute. I stretched my hand out to them. They smiled benignly at me and gave me a hearty handshake as if we had been friends for years. I thought this was a comforting and reassuring reception for a CP, and a foretaste of an enjoyable stay at Calabar.

But before I tell the story of my 25 months' sojourn at Calabar Prison, the bizarre background to my transfer from Ikoyi must be related.

Shortly after my imprisonment, there was a rumour that my adversaries in the NPC and some in the NCNC were making active plans to poison me. As time went on, the rumour became widespread and persistent.

When I heard the rumour, I was indifferent. I did not put the intended villainy beyond my foes, but there was nothing I personally could do to prevent the act. As it was, I was completely at the mercy of my foes who were in power, and who would not scruple to procure a prison officer or warder to inject poison into my food. Besides, there was at that stage, no substance in the rumour. Even if there was, I was still powerless. My only armour was God. I, therefore, refused to discuss the rumour at any length with my visitors. But, in due course, an indirect substantiation of the rumour came from two sources.

The first was a very good and loyal friend of mine. He was Chief Akinyele, the Otun of Itoku in Abeokuta (of blessed memory). He was also an intimate friend of Chief M. A. Majekodunmi, who was the administrator of the Western Region from 29 May to 31 December 1962, when the region was administered under a state of emergency. He it was who ordered my restriction and lastly my house arrest from 29 May to 2 November 1962. Chief Akinyele paid me a visit at Ikoyi in about February 1964. It was his first since my incarceration. He was accompanied by Chief Toye Coker who also, at that time, was a good and loyal friend of mine.

Chief Akinyele was an ebullient character. When we met and embraced each other, I was jovial but he was melancholy. After he had been seated, he burst into tears.

About one minute or so passed before he was able to speak. He had been very much disturbed by the rumour that I was going to be poisoned. At first he had discounted it, but when it persisted and gained wide currency, he had spoken frankly to Chief M. A. Majekodunmi about it. To his dismay and utter depression, the latter neither confirmed nor denied the rumour. All he said, by way of advice, was that it would be in Chief Awolowo's interest if his admirers and fanatical supporters desisted from shouting his name and singing his praise all over the place. The Otun burst into tears again.

I was moved. But I had to tell him, quite bluntly, that there was nothing he or I or anyone could do to prevent the act, if my foes were determined to carry out their evil intention. For instance, he could not take me with him, on his departure, to put me out of danger. I pointed to the high walls surrounding the prison with barbed wires on top of them, and remarked that I could not climb the walls to escape. Even if I could, it would be an extremely cowardly act which I should not contemplate or attempt. And even if I did, and escaped to the other side, I would soon be recaptured with the unsolicited aid of young persons and others who would shout 'Awo, Awo, Awo!' on my trail.

However, I gave him a positive and categorical assurance. Whilst no human being could help, there is always a Providential Intervention in times of dire need which never fails. Therefore, what he and others and all of us should do was to pray fervently for that Divine Intervention.

The second source of indirect substantiation was Prophet B. A. Otubogunwa. When the rumour was at its peak, he made a prediction which was published in the *Drum Magazine* of March 1964, stating that 'Towards the end of the year the death of a prisoner will cause unrest and rioting in Nigeria'. Though no name was mentioned, yet it was generally believed that I was that prisoner. To enhance the stature of the prophet and add credibility to his prophecy, there was a full-page colour portrait of the prophet in the *Drum Magazine*.

Unfortunately, after this prophecy, one of my colleagues, Mr Sunbo Jibowu, who was serving his jail term at Kirikiri Prison, died. There was no rioting. The prophet was, therefore, questioned by a *Drum Magazine* correspondent. His reply was as follows:

> I am very certain that another important political prisoner will die before the end of this year. His death will lead to very serious political unrest and rioting.
>
> (*Drum Magazine*, October 1964, Ghana Edition)

The prophet was now more direct. All lingering doubts disappeared. I was the only 'important political prisoner' in Nigeria at that time. Consequently, I was satisfied that the prophecy had been induced by a cabal within the NCNC to excuse my eventual death as natural; and as an act of God, already foreseen by one of His prophets. The cabal was, of course, acting in pursuance of the common design of the NPC NCNC coalition.

When the rumour persisted the director of prisons, unknown

to me, gave imperative instructions to the superintendent at Ikoyi as follows.

1. Only trusted first-timer prisoners from areas known to be loyal to me in the country should prepare and serve my food.
2. Such prisoners should be put into individual cells and should not be allowed to mix with other prisoners whether first-timer or habitual.
3. Food and water intended for me should be tasted not by a junior warder but by an officer not lower in rank than a cadet officer.

The rumour started and gained currency when Mr Ogundahunsi was on leave. Mr J. S. Ebili, a superintendent, who took charge in Ogundahunsi's absence, carried out the instructions faithfully without breathing a word to me. When Mr Ogundahunsi returned, Messrs Sasore, Akinsanya, and Umoren constantly accused him of being inconsiderate in changing our cooks and stewards every so often. With the result that, with regard to our food, the style of cooking was always changing. We could not anticipate what was coming for lunch or dinner. I did not complain. However, one day Ogundahunsi had to disclose to me in confidence the reason why constant changes had to be made. After some time a permanent arrangement was made, and my colleagues were satisfied.

I am still on this poison episode. Exactly a fortnight after I had arrived in Calabar, Chief Osagie ostensibly paid an official visit. He had actually paid the visit to explain to me why he had to transfer me from Ikoyi, and, to ensure that I was as comfortable as prison regulations and a liberal interpretation of them permitted.

With regard to my transfer, he had acted swiftly in order to forestall the federal government. There had been a powerful move to transfer me to somewhere in the Northern Region. But on reflection, it had been thought more prudent to postpone the transfer until my appeal was disposed of.

After judgement in the appeal, he had feared that one day he might be instructed by the Minister for Internal Affairs, who was a rabid enemy, to transfer me to one of the northern prisons which, at that time, were all under the Native Authorities, and badly run. I would be most uncomfortable in any of them.

There had been complaints in official circles that I was holding political meetings at Ikoyi to plan the overthrow of the federal government, and that it was necessary to transfer me out of the easy reach of my political associates. There was no iota of truth in this allegation. He had no doubt that it was just a pretext for what looked to him like an ulterior motive. He therefore decided to forestall the minister before the latter gave him an order which he would have to carry out whether he liked it or not. He said nothing about the poison episode. However, his action was clearly and unerringly suggestive.

Much later, an authentic and direct substantiation of the attempt to poison me came. It was from no less a person than Dr Nnamdi Azikiwe who was the president of Nigeria at the time the rumour was rampant and loud.

The *Punch* of Thursday 26 April 1979, carried a report on Dr Azikiwe in the following words.

> Dr Nnamdi Azikiwe, the presidential candidate of Nigeria People's Party (NPP) has described his colleague in the Unity Party of Nigeria, Chief Obafemi Awolowo, as an ungrateful person. He said but for him, Chief Awolowo would not be alive today. Dr Azikiwe told newsmen in Lagos yesterday of a time when Chief Awolowo was to be detained during the treasonable felony trials at a place where he would have been killed. He said he insisted that

Chief Awolowo should be detained at Calabar where Chief Awolowo was later released in 1966 by Mr Yakabu Gowon.

'The tragedy of the situation is that it is the same Chief Awolowo who was reported to have accused me of being a tax dodger, unfit to lead,' he declared

For my safety in prison, I owe a huge debt of gratitude to Chief Giwa Osagie, together with his subordinate officers and men who faithfully carried out his instructions to protect me from harm. Chief Osagie and I never met until that night at Broad Street Prison when my colleagues and I refused voluntary lock-up. And that was an unfriendly meeting. I was therefore over-whelmed by the kindness and humanity which he exhibited towards me when my life was seriously threatened, and I was powerless to defend myself against my inveterate enemies.

Paul the Apostle in his second letter to Timothy (2 Timothy 4:14) says, 'Alexander the Coppersmith did me much evil: the Lord reward him according to his works.' The best way, I think, I can phrase my deep sense of gratitude to Chief Osagie is to adapt, in reverse, Paul's reference to Alexander the Copper-smith, and say loud and clear, 'Chief Giwa Osagie, the Director of Prisons in 1964–1966, did me much good: may God reward him munificently, and bless him all the days of his life.'

Until he spoke in 1979 – fifteen years later – I did not know and I had no means of knowing what part Dr Azikiwe had played in the odious and inhuman attempt to kill me. I still have no means of knowing. However, I now have his *ipse dixit*, which I accept. And so, I am sincerely grateful to him for his kind contribution, and, particularly for letting the world know the truth that a serious attempt was actually made by my political opponents to destroy me physically in prison.

EDDISON J. ZVOBGO: ZIMBABWE

Upon the Sixth Anniversary of My Detention

August 26th, 1964 – August 26th, 1970

> The hour-glass
> Mumbles on
> Dropping the tiny grains
> Of sand
> Beneath,
> Measuring the pulse
> Of the universe
> For kicks.
>
> It's midnight
> Now
> As I sit all alone
> Playing a game
> Of patience
> With back against the wall
> And manacled hands
>
> My eyes are blindfolded
> With a coarse cloth
> Of time-cataract
> Which reveals, teasingly
> What was,
> And may yet become.
>
> The cigarette fumes
> Rise higher and higher,
> Breaking apart
> As they dissolve

And disappear
Into the masses of time
Beyond.
Only the butt stands
On my Ricory Instant coffee holder,
Ashamed of what it
And I have become.

Thoughts breed
In my mind,
Defying the laws
Of supply and demand;
Most descend
From outer-space
But ricochet
Upon registering their sense
To quickly vanish
Beyond
To the seas of time.

That's just as well;
Yesterday, I stood-up
To shake hands
With thoughts
And ideas;
There was the sense
Of justice,
Glory and freedom,
The purity of truth,
The excitement
Of cause and effect,
The virtue of service
And the virginity
Of love.

I dated ideas,
And we romanced.
But each time
I proposed marriage
To ideas,
Man brandished
Hand-cuffs,
And said, 'don't or else'.

MOLEFE PHETO: SOUTH AFRICA

And Night Fell

On the 16th, the sun rose in a halo of glory. I felt as if I were the only man in the universe waiting for it, and through the window of the ten-by-twelve-paces cell, I saw its rays. It promised to touch the window of my confinement as it played in the ten-by-twenty ceilingless courtyard outside the cell. It did not matter that I was not allowed out of the cell, as long as the sun could kiss the window momentarily and perhaps my face and hands, through the iron bars, the only exposed parts of me.

As it rose higher, I realized its rays slanted southward, touching the entire south wall, signalling its move towards me. By midday, it began to dance away from me, its rays receding eastward on its journey westward, taking a course north of the cell. At about two in the afternoon I had given up hope. Its light was south-east, nowhere near where I was. Towards five o'clock, I saw the shadows made by my cell rising upwards on the east wall, by which time the sun was behind me, growing weaker, about to set. A lonely bird in the nearby park sang its farewell to day, to sun, to man and life and to me, as it went: *Phez'ko mthwal', Phez'ko mthwal', Phez'ko mthwal'.*

I remembered hearing this bird in Vendaland, in the northern Transvaal, during my music research projects, and I was to hear it too in Mozambique and in Swaziland, where I went to rest after prison. Khosi Noge, my hostess, explained the lyrics of the bird-tune to me. *Phez'ko mthwal'* meant 'up and onto your burden'.

From *And Night Fell: Memoirs of a Political Prisoner in South Africa*, Allison and Busby, 1984

I sank on the mat, spread out three grey blankets, folded my black jersey to make an uncomfortable pillow and prepared myself to sleep at 5.30 in the afternoon . . . And, in a little while, night fell.

KOFI AWOONOR: GHANA

On Being Told of Torture

For each hair on man, there is
a ledger in which the account
   will be written.
Time is not measured by the hourglass
but by the rivulets of blood
     shed
   and will be shed
Even though our bones crunch
our spirits will not break
     until we make a
        reckoning in the red bright book
        of history.

He said he saw him lying
on the floor in his own blood
     unconscious
     delirium was his refuge
     from pain. In that state,
     my mother will bear arms
     and urge me to topple a govt.
But, no matter what,
there is still a tree blossoming
now this New Year,
there is goodwill on earth
     children still laugh
        lovers hold hands in dark corners,
        and the moon is new on all of us.

Weep not now my love
for as all die, so shall we

but it is not dying that should pain us.
It is the waiting, the
            intermission when we cannot act,
        when our will is shackled by tyranny.

That hurts.
Yet somehow, I know
the miracle of the world
will be wrought again.
            The space will be filled
            in spite of the hurt
            by the immensity of love
            that will defy dying
                and Death
                    Good night, my love.

EDISON MPINA: MALAWI

The Men Next Door

The ten men next door are going to die
tomorrow. They are singing their last hymn:
'A pilgrim was I wandering . . .'
in their cell without an outside. At this final
hour, God seems to be where they have been
going all this time. If so, they have arrived.
Their cell, like mine has three corners. In one,
imitating Lazarus, God is squatting, holding his
    chin.
He's listening to the most solemn final
wishes. But he is not moved; it is true, I believe
    now,
that God does leisurely watch his own creations
being destroyed. In another corner, the radiogram
that Reverend Father Charles bought from his own
    savings
and brought into the cell next door
– so the reports go,
is bleating *skokiaan*.[1] But none of the men is
dancing. I can't see what's in the third corner
now, my eyes have grown so bad during this
    sojourn
in a condemned cell.
Yesterday the ten men were given huge mutton,
spinach and brown beans, but the food lies on the
floor, putrefying. Today, on the eve of their death,

---

[1] Popular music that originated from South Africa and also symbol of the gallows. [Ed.]

the ten men were allowed warm baths. They have
   taken none
of it, vowing that they are not just pigs reared
for their bacon. They sing to beat *skokiaan*.
By my side, Victor Ndovi cannot sleep. Indeed no
   one
is sleeping in my baggy cell of forty, the size of the
   cell
occupied by the ten men who are going to die
   tomorrow.
The windows are shut, but Victor and I have
   heard
it pour in the condemned cell next door
since its occupants, the ten men who are going to
   die
tomorrow were admitted there.
To do them homage the whole world is quiet; but
the Kings African Rifles memorial clock
at the square outside still whirs, lest we forget
our own condemnation.
Next week, next month or next year
(for events take their own time in these precincts)
I will be moved next door with nine others.
I shake at how I shall perform; for I'm
dead, already dead
in this.

                                 Zomba Central Prison, August 1973

TSHENUWANI SIMON FARISANI: SOUTH AFRICA

The Wait Is Over

It was morning . . . afternoon . . . evening . . , March 27. There were footsteps in the passage, voices, then a light in my cell. The door opened. This was my turn. After fourteen days of waiting, blank waiting, now they were here. Before sunrise, the clean sheets would be blue with ink, and a lot of nonsense.

'Are you Tshenuwani Farisani?'

'Yes sir, I am.'

'What is your profession?'

'Dean of the Evangelical Lutheran Church in Southern Africa.'

'What is your profession, man? Do not waste my time, what kak is this din? Do you . . .'

'I preach and supervise . . .'

'You are dominie . . . a pastor . . . a kaffir dominie?'

'Yes, I preach, I am a pastor.'

His colleagues watched. He grinned. 'Get dressed. Quick! We go!' I reached for my Bible. 'Leave it!'

For a moment I hesitated, then almost involuntarily I murmured, 'But I need it. I shall need it.'

'Let him take it, Captain. By midnight he will have forgotten about it. It may be interesting to the Bible to watch what we can do to its dean!'

Handcuffed, I was led through the innumerable doors and gates. It was good to walk outside, good to watch the stars and the clear sky. The feeling of being free from the dulling atmosphere of the cell, my home for the previous two weeks, made

---

From *Diary from a South African Prison*, Fortress Press, 1987.

me forget about what awaited me. Handcuffed to the back of the pickup, legs manacled in irons to a cross-bar. The pain began to sting. I pleaded that my legs not be crossed. Captain White barked, 'He knows how to handle communists. You will not teach him his job!' Indeed, the lackey did a perfect job. 'If you like you can jump off the van and run to your communist brothers in Tanzania.' The lackey leaped into the back of the van and sat next to me. 'You have done an excellent job last night,' said Captain White, 'today, and also now. Come, three of us can sit in front.' Then, turning to me, grinning his white, shining teeth menacingly in the dim street lighting, the captain said, 'Dean, be comfortable. We apologize that the state cannot afford a canopy for this bakkie[1] as the money goes to combating terrorism. Keep the wind out of the bakkie with your prayers. I wish you a good trip.'

We sped away from Pietermaritzburg, at perhaps 140 kilometres per hour. I froze in the ice-cold wind and wriggled as the handcuffs cut into my flesh and pain seared my twisted limbs. Contradictory desires clashed in my mind: 'The sooner we reach our destination, the better. I cannot bear these pains any longer ... The longer it takes to reach our destination, the better. The wind is cold but fresh, the present pains nothing compared with what I may suffer once we reach our destination.'

We followed the arrow to Howick police station. Handcuffed and leg-ironed, I struggled up the steps to the third floor. My legs felt numb. Three were waiting for me. 'Let him sit on this chair, like a *gentleman*.' I sat. Before me stood the officer in charge, this hefty tower of white muscles, eyes half-closed, the large nostrils pulling in 87 per cent of the oxygen between us. I was worried more by what I could not see than by what I could

---

[1] Pickup truck. [Ed.]

see. The two bullies behind me kept stamping the floor and saying between themselves, 'Let us wait and see if we shall be needed'. Now it was the turn of the white giant: 'Can you tell us something about amalgamation?'[2]

Astonished, I reacted, almost involuntarily: 'Amalgamation! What is amalgamation?'

The officer turned round and shouted as if possessed, 'Gentlemen! Come! Come, gentlemen! We shall need your services!' Punches. Kicks. Punches. Kicks. Punches. Kicks. Pushed. Pulled. Pushed. Pulled. Pushed. Pulled. Hair pulled out. Beard uprooted. Carried in the air by my hair. I was thrown on the floor, then commanded to stand. Thrown on the floor. Commanded to stand. It was a long, very long, hour. Perhaps two, perhaps three. Perhaps thirty minutes. The thunders of the blows and the thuds were punctuated by my groaning and the occasional shouts by the possessed three: 'Enemy of my country! Communist! Terrorist! Die! Die! Die! Kill! Kill! Amalgamation! Botswana! Amalgamation! Botswana boys![3] Enemy of my country! Subversive! Communist church! Die! Smelling kaffir! Swine! Skunk! Political donkey! Will you speak? Will you speak? Will you speak?' Stop. Dead silence. No movement. One frightening, long minute.

'Window! Let the dirty swine see the bowels of the earth. If we cannot get anything out of his live body, we shall get something out of his corpse.' The officer moved from the window.

The two whites, now joined by a black, grabbed me, dangled me upside down through the window, and demanded, 'Amalgamation! Amalgamation! Botswana! Botswana boys! If we cannot get satisfactory answers, we will let you fall to the ground

---

[2] The South African government suspected that several black political groups were coming together.

[3] They were accusing me of recruiting schoolboys to go to Botswana to join the liberation movement against apartheid.

below, breaking your spinal cord and scattering your cheeky brains all over the place, and we'll tell the world that you jumped through the window.'

Thank God I had been fasting since Thursday, for a full stomach would have added weight to the hopelessness of the situation. I said a prayer at that moment. I could even afford to speak softly and move my lips. My mouth was at a safe distance, though my life as a whole was in danger. 'If I must hang in the air, Lord, let it be. Your Son hung on the cross. Who am I to be identified with his suffering! What an honour! Your Son suffered to regain the life – the rights of all people enslaved and oppressed by death and the devil. He died for the whole world.'

'Now, kaffir, are you ready to tell the truth if we pull you in?'

'Oh Lord, I am only one of many in South Africa who must hang for the liberation and freedom and rights of the oppressed whose only wrong is their skin, painted by you. If I must die, let it be; but one thing I ask of you, let not the hope for freedom die in my people. Amen.'

Once the window-on-the-bowels-of-the-earth exercise was over, the officer in charge demanded that I tell about the underground activities of all black organizations, banned and unbanned, of my church activities, of the SACC, SASO, the CI, the Bold Evangelical Christian Organization (BECO), the Lutheran World Federation, the escape routes to Botswana, Lesotho, Swaziland, Mozambique. He demanded to know my personal and family history; he wanted me to write down all the sermons I had preached and all the speeches I had ever delivered. Yes, he demanded to know my connections with trade unions, my involvement in student riots, and all about other connections. When all my verbal answers could not satisfy them (I was all the time forced to stand), they handcuffed me, having made sure to place newspapers round my wrists to prevent visible marks, forced my legs through my arms, and pushed a stick in between, placing it on two high chairs. And there I was, hanging in the air. The pains were indescribable. The black bully disappeared, followed by the two white bullies and finally by their leader.

I was the loneliest man in the world. Next door I could hear the white giant: 'Take off your dress. Your smelling petticoat. Show us your terrorist thing which makes your terrorist boyfriends go mad.' There was a struggle. Some thuds. The walls shook. Silence, very uncomfortable silence. Heavy breathing, staccato pace. Another struggle. Then, 'She's trying to bite me. Bring those pliers. We shall pull her thing out.' A long, long struggle. How could a young girl, judging by her voice, keep these white giants and the black bully struggling? It sounded like the Third World War. Like the superpowers allied against tiny Lesotho.

'NO. No. NO. *Ngiyafa baba! Ngiyafa baba* [I'm dying, Daddy!] NO. NO . . . NO . . .' For some time her screams had miraculously healed my pains. When her screams subsided, I had started groaning, and when nothing could be heard from her, I continued exactly where she had left off. For the first time in 20 years I cried like a young girl, letting loose all the tears that had been clogged for years by the artificial pride of masculinity. I was actually surprised when Thick Bully shouted a message to Thin Bully (as I came to call the two bullies, '*Kerels, kom julle hoor; hy kraai soos'n haan*' ('Chaps, come, here; he crows like a cock'). I had thought I was cackling like a hen. All four were back in my room. Each took a can of beer from a small refrigerator, and as if responding to the movements of a choir conductor, they opened the cans at the same time, drank at the same pace, and emptied the cans as if a voice had shouted, 'Stop.' In a chorus they shouted, 'Are you going to speak? Speak the truth! Nothing but the truth! Stop telling lies in this room of truth [*waarkamer* or *waarheidkamer*].'

I agreed that I would tell the truth, hoping I would be let off the hook. I was wrong. 'First you must tell the truth on the cross; thereby we shall know that you can tell the truth on the floor.' Having said this, the white giant let the group out, but before he closed the door, he said, 'Some friendly advice to my dean: arrange all your facts concerning all our questions in order to tell them all without explanation in five minutes. Remember, we cannot free you, only the truth can make you free. You are a man of the Bible, you should know that.' This time my silent pain had the upper hand over the screams in the adjoining offices, the rooms known as truth rooms when interrogations were in session. Again I was alone, and lonely . . . except for the uncompromising pain. I arranged my screams in a meaningful chorus, directed at a real target, clothed in the words of Calvary, in Hebrew and Aramaic, in Venda and in Sotho: *Eli, Eli, lama sabachtani! Eloi, Eloi, lama sabachtani! Mudzimu wanga wo ntutshelani! Modimo waka O nthogeletseng!* (My God, my God, why have you forsaken me?) My God! My God! Never in my life had these words been so meaningful.

When I regained consciousness only the black fellow was in the room. 'Welcome to the land of the living, black brother. Do you remember me? Sit up and look at me properly.' I had only leg irons. The stick and the handcuffs had been removed, leaving rings of blood on my wrists and ankles. At one stage or another the newspaper slips must have moved, allowing direct contact between iron and flesh. The face before me was familiar. I had seen it at many BPC and SASO conferences and seminars. Most recently I had seen him at Sibasa during student riots. Near Sibasa police station he had stopped to greet me, raised a clenched fist and shouted, 'Power to the people,' to which I responded, 'Power to Azania [South Africa].' He had then indicated, 'The Soweto struggle continues and is even growing; how are you managing in this part of Azania? I must already say that we are very much impressed by your performance this side.' When he uttered the last word, I was already more than three metres from him, so that he had to half-shout it. Here he was today, dressed as he was at Sibasa: blue jeans, a black afro-shirt with a clenched fist on the breast and a map of Africa on the back with the word 'Azania' on the southern tip, smart boots, their colour lost in dirt, unaccompanied by socks. His hair was like dusty wild grass, long, uncombed, and uncared for.

'Now, brother,' he added in faltering Venda, 'I have been one of you. I can assure you that we are fighting a stupid war, a lost cause. I am now several years with the security police. I enjoy my job. I have seen the light. During my many years of service all the political die-hards that we detained ultimately cracked like nuts under pressure. Some, within minutes of detention, on their own initiative would say, "I want to tell you now. I will not wait for interrogation." They would sing like birds. Others crack after an hour, a day or two, a week or a month, even more, but one principle is clear: they all crack sooner or later. No person can carry the Drankensberg[4] and survive. Now you should make up your mind: tell all with the minimum of suffering or spill all the beans in the bottom of hell. Perhaps you should know,' he went on, 'that your friends were also detained immediately after you. For the past two weeks we have been working on them. We now know all about you. We also know that you were influenced and misled. We do not want to punish you, but those who misguided you to misguide other people who in turn misguided other people, particularly the young. I do not want to see the white police deal with you again. You are mine, but only if you co-operate, if you play ball. It is now one in the morning. They come back at eight. Here is a pen and

---

[4] The largest mountain range in South Africa.

some paper. Let the river flow, do not dam it up, let it burst and carry you into the ocean. Good luck, black brother, do a good job.'

I sat on a comfortable chair, table and stationery before me. The most distasteful task stared me in the eyes. I tackled the bull by the horns. I wrote and wrote, and wrote and wrote and wrote and wrote and wrote. Every time I filled a page, he would take the leaf for examination. 'You should improve your details. Names of persons, places, dates, motives, things minuted and unminuted, who proposed what motion, who seconded, who opposed – all these things must come in.' I wrote . . . and . . . wrote . . . for hours on end. Before he left, at about eight in the morning, I overheard him say to the whites who had just arrived, 'The dean has written a lot of rubbish. It is lying on the table.'

Two bullies marched in, a completely new lot. The one walked behind me and landed a deafening hot punch on my right ear. Simultaneously the other removed the chair from under me, shoved me to the ground, and kicked the table over me. Another kick, this time to my groin, followed by another, three . . . five . . . innumerable. A hundred pages of statement lay scattered all over the floor. I was forced to stand up, but halfway, a blow to my face left me tumbling backwards. One bully put his boot on my neck while the other placed his boot on my genitals. I was allowed to stand, and then forced to carry the 'liberation stick', with weights attached to both ends. Carrying this stick with hands raised, I was forced to jump into the air without rest, singing loudly, 'Amandla Awethu! Power to the people! Power to Azania!' I sweated like a horse and groaned like a hungry pig. Totally exhausted, I let the stick fall on the floor and collapsed. Heaving like a heavyweight boxer in the fifteenth round, I managed to mumble a few words, syllable by syllable: 'I . . . am . . . tired . . . I . . . am . . . dying.'

The same officer from hours before, the white giant, had arrived in the meantime and instructed that cold water be poured over my head. I managed to gulp two or three mouthfuls, mixed with dirty, salty sweat. But who cared? I was helped into a standing position, and then forced to sit on an 'imaginary chair', that is, to squat, arms stretched out to the sides, unsupported.

My energy exhausted, I collapsed. They kicked . . . pummelled . . . rolled and spat on me. They pulled me up on my knees, supporting me on both sides. I collapsed.

When I regained consciousness I was being treated by a white doctor. 'Why are you sweating?' the doctor enquired. Before I could say a word, the security policeman said, 'He is just excited.'

The doctor gave me some medicines and then said in Afrikaans, '*Hy is baie swak; hy mag vrek; moenie hom harde oefening gee nie*' ('He is too weak; he may die; do not give him hard exercise'). After his departure, the interrogation continued. I had to stand the whole time.

Next came the 'liberation broom', a very broad, heavy broom. I was forced to sweep aimlessly in the room. In the process I would now get a hard kick from behind, a surprise punch below the belt, another on the chest or stomach, then on the head, or a chop at the back of the neck. It had already been two days with no food, and no sleep. No water, no rest, no peace, no love, no sense, no mercy . . . perhaps no God. Several times I would fall asleep standing, only to be awakened by a hot slap that sent me flying across the room.

Occasionally the white giant would pretend to be very friendly, saying, 'Stop your nonsense, you youngsters. This man is a pastor. You need not be rough with him. He will co-operate.' Then he would command me to sit on the floor. 'Do you have any confessions to make?' When my answer did not

165

satisfy him, he would jump in fury. 'You kaffirs are stupid. An adult kaffir does not even have the brains of a five-year-old white child. Yet you say you do not want Bantu education. If you are doing so badly in Bantu education already, how do you think you will manage with the white man's education?' I wrote and wrote. And wrote. And wrote and wrote and wrote and wrote and wrote. And wrote. 'You continue to write all this rubbish, and you will see what will happen to you. You and Steve Biko have corrupted the youth of this country. You preach that apartheid is the policy of the devil and that those who practise this policy are agents of the devil. We want to tell you once and for all, if we must choose between sharing power with non-whites or obliterating them, we shall choose the latter. If you do not like apartheid, you'd better pack your bags and be off to Tanzania to live with your communist brothers.' After this lecture the officer went through my statement, popularly known as a 'confession'. A tall, slender white man came in, most probably senior to all present. They all stood up and saluted him. The white giant greeted him, 'Good afternoon, Major.' 'Afternoon, Captain. But why does this baboon not stand up? Is this what you are teaching him, giving him soft porridge[5] just because he is a bloody pastor? *Laat hy gaan kak* [Let him fuck off]. He is smelling terribly. Take him out of this office; it is not a pig sty!'

I was led out by both security policemen, to some holding cells nearby. 'Come out, *madala* [old man]!' one called out contemptuously. Out came an old man, as pale as a ghost, lips cracked, and apparently very weak physically. 'Do you know this man, *madala*?' Instead of responding to the question, the man raised a clenched fist and saluted me: 'Power to the people.

---

[5] Light treatment.

Power, brother! You are fine. I am fine. Power!' I knew him. I recognized him – once we were both guest speakers at a student conference in Wilgespruit – old man Muthuping. Some call him Justice.

ABDELLATIF LAÂBI: MOROCCO

Dream of a Wake

The warders had begun to clink their keys against the bars which separated you, and to knock on the door at the entrance to the visiting room. You had to hurry up and end the visit. You noticed your wife hesitate for a moment. Then her eyes filled with tears and you knew by a slight tremor and pursing of her lips that something was wrong. She turned her head away, unable to stand your questioning look.

'What's the matter?'

'You know, I had something to tell you. I'm sorry I didn't do it sooner.'

'What is it?'

'Your mother is dead.'

'When?'

'The twenty-seventh of July.'

'How did she die?'

'You know she already had high blood pressure. Then she became sort of anorexic. For some weeks she had refused to eat.'

'Why didn't you tell me about it when it happened?'

'Your family begged me not to, to wait until the trial ended.'

'Did you think it would have changed anything in my behaviour, had some effect on my morale?'

'No. You know that. But I had promised. Do you forgive me?'

'Yes. Of course.'

The warders brutally pulled the curtain. You had scarcely

From *Rue de Retour*, translated from the French by Jacqueline Kaye, Readers International, 1989.

time to see another tear run down your wife's face. Then nothing. The curtain hid everything. Your eyes were dry.

'Goodbye,' your wife was still saying on the other side of the curtain.

'Goodbye. Don't worry,' you said finally.

You took your basket and went out of the visiting room. In the exercise yard the light was blinding. Your eyes were still dry. There is a feeling of emptiness in your brain and heart, a kind of irritation – as if you had not had and could not have the right kind of reaction. It was true you had learned not to dramatize anything any more. From the beginning of the ordeal you had collected and received so many hard knocks. In its recurrence death no longer had the bitter taste of the destructive unknown. It had become familiar, an ordinary actor in the collective drama.

You returned to your cell with two comrades (at that time you were three to a cell). You took out the food brought by your families. You ate while chatting about the week's events. After drinking tea, each one resumed his place. Each of your comrades got a book out and began to read.

Unlike other occasions, you did not begin a letter to your wife, talking about the visit, so as to prolong the gracefulness of the meeting. You lay down. You unfolded a blanket. You used it to cover your whole body, even your head. Then you opened your eyes in the darkness. You stayed like that for a long time . . . Quite a bit later – you must certainly have sobbed – you felt a hand being placed on your head. A comrade was calling you. You lifted the blanket.

'What's the matter with you?' he asked. 'Are you ill?'

'Yes . . . No. It's nothing. Some bad news.'

'What is it?'

'My mother is dead.'

At these words, the other left his place and came up to you.

He took your hand while the other continued to stroke your head. None of the three of you knew what to say. Silence filled the cell until the moment the warder came round to put out the light. You remained like that in the darkness. Then one of your friends murmured in a quiet warm voice:

'Courage, comrade, courage!'

'Thank you, comrade. I'll be all right.'

Your friends returned to their places. You opened your eyes again in the darkness of the cell which had now become total. Silence reigned, broken from time to time by the noise the rats made scratching the bottom of the bucket which you had filled with water to make it heavy and which you placed over the hole of the W.C. to protect yourselves against these nocturnal pests. The rats knocked against the bucket, got mad, moved it a bit, but could not overturn it. They finally left, hoping to find a way out somewhere else.

You stared into the darkness. You were looking for something. Yes: you were trying to recover the colour of your mother's eyes. She had eyes of a particular greenish-blue, more green than blue, like marjoram when it is still fresh. You can't tell how you fell asleep. A knock-out blow to the head which immediately plunged you into the vortex of a dream.

The scene opens on the small house of 'Ayn al Khayl where you first saw the light of day, where you spent the first days of your childhood. All the neighbourhood is gathered to help at a double ceremony. The family is all there. But this is no longer the small clan whose ranks were scattered more than 30 years ago. It's a veritable tribe that parades before you, nephews and nieces, children of cousins, husbands and wives of all that progeniture. Faces you cannot put a name to but who all have what one might call a familiar air.

You are there, in the middle of the crowd, in the splendid clothes of the newly circumcised. You are wearing a green embroidered tarbouch on your head, with a kaftan and babouches of the same colour and with the same embroidery. You are enthroned on a chair of painted wood. You pay no attention to the pain which radiates out from your new scar because there's so much going on. In response to the sounds of the *ghaitas* and the wild beatings of the tambours, come the piercing cries of the chorus of wailing women. All around you faces are impassive. They express neither sorrow nor joy. You look in vain for your father in the midst of the crowd. You can't find him.

The wailing women suddenly appear. They come out of your parents' bedroom. But instead of uttering cries, they begin to let out youyous and to recite propitiatory formulas that are only pronounced on happy occasions. They are bearing on their shoulders a mortuary slab on which a corpse is stretched out. They parade around a central courtyard of the house and then put down their burden. Their youyous rise up more beautifully. The *ghaitas* bawl out amid the mad beating of the tambours.

It is your mother stretched out on the slab, rigid, but with a strange beauty. Made up, wearing her bridal dress, she looks as if she has just closed her eyes like any bride during the wedding ceremony. Relatives and neighbours come closer and take out of their pockets banknotes which they wave around ostentatiously before slipping them into the embroidered golden waistband, four fingers wide, around your mother's waist. Each gift provokes more youyous. Finally your father emerges from the crowd.

He is crying. You notice he is the only one who is crying. He goes up to your mother, takes the banknotes and gives them to the woman who appears to be the chief mourner. At the same time the women mourners lift up the slab and go towards the door of the house. Once there, they try unsuccessfully to pass through it but the door is too narrow. They try in every possible way. Nothing works. In a final attempt, they lift the slab up as if it were a wheelbarrow. The body slips and is on the point of tipping out onto the steep road.

You feel your heart beating wildly. You are suffocating. Your body does not obey you any more. It's getting heavier and heavier as if it's being crushed by a gigantic press. You want to cry out and call for help but you can't speak any more. You know that you simply must call out to free yourself from being crushed and to recover the use of your limbs. You struggle with yourself for a long time before you marshal sufficient energy to release your cry . . .

'Are you all right? Shall I call the warder? Do you want a drink?'

Your comrade goes to the tap in the darkness. You take the water. You drink it and lie down again . . .

Bit by bit you get your breath back. Your heartbeat recovers its normal rhythm. You lie on your back. You think about your dream. You don't try to decipher it. You look at it as a work of art by the double who lives in your body, ceaselessly weaving the weft of the dark places of your fears and your obsessions. Then a single idea arises from the labyrinth of your terror, a promise. Yes. You promise that the first thing that you will do, if one day you should go free, is to take yourself to the grave of your mother in Fes.

NAWAL EL SA'ADAWI: EGYPT

Solitude

I had imagined prison to be solitude and total silence, the isolated cell in which one lives alone, talking to oneself, rapping at the wall to hear the responding knock of one's neighbour. Here, though, I enjoyed neither solitude nor silence, except in the space after midnight and before the dawn call to prayer. I could not pull a door shut between me and the others, even when I was in the toilet.

If Boduur ceased quarrelling with her colleagues, she would begin reciting the Quar'an out loud. And if Boduur went to sleep, Fawqiyya would wake up and begin to discuss and orate. If Fawqiyya went to sleep, Boduur would wake up to announce prayertime and the onset of night.

One night, the quarrel between Boduur and one of her comrades continued until dawn, ending only when Boduur fainted after she'd been hit by violent nervous convulsions. She tore at her hair and face with her fingernails, screaming until she lost consciousness.

As soon as the *shawisha* had opened the cell door in the morning, I called out to her, 'I want to be transferred to a solitary cell. I don't want to stay in this cell any longer.'

But the prison administration rejected my request. I came to understand that in prison, torture occurs not through solitude and silence but in a far more forceful way through uproar and noise. The solitary cell continued to float before me like a dream unlikely to be realized.

Since childhood, I've had a passion for solitude. I've not had

From *Memoirs from the Women's Prison*, translated from the Arabic by Marilyn Booth, The Women's Press, 1986.

a room in which I could shut myself off, for the number of individuals in every stage of my life has been greater than the number of rooms in the house. But I have always wrested for myself a place in which I could be alone to write. My ability to write has been linked to the possibility of complete seclusion, of being alone with myself, for I am incapable of writing when I am unable to give myself completely to solitude.

After midnight, when the atmosphere grows calm and I hear only the sound of sleep's regular breathing, I rise from my bed and tiptoe to the corner of the toilet, turn the empty jerry can upside down and sit on its bottom. I rest the aluminium plate on my knees, place against it the long, tape-like toilet paper, and begin to write.

◆

In prison, a person's essence comes to light. One stands naked before oneself, and before others. Masks drop and slogans fall. In prison, one's true metal is revealed, particularly in times of crisis.

The warden gave one of our cellmates a body search and came upon a small piece of paper. It was nothing more than a short letter that she had written to her family, asking after their health and reassuring them of hers. However, the prison administration raged. There must be a pen and paper in the political cell! The search team attacked us – opening suitcases, overturning mattresses, stripping off *higaabs*, *niqaabs*, and cloaks.

One of the *munaqqabas* let out a scream – 'Infidels!' – when they uncovered her hair in front of the male prison administrators. They took her away to the disciplinary cell. From afar, we heard her screaming and we knew they had beaten her. We threatened collectively to go on a hunger strike until she was returned to us, and as a sort of protest against her beating. Collectively, that is, except Boduur and Fawqiyya.

174

'Going on strike is a type of protest and I do not participate in any protest against the authorities,' said Boduur. 'I do not address the tyrant – I only speak to God. I complain to no one. Complaining to anyone but God is a debasement!'

'They will face the strike by oppressing us still more,' was Fawqiyya's comment. 'Maybe they will put us all in correction cells and beat us.'

However, the group rejected Boduur's logic and that of Fawqiyya alike. The prison regulations do not permit beating or body searches. We must proclaim our rejection of this treatment and our protest. If we are silent this time, our silence will encourage them to repeat the insulting treatment and the beating. Let us use any weapon which we have between our hands. Even if it is merely depriving ourselves of food.

We failed to persuade Boduur. 'There is no point in making any protest,' she said in a tone of finality. 'They are tyrants. God will crush them if it is His wish.'

But Fawqiyya was more frank. The cellmates surrounded her with questions and asked how she could not submit to majority rule, when it was she who had touted the slogan of collective work and sacrifice for the sake of others. She said in a feeble voice, which was unlike any tone we'd heard from her previously, 'I am ill and I can't endure the strike.' She lay down on her bed moaning and complaining of a pain in her chest.

The door of the cell opened suddenly and we saw the *shawisha* entering, followed by our cellmate. We all jumped up to hug her, happy to see her return to us.

Fawqiyya jumped out of bed and embraced her, too, and in the act of leaping she forgot that she was ill.

◆

Before dawn, I awoke to Boduur's voice.

'Get up! Arise for prayer! Prayer is better than sleep!'

'I'm not asleep,' she said in a listless voice. 'I'm sick. They beat me here . . . on my head . . . Men and women carrying thick, heavy sticks . . . I didn't see their faces . . . I heard their voices, though . . . They pulled off my *niqaab* and *higaab* . . . my hair came down in front of them . . . I hid it with my hands, my arms. Let them beat me to death but I will not allow men to see my hair! They pulled me by the hair down on to the ground, and put their hands all around my neck so I nearly choked. They stamped on my glasses . . . and I can't see at all without my glasses . . . I have an awful headache . . . my whole body is aching . . . my head . . . my neck . . . my spine . . .'

Boduur's voice came back. 'Get up and wash so you can perform the prayer, and don't say that you're ill! Prayer cures you of sickness. It is God who heals. Don't write any complaint to anyone. God is present. If you are innocent, God will make you victorious. Do not say that you didn't do anything wrong: you must have done something sinful in your life and then forgotten about it. God could not possibly expose you to pain or torture or prison or beating without a sin on your part. A human being is always sinful and you must ask God's forgiveness. Repentance is an obligation, whether you've committed a sin or not. Since God has requested us to ask His forgiveness, we must have committed sins. Human beings are sinful by nature – otherwise, there would be no such thing as repentance or forgiveness. Say "I beg God's forgiveness" three times, and get up to pray! You absolutely must stay up all night to pray – the five obligatory prayers are not enough. If you find the water cut off, intention is enough. The religion makes things easy, not difficult, and washing with water is not obligatory. Water is not important. It is important, though, that you keep God in your mind and speech, day and night. Staying up at night to pray is better and more enduring than sleep. You went to the correction cell because you were not staying up at night to pray and because you haven't memorized the Qur'an. I've told you more than once that you must learn two chapters of the Qur'an by heart every week. This is a sacred duty. Whoever does not fulfil it must have her feet whipped fifty times. Who knows, maybe it was God's will that you were beaten by the hands of others so you would atone for your sins. It's not enough that you cover your face with a *niqaab*. You must cleanse your heart of Satan's whisperings. Woman is nearer to Satan than man – through Eve, Satan was able to reach Adam. Woman was created from a crooked rib and she becomes straightened only through blows which hurt. Her duty is to listen and obey without making any objections – even a blink or a scowl. A scowl calls for 30 lashes on the feet.'

I saw the girl rise from her bed. I saw her walk, her back stooped, in the direction of the toilet, groping for a way with her hands, for she had lost her glasses. She put on her cloak and *niqaab* . . . and stood behind Boduur, praying and asking God's forgiveness for her sins.

◆

Shawisha Nabawiyya astonished me sometimes by taking courageous stands in which she stood firmly on the side of right and showed no fear of the prison administration's power. Unlike the other *shawishas*, she did not accept any bribery. Nor did she allow a prisoner to be beaten, even if the senior official in charge ordered her to do so.

'Once I obeyed the order and beat a prisoner in the correction cell,' she said. 'Then I went home, and I felt pain around my heart. I stayed home for a week, sick, and since then I have not beaten any prisoner. Even if they threatened to dismiss me, I would never beat a prisoner. I quarrel with my son when he beats a cat or dog – so what about a human being?'

Boduur was sitting beside her, listening to her words. 'You have a good heart, *Shawisha* Nabawiyya, and God will reward you well. God has requested us to show gentleness towards animals and human beings and all of God's creatures.'

'Except for one,' I remarked. 'Woman.'

'Why woman?' asked the *shawisha*.

'Because she was created from a crooked rib,' I replied, 'and only straightens up through beating.' I laughed, and so did the *shawisha* and the others in the cell – all except Boduur. Without delay, the scowl appeared on her forehead in the form of a deep, vertical line. 'Woman lacks intelligence and religion,' she said.

'And you? Aren't you a woman?' asked the *shawisha*.

'No!' she shouted.

SYL CHENEY-COKER: SIERRA LEONE

The Night of the Beasts

Seven feet by seven when the night
invades threateningly the walls of the cell
and the warden performs his monotonous habit of
    praying
before locking up his charge; seven feet sculptured
    in stone
set to perfection like that other six feet dug in the
    earth;
again they have imprisoned him, whipped him in
    profile
held him up, his heart beating, facing the brazier
so that thinking of his mother in the night of the
    beasts
the son of woman shakes convulsively
before covering his face to cry

burnt out in skeleton, this country's image
has a vicious look it resembles a dagger's edge
it speaks chapters of brutality of villages nakedly
    scarred
of rivers infested with corpses of graves hurriedly
    covered
this country whose heart has the beat of a river
amazed at the size of its own flood
whose history born out of the vertical rupture of
    the earth
no longer remembers the rape of its own pulsating
    female

prisoner of conscience, the man paces seven feet
by seven, resembling a deranged civet

the beasts have beaten out his brain, only his
nightmare is left flowing from a sea of dead
   urchins
a lava of bad blood gushing from the head of his
   country
and reliving it all over again he hears a tune like
death's larghetto into the dawn where his beloved
waits in tears holding a bouquet of flowers.

KOIGI WA WAMWERE: KENYA

A Massacre of Prisoners

'To the extent that you did it to one of the least of these my brothers, you did it to me.'

The massacre started with grains of sand in maize flour. The first time *ugali* with sand came, I tried to eat and did not complain, thinking its presence a mere accident. The following day, the same meal was served. Now I complained and refused to eat. It continued coming and I continued to complain. Finally, I was given more potatoes instead of *ugali*. When I asked why they were not cooking with clean maize flour, I was told it was because flour with sand could not simply be thrown away. It had to be eaten because there was no money to replace it.

On the other side of the fence, in the compounds of ordinary criminals, without my knowledge, complaints against *ugali* with sand had been growing and would soon culminate in prisoners' refusal to eat, with terrible consequences.

The night of 31 May 1984 was among my worst in prison. I did not sleep worrying about the possibility of release on 1 June, which was a public holiday. During the day, I had heard names of prisoners who might be released being called out and this had given me the hope that I too might be set free. Dawn found me awake, eyes wide open, red and terribly tired. I simply could not sleep.

At about seven, I heard names of those who would be released being called out. In the meantime, I strained my ears for any sign of my own pardon, but there was none.

From Koigi wa Wamwere's forthcoming prison memoirs.

That morning they were late in opening the cell to allow me to go to the toilet. Suddenly I heard a loud gunshot, another and another and I began to count 4, 5, 6, 7, 8, 9, 10, 11.

There was a lot of screaming, wailing and shouting:

'Stop or I will shoot. Go there, all of you. Line up. *Kaba*.'

'Lie down. Lie down. Squat in line. Squat in line. *Kabeni Kabeni*.'

In compound 14 next to the detention block, I heard a prisoner crying in great pain. A prison officer shouted:

'Death is what those who bring politics to prison get. If you refuse to obey orders to eat, we cannot just sit by and watch. We do what we must. Wake up, move there. If you are hurt, it is your fault, *shauriyako*. Blame politics, not prison. *Ingia*, move in. Without politics, those who have died would not have to die.'

When an *askari* opened my cell, I asked: 'What is going on?'

'Nothing!'

'I heard shooting.'

'Yes, of elephants that had strayed onto the prison farm.'

'The shooting and shouting did not come from the farm. It came from the kitchen area.'

'They are stupid! It is their fault!'

'Who is stupid?'

'Prisoners who refused to drink porridge.'

'Why did they refuse?'

'They said it had sand, but this is prison.'

'So what happened?'

'Each bullet shot you heard took away a life.'

'You mean eleven prisoners were killed?'

'Yes, it was their fault!'

◆

My stay in Manyani ended with the slaughter of eleven souls.

It was smaller than the massacre that had taken place at Naivasha. A prisoner there called Kairu, driven insane by the brutality of guards, reacted to the beating of another prisoner by an *askari*, bashed him on the head with a hammer, chiselled out his brain and ate it. The guards at Naivasha organized a retaliatory raid, slaughtering tens of prisoners.

The Manyani massacre was not reported in the Kenyan press and there was no public or international reaction, as there had been about the Hola massacre in 1959, when colonial guards killed a similar number of prisoners.

MAINA WA KĨNYATTĨ: KENYA

The Prison Catechist

You saw the two old torn blankets
On the floor
You saw the stinking bucket of shit
In the middle of the cell
You saw the garbage they feed me
Vermin crawling the walls
The cell an ice box

You heard a scream
Through the barred windows
You saw the torturers with nightsticks
You smelt the stench of death
In the corridor
Yet you insist
I forgive my captor
And believe in your God
A God who has betrayed millions

I know
You cannot see your perfidy
You cannot understand your pernicious act
You are a tool
In the hand of a dictator

21 November, 1984
Kamĩtĩ M. S. Prison

JACK MAPANJE: MALAWI

Skipping Without Rope[1]

I will, I will skip without your rope
Since you say I should not, I cannot
Borrow your son's skipping rope to
Exercise my limbs, I will skip without

Your rope as you say even the lace
I want will hang my neck until I die
I will create my own rope, my own
Hope and skip without your rope as

You insist I do not require to stretch
My limbs fixed by these fevers of your
Reeking sweat and your prison walls
I will, will skip with my forged hope;

Watch, watch me skip without your
Rope watch me skip with my hope
A-one, a-two, a-three, a-four, a-five
I will, a-seven, I do, will skip, a-ten,

Eleven, I will skip without, will skip
Within and skip I do without your
Rope but with my hope; and I will,
Will always skip you dull, will skip

Your silly rules, skip your filthy walls
Your weevil pigeon peas, skip your

---

[1] Prisoners were not allowed to bathe until they stank; they created stench by
skipping.

Scorpions, skip your Excellency Life
Glory; I do, you don't, I can, you can't,

I will, you won't, I see, you don't, I
Sweat, you don't, I will, will wipe my
Gluey brow then wipe you at a stroke
I will, will wipe your horrid, stinking,

Vulgar prison rules, will wipe you all
then hop about, hop about my cell, my
Home, the mountains, my globe as your
Sparrow hops about your prison yard

Without your hope, without your rope
I swear, I will skip without your rope, I
Declare, I will have you take me to your
Showers to bathe me where I can resist

This singing child you want to shape me
I'll fight your rope, your rules, your hope
As your sparrow does under your super-
vision! Guards! Take us for the shower!

MUHAMMAD AFIFI MATTAR: EGYPT

Testimony

At 2.30 in the morning of 2 March 1991 my home and bedroom in Ramlat al-Angab (my village in the district of Ashmoun in Manufiyya province) were raided by forces armed with sub-machine guns, batons and bulletproof vests. Members of this force, led by officers in both civilian dress and uniform, meticulously searched my house, my books and my personal papers. They neither presented an authorization from the State Prosecutor or any other legal body nor gave any reason for this terrifying armed assault. Following the search, I was led, shackled and between two rows of soldiers poised to fire, to a transport vehicle. The vehicle set out, followed by several others guarding it, with neither myself nor my family knowing my destination. I was held until noon that day in the police station of Shibeen al-Kom where I went through the routine police procedures of being photographed and fingerprinted, filling out forms, etc. I was then taken by the transport vehicle to Lazoughly Square in Cairo and transferred to officials of the State Security Intelligence. Immediately the brutal torture and dehumanizing practices against me began. These took the following forms:

1 Sophisticated metal fetters were placed around my wrists, the kind that would tighten at the slightest movement of the hands, with the effect that hands, arms and shoulders combined into a mass of intertwined pain, numbness and unbearably slow-moving insensibility. These fetters were kept on me for the entire ten days of my stay at Lazoughly headquarters.

From PEN International *Newsletter*, Vol. XCII, No. 1, 1992. Translated by Barbara Harlow.

2 Both my eyes and ears were bound with a hard, pressing band that was never removed, causing an accumulation and hardening of pus under my eyelids that made my eyes feel as if they were filled with small bits of broken glass. Any sudden movement of eyes or closed eyelids became extremely painful. The band also caused my ears to swell, gluing them painfully to my head. Continued beatings and being knocked to the floor forced the knot of the band to break the skin of my head, leaving a deep wound, two fingers wide. This wound bled for 45 days before it finally healed leaving a scar still visible today. All the above affected and weakened as well the vision of my right eye.

3 I was forced on more than one occasion to swallow two small unidentified tablets that caused severe mental disorientation, visual and auditory hallucinations and a total loss of any sense of time and place. I was prey to confused dreams, the most painful of which was that my children and other members of my family were assembled to watch me being tortured, dehumanized and threatened with murder and sexual assault. Under the band covering my eyes and ears, I would imagine that I saw and heard them. This was the effect of the drug that I was forced to take, a drug given in order to deprive a person of will and judgement, to uncover what is hidden in the mind, and to destroy any self-control.

4 I was hung by my bound hands like an animal for the slaughter. My feet were tied, so preventing me from standing or moving and concentrating the weight of my body on those two wrists hung high in a place I could not see. In this position I would be beaten with batons and other instruments. My pain and terror were intensified by the fact that my body was thrown back and forth by the beating, and by the threat that the baton would be forced to penetrate between my thighs.

5 Both my hands were subjected to electric shocks that made me scream like a wounded wolf for long hours and caused my whole body to tremble with pain. My fingers were burnt, black and raw. The tips of my fingers and the back of my hands have still not completely regained their sensitivity.

6 I was stripped and held naked in the cold wind for a long period of time, until I nearly lost consciousness.

7 I underwent severe and savage beatings that would strike at all parts of my body in a rapid and terrifying rhythm, as well as quick painful slaps to the face and more professional blows that bruised my entire body. One of these wounds cut to the very bones of my nose, leaving a visible scar – the mark of the poet's standing with the authorities in our time.

8 I was denied food and life necessities, except in minimal amounts, for long periods of time. No attention was paid to the human needs of a sick person for medicine or blankets. Going to the toilet gave my tormentors an opportunity to humiliate whatever was left of my sense of being human.

This, then, is what happened to me during ten days of continuous torture. 'Ten days' are words, but I experienced them as a prolonged dark age of despair that I faced alone against an unforgettable brutality.

Following those ten days, on 12 March 1991 I was removed to Tara Istiqbal prison and placed in cell no. 2912B, where I was held until my release on 12 May 1991. I never stood before any prosecuting body, nor was I charged, and I was never given a chance to defend myself.

Survival

TAHAR DJAOUT: ALGERIA

March 15, 1962

how to curb their rage to dissolve the stars
and to birth eternal night
I challenge their iron
and the enraged ire with which they multiply the
    chains

in the blue smile
of the Admiralty open on the promises
today in long swallows I gulp
– sun thundering over Algiers –
the joys of a feasting
where resurrected dawns gambol
and yet I think on the holocausts
unleashed to make dawn break
I think of Feraoun
– smile frozen in the sun's circumcision

they are afraid of the truth
they are afraid of the straight pen
they are afraid of truly human humans
and you, Mouloud, you insisted and spoke
about wheat fields for the sons of the poor
and spoke of pulverizing all the barbed wire
that lacerated our horizons

they speak of you and say that you were too good
that you felt revolted
hearing shells greet each dawn

Translated from the French by Pierre Joris.

that you believed human beings to be born so as to
  be brothers
and though challenging all the orgies of horror
you were incapable of hatred

one day, Mouloud, goodness finally triumphed
and we could wear the sun's trident
and we could honour the memory of the dead
because
    with
        your hands, those gleaners of dawn's
            mysteries,
and your dreamy inveterate poet's face,
you have known how to fulfil our truths
written in sun scraps
on the breasts of all those who revolt

NELSON MANDELA: SOUTH AFRICA

Rivonia

Prison not only robs you of your freedom, it attempts to take away your identity. Everyone wears a uniform, eats the same food, follows the same schedule. It is by definition a purely authoritarian state that tolerates no independence or individuality. As a freedom fighter and as a man, one must fight against the prison's attempt to rob one of these qualities.

From the courthouse, I was taken directly to Pretoria Local, the gloomy red-brick monstrosity that I knew so well. But I was now a convicted prisoner, not an awaiting-trial prisoner, and was treated without even the little deference that is afforded to the latter. I was stripped of my clothes and Colonel Jacobs was finally able to confiscate my *kaross*. I was issued the standard prison uniform for Africans: a pair of short trousers, a rough khaki shirt, a canvas jacket, socks, sandals and a cloth cap. Only Africans are given short trousers, for only African men are deemed 'boys' by the authorities.

I informed the authorities that I would under no circumstances wear shorts and told them I was prepared to go to court to protest. Later, when I was brought dinner, stiff cold porridge with half a teaspoonful of sugar, I refused to eat it. Colonel Jacobs pondered this and came up with a solution: I could wear long trousers and have my own food, if I agreed to be put in isolation. 'We were going to put you with the other politicals,' he said, 'but now you will be alone, man. I hope you enjoy it.' I assured him that solitary

These extracts are from *Long Walk to Freedom*, Little, Brown & Company, 1994.

confinement would be fine as long as I could wear and eat what I chose.

◆

For the next few weeks, I was completely and utterly isolated. I did not see the face or hear the voice of another prisoner. I was locked up for 23 hours a day, with 30 minutes of exercise in the morning and again in the afternoon. I had never been in isolation before, and every hour seemed like a year. There was no natural light in my cell; a single bulb burned overhead 24 hours a day. I did not have a wrist-watch and I often thought it was the middle of the night when it was only late afternoon. I had nothing to read, nothing to write on or with, no one to talk to. The mind begins to turn in on itself, and one desperately wants something outside oneself on which to fix one's attention. I have known men who took half-a-dozen lashes in preference to being locked up alone. After a time in solitary, I relished the company even of the insects in my cell, and found myself on the verge of initiating conversations with a cockroach.

I had one middle-aged African warder whom I occasionally was able to see, and one day I tried to bribe him with an apple to get him to talk to me. '*Baba*,' I said, which means Father, and is a term of respect, 'can I give you an apple?' He turned away, and met all my subsequent overtures with silence. Finally he said, 'Man, you wanted long trousers and better food, and now you have them and you are still not happy.' He was right. Nothing is more dehumanizing than the absence of human companionship. After a few weeks I was ready to swallow my pride and tell Colonel Jacobs that I would trade my long trousers for some company.

During those weeks I had plenty of time to ponder my fate. The place of a freedom fighter is beside his people, not behind bars. The knowledge and contacts I had recently made in Africa were going to be locked away rather than used in the struggle. I cursed the fact that my expertise would not be put to use in creating a freedom army.

I soon began to protest vigorously against my circumstances and demanded to be put with the other political prisoners at Pretoria Local. Among them was Robert Sobukwe. My request was ultimately granted, accompanied by a stern warning from Colonel Jacobs that serious consequences would result if I returned to my impudent ways. I don't think I ever looked forward to eating cold mealie pap so much in my life.

◆

Apart from my desire for company, I was keen to talk with Sobukwe and the others, most of whom were PAC, because I thought that in prison we might forge a unity that we could not on the outside. Prison conditions have a way of tempering polemics, and making individuals see more what unites them than what divides them.

When I was taken to the courtyard with the others, we greeted each other warmly. Besides Sobukwe, there was also John Gaetsewe, a leading member of the South African Congress of Trade Unions; Aaron Molete, an ANC member who worked for *New Age*, and Stephen Tefu, a prominent communist trade unionist, and PAC member. Robert asked me to give them an account of my African tour, which I did gladly. I was candid about how both the PAC and the ANC were perceived in the rest of Africa. At the end of my narrative I said there were issues that I wanted us to examine. But after initially allowing Sobukwe and me a certain proximity, the authorities took pains to keep us apart. We lived in single cells along a corridor and he and I were put at opposite ends.

Occasionally we did have a chance to talk as we sat next to each other on the ground of the prison courtyard sewing and patching up shabby old mailbags. I have always respected Sobukwe, and found him a balanced and reasonable man. But we differed markedly about the principal subject at hand: prison conditions. Sobukwe believed that to fight poor conditions would be to acknowledge the state's right to have him in prison in the first place. I responded that it was always unacceptable to live in degrading conditions and that political prisoners throughout history had considered it part of their duty to fight to improve them. Sobukwe responded that prison conditions would not change until the country changed. I completely agreed with this, but I did not see why that ought to prevent us from fighting in the only realm in which we now could fight. We never resolved this issue, but we did make some progress when we submitted a joint letter to the commanding officer setting out our complaints about prison conditions.

Sobukwe never broke in prison. But in Pretoria he was a bit sensitive and testy, and I attribute this to Stephen Tefu. Tefu had become a kind of goad to Sobukwe, teasing, taunting and challenging him. Even at the best of times, Tefu was a difficult fellow: dyspeptic, argumentative, overbearing. He was also articulate, knowledgeable, and an expert in Russian history. Above all, he was a fighter, but he would fight everyone, even his friends. Tefu and Sobukwe quarrelled every day.

I was keen to discuss policy issues with Sobukwe, and one of the matters I took up with him was the PAC slogan 'Freedom in 1963'. It was already 1963 and freedom was nowhere to be seen. 'My brother,' I said to Sobukwe, 'there is nothing so dangerous as a leader making a demand that he knows cannot be achieved. It creates false hopes among the people.'

I said this in a most respectful manner, but Tefu jumped in

and started to berate Sobukwe. 'Bob,' he said, 'you have met your match with Mandela. You know he is right.' Tefu continued in this vein, annoying Sobukwe to the point where he would tell Tefu, 'Leave me alone.' But Tefu would not stop. 'Bob, the people are waiting for you. They are going to kill you because you have deceived them. You are just an amateur, Bob. You are not a real politician.'

Tefu did his best to alienate me as well. Every morning, when we were visited by the warders, he would complain to them about something – the food, the conditions, the heat or the cold. One day an officer said to Tefu: 'Look, man, why do you complain every morning?'

'I complain because it is my duty to complain,' Steve said.

'But, look at Mandela,' the officer said, 'he does not complain every day.'

'Ah,' said Tefu with disgust, 'Mandela is a little boy who is afraid of the white man. I don't even know who he is. One morning, I woke up and found every newspaper saying "Mandela, Mandela, Mandela", and I said to myself, "Who is this Mandela?" I will tell you who Mandela is. He is a chap built up by you people for some reason that I don't understand. That is who Mandela is!'

◆

We were joined for two weeks by Walter Sisulu, who had been on trial in Johannesburg for incitement to strike while I had been in Pretoria. He was sentenced to six years. We had a number of opportunities to talk in jail and we discussed Walter's application for bail while his appeal was pending, a move I wholeheartedly supported. After two weeks he was released on bail, and he was instructed by the movement to go underground, from where he was to continue to lead the struggle, which he ably did.

Not long after Walter left, I was walking to the prison hospital with Sobukwe when I spotted Nana Sita in the courtyard about 25 yards away. Sita, the distinguished Indian campaigner who had led our defiance at Boksburg in 1952, had just been convicted by a Pretoria magistrate for refusing to vacate his house – the house he had lived in for more than 40 years – which was in a neighbourhood that had been proclaimed 'white' in terms of the Group Areas Act. He was hunched over, and the fact that he was barefoot despite an acute arthritic condition made me uncomfortable in my own sandals. I wanted to go over to greet him, but we were marching under the eyes of half a dozen warders.

Suddenly and without warning, I suffered a blackout. I crumpled to the concrete and sustained a deep gash above my left eye, which required three stitches. I had been diagnosed back in the Fort with high blood pressure and had been given certain pills. The cause of the blackout was evidently an overdose of these pills; I was taken off them and put on a low-salt diet; this solved the problem.

That afternoon was my first scheduled visit from Winnie since I had been sentenced. Stitches or no stitches, I was not going to miss it. She was extremely concerned when she saw me but I assured her I was fine and explained what happened. Even so, rumours circulated that my health had broken down.

Gathering Seaweed

One morning, instead of walking to the quarry, we were ordered into the back of a truck. It rumbled off in a new direction, and fifteen minutes later we were ordered to jump out. There in front of us, glinting in the morning light, we saw the ocean, the rocky shore, and in the distance, winking in the sunshine, the glass towers of Cape Town. Although it was surely an illusion, the city, with Table Mountain looming behind it, looked agonizingly close, as though one could almost reach out and grasp it.

The senior officer explained that we had been brought to the shore to collect seaweed. We were instructed to pick up the large pieces that had washed up on the beach, and wade out to collect weed attached to rocks or coral. The seaweed itself was long and slimy and brownish-green in colour. Sometimes the pieces were six to eight feet in length and thirty pounds in weight. After fishing out the seaweed from the shallows, we lined it up in rows on the beach. When it was dry, we loaded it into the back of the truck. We were told it was then shipped to Japan, where it was used as a fertilizer.

The work did not seem too taxing to us that day, but in the coming weeks and months we found it could be quite strenuous. But that hardly mattered because we had the pleasures and distraction of such a panoramic tableau: we watched ships trawling, stately oil tankers moving slowly across the horizon; we saw gulls spearing fish from the sea and seals cavorting on the waves; we laughed at the colony of penguins, which resembled a brigade of clumsy flat-footed soldiers; and we marvelled at the daily drama of the weather over Table Mountain, with its shifting canopy of clouds and sun.

In the summer the water felt wonderful, but in winter the icy Benguela Current made wading out into the waves a torture. The rocks on and around the shore were jagged, and we often cut and scraped our legs as we worked. But we preferred the sea to the quarry, although we never spent more than a few days there at a time.

The ocean proved to be a treasure chest. I found beautiful pieces of coral and elaborate shells, which I sometimes brought back to my cell. Once someone discovered a bottle of wine stuck in the sand that was still corked. I am told it tasted like vinegar. Jeff Masemola of the PAC was an extremely talented artist and sculptor and the authorities allowed him to harvest pieces of driftwood, which he carved into fantastic figures, some of which the warders offered to buy. He constructed a bookcase for me, which I used for many years. The authorities told visitors that they had provided me with it.

The atmosphere at the shore was more relaxed than at the quarry. We also relished the seaside because we ate extremely well there. Each morning when we went to the shore, we would take a large drum of fresh water. Later we would bring along a second drum, which we would use to make a kind of Robben Island seafood stew. For our stew we would pick up clams and mussels. We also caught crayfish, which hid in the crevices of rocks. Capturing a crayfish was tricky; one had to grab it firmly between its head and tail or it would wriggle free.

Abalone, or what we call *perlemoen*, were my favourite. Abalone are molluscs that cling tenaciously to rocks, and one had to prise them loose. They were stubborn creatures, difficult to open and if they were the slightest bit overcooked, they were too tough to eat.

We would take our catch and pile it into the second drum. Wilton Mkwayi, the chef among us, would concoct the stew. When it was ready, the warders would join us and we would all sit down on the beach and have a kind of picnic lunch. In 1973, in a smuggled newspaper, we read about the wedding of Princess Anne and Mark Phillips, and the story detailed in the bridal luncheon of rare and delicate dishes. The menu included mussels, crayfish and abalone, which made us laugh; we were dining on such delicacies every day.

One afternoon, we were sitting on the beach eating our stew when Lieutenant Terblanche, who was then head of prison, made a surprise visit. We quickly pretended to be working, but we had not fooled him. He soon discovered the second drum containing a mussel stew bubbling over the fire. The lieutenant opened the pot and looked inside. He then speared a mussel, ate it, and pronounced it '*smaaklik*', Afrikaans for 'tasty'.

DENNIS BRUTUS: SOUTH AFRICA

Letters to Martha

1
After the sentence
mingled feelings:
sick relief,
the load of the approaching days
apprehension –
the hints of brutality
have a depth of personal meaning;

exultation –
the sense of challenge,
of confrontation
vague heroism
mixed with self-pity
and tempered by the knowledge of those
who endure much more
and endure . . .

2
One learns quite soon
that nails and screws
and other sizeable bits of metal
must be handed in;

and seeing them shaped and sharpened
one is chilled, appalled
to see how vicious it can be
– this simple, useful bit of steel:

and when these knives suddenly flash
– produced perhaps from some disciplined anus –
one grasps at once the steel-bright horror
in the morning air
and how soft and vulnerable is naked flesh.

WOLE SOYINKA: NIGERIA

I Anoint My Flesh (Tenth Day of Fast)

I anoint my flesh
Thought is hallowed in the lean
Oil of solitude
I call you forth, all, upon
Terraces of light. Let the dark
Withdraw

I anoint my voice
And let it sound hereafter
Or dissolve upon its lonely passage
In your void. Voices new
Shall rouse the echoes when
Evil shall again arise

I anoint my heart
Within its flame I lay
Spent ashes of your hate –
Let evil die.

EDDISON J. ZVOBGO: ZIMBABWE

My Companion and Friend: The Bare Brick in My Prison Cell

The surface shines
Causing my eyes to flee
To the edges
Where the dull grey mortar
Mounts the brick
Marrying it to its neighbours.
But as I gaze
At this brick over seven years
Lying in my cage
Which measures four strides by three
An entire universe has sprung
All over its dreary burnt-out terrain.

Slowly, the erstwhile smoothed
Face blossomed with islets
Ravines and dongas:
Here a Kariba, there a volcano
And then a Grand Canyon
Running westward Maluti mountains.
No gales of wind blow
And no birds sing.
I have yet to discern cities
And highways, nor do I see
Lush green fields of maize and wheat.
But, the whole globe is here.

We have become friends
Over the long years;
Both of us are deportees

From our homes and friends;
Both of us long to return from death
To the councils of our peers.
Does nobody care to remember
That perhaps these caked grains
Have fed some plant which gave forth
Grain or fruit for man?
Is this banishment to these wedges
Through form and fire deserved?

I have counted thousands
Of hungry granules on its face
Which cry for water
And hope, hoping that they, too,
Might be fulfilled
As I long to be free and fulfilled.
Next year, as I look
At the brick much more closely,
I shall be able to travel
On its terrain to the Louvre
In Paris and perhaps even go down
To the Riviera before I die.

Perhaps those sullen edges
May soon become the very
Outerspace that still remains
To be charted by modern
Technology and astronautics,
And I, share glory with Armstrong.

This brick insulates me
From myself, rendering me
As cold as salad.
I bear no grudge against it;
All I seek is a sworn treaty

Between us, so that when its purposes
And mine are done, it may
Cover my bones and, consummate
Our seven year romance.

ANTÓNIO JACINTO: MOZAMBIQUE

Monte Gracioso

Beyond the gratings
    The barbed wire
    The trench
Beyond the turrets
The soldiers, the sentry boxes, the sentries
    Gracioso

Called the
    'dry, fierce, sterile mountain' by Camões
        Gracioso
The breadth of the sparrow hawks and xinxerotes
And the unconquerable imagination of the poet

Between earth and sky
Atop the pinnacle of the mountain
You Poetry, with a halo of clouds
Swept by winds from the Sahara
You Poetry
With a nod just for me.

Translated from the Portuguese by Don Burness.

209

WINNIE MADIKIZELA-MANDELA: SOUTH AFRICA

That Grim Time

In mid-1976, following the pupils' revolt in Soweto, eleven women – largely members of the newly formed Federation of Black Women – were detained under Section 6 of the Terrorism Act and placed in solitary confinement. When that piece of legislation was revised as Section 29 of the Internal Security Act, we were removed from solitary confinement and allowed to be together, to have newspapers and to receive visitors twice a week.

We were not all detained together; neither were we all released together, but we spent most of that time together – Jeanie Noel, Sibongile Kubeka, Sally Motlana, Cecily Palmer, Joyce Seroke, Vesta Smith, Jane Phakati, Deborah Mashoba, Fatima Meer, Lorraine Tabane and I. We also found four other women in prison who had been charged under the Terrorism Act and were awaiting trial: Elizabeth, Ethel Mafunya, Mali Mokoena and Edith Mbala.

As recorded by the SA Institute of Race Relations, the Minister of Police reported in September 1976 that 2,430 people had been detained in the three months since June that year – excluding those detained in the homelands. Among the detained were 160 schoolchildren.

Those of us who were in the front line of that liberation struggle never trusted the minister's figures. We knew that the government used statistics for damage control. We multiplied their figures by three to arrive at reality.

Our treatment in 1976 was relatively humane when I compare

From the Foreword to Fatima Meer's *Prison Diary: One hundred and thirteen days*, Kwela Books, 1976.

it with the brutal treatment I suffered during my eighteen months of detention in 1969. Throughout that period, I was interrogated, tortured and kept in solitary confinement.

Others still, detained in 1976, never left the prison alive. The public was expected to accept that those who died in prison were not killed, but had committed suicide due to psychological factors or under instructions from the Communist Party. White South Africa comforted itself with such explanations. Black Africa did not; it waited its day – not for revenge, but for the elimination of the racist torturers and for the reconstruction of South Africa on the foundation of democracy.

◆

I list some of these so-called suicides.

The passing of Steve Biko, above all, demonstrates the brutality of detention without trial, its inhumanity and injustice. Steve Biko was detained three days before I was detained; 24 days later he was dead. The Minister of Police, Jimmy Kruger, said he died as the result of a hunger strike. Another official claim was that he had fallen while resisting police during interrogation.

Twenty-six-year-old Hoosen Haffejee was detained on 2 August, about three weeks before Fatima and probably in the same cell where she spent her first night. He was found dead the following morning. The police claimed he had hung himself with his trousers knotted around his head from the bars of his cell door.

On 13 August, Bayempin Mzizi was found dead after a month in detention. Police claimed he had hung himself by a strip of cloth from his jacket, tied to the bars of his cell window.

Eighteen-year-old Sipho Malaza, a schoolboy in detention since July 1976, was found dead on 16 November. Police reported that he had hung himself with his belt.

Dr Nanaolth Ntshuntsha was detained on 14 December, 1976; he was dead on 11 January. Police claimed he had torn his vest into strips and hung himself.

Ernest Mamashila, 35, detained on 16 November, 1976, was found hanging from strips torn from a cell blanket on 19 November. The magistrate returned a verdict of suicide.

Luke Mazwembe, 32, was dead on the same day he was detained – 2 September, 1976. Police claimed he had hanged himself with strips of a blanket cut with a razor blade and tied into a noose with twine. They could not explain how and where he had got the blade and twine. The *post mortem* revealed several wounds on his body, but the magistrate ruled he had committed suicide.

Aaron Khoza, 35, detained on 9 December, 1976, was found dead in his cell on 26 March, allegedly having hung himself by winding his jacket around his head and fastening it to the bars of the window.

Joseph Mdluli died in detention due to force applied to his neck. The police alleged he suffered the force when policemen tried to restrain him in a suicide attempt.

Elmon Mohele was detained on 7 January, 1976, and died on 20 January in a nursing home after two brain operations. Police claimed he fainted during the interrogation and hit his head against a desk. The magistrate ruled he had died as a result of hypertension and spontaneous intra-cerebral haemorrhage.

Mathews Mabelane, 23, died on 23 February, 1976, allegedly due to an accidental fall from the 10th floor of John Vorster Square. He apparently dashed to the window, walked on the ledge and slipped.

Phakamile Mabija died in detention, allegedly by falling from the sixth floor of John Vorster Square on 7 July.

Essop Timol also fell to his death, allegedly from the same building.

Elija Loza, 59, detained at Victor Verster, died on 1 August at Tygerberg Hospital while in police custody. His family was told he had died three weeks earlier after suffering a stroke.

George Botha, 30, a coloured teacher, was detained on 10 December, 1976. He was dead on 15 December, allegedly after falling from a multi-storey building.

Dumisane Mbatha, 22, died while being detained at Modderbee Prison. It was claimed he had died of natural causes.

Samuel Malinga, 45, was detained on 3 January, 1976. He was dead on 22 February. According to the government pathologist, Professor I. Gordon, he died of natural causes.

Trade unionist Lawrence Ndzanga, 52, was detained on 18 November, 1976, as was his wife Rita. Lawrence died in prison, allegedly of heart failure. His wife was not allowed to attend his funeral, although all charges against her had been withdrawn.

Wellington Tshazibane, 30, was detained on 10 December. He was found dead on 11 December – allegedly due to hanging, as confirmed by the magistrate. His family never accepted the official reason.

◆

All these deaths were murders, as we knew at the time and as were confirmed later ...

We thank God that we have lived to tell our story. The story must be read against the background of the brutalities suffered by hundreds, maybe thousands, and it must be read in commemoration of those martyred during that grim time; and the story must be read in condemnation of all those magistrates and state pathologists who so callously and opportunistically declared these murders to be suicides. Their co-operation emboldened the apartheid system to continue detaining innocent people with impunity.

ABDELLATIF LAÂBI: MOROCCO

Hunger Strike

So let's talk about this hunger strike
it's a form of struggle
that those in my position
have used throughout the long history
of mutilation
Very true, it's only passive
but when you only have your naked stomach
with which to take on
the whole arsenal of despotism
you use your only weapon
this irrepressible spirit within yourself
you use it to the point of exhaustion
even risk its extinction
to protect your dignity

the sun is tasteless
when you're hungry
and the sleepless nights are icy
you think of so many things
both serious and funny
I swear that when I was really ill
I was tormented by the idea of real food
I used to imagine delicious meals
all my gastronomic inheritance passed
before my eyes
but all right, I'm not ashamed of these thoughts
for what's crucial

Translated from the French by Jacqueline Kaye.

is this trial
this voyage into the unknown
is the feeling of great power at the heart of
the greatest weakness
the superiority of he who resists
when confronted with he who oppresses
Yes, life itself is a formidable weapon
which will always amaze
the armed corpses
What's crucial
is to always share the suffering
of those tortured by hunger
that is this rotten, bloody taste in the mouth
these rolling cold eyes in the foggy day
these guts which twist and snake
with the despair of emptiness
What's crucial
is once again the brotherhood of suffering
profound ideas arise in the night
become real
they are not mine or his or his

but they belong
to all those deprived of the sun
What's crucial
is once again the brotherhood of suffering
for our hunger
is not for wealth
it's not the greed of the monster
on his knees
before the golden calf of debauchery
our hunger is for a new world
inhabited by new men

of a sun shared
limitlessly
of an incurable peace
which can only hurt the division makers
Also
in these days of abstinence
it was a source of pride to me
to be hungry
and so to disturb a little
the shameful peace
of those who starve our people.

BREYTEN BREYTENBACH: SOUTH AFRICA

Seasons and Storms

It is 25 November 1975, when I am sentenced. I shall not be seeing the stars again for many years. In the beginning I don't realize this, I don't miss them. And then suddenly it becomes very important, like chafing sores in the mind – something you've taken for granted for so long and that you now miss, the way you'd miss a burial site if you died in space. It is not natural never to see stars, or the moon for that matter – it is as cruel as depriving people of sound. I see the moon again for the first time on 19 April 1976 when, at about twenty-three minutes to four in the afternoon, I am in the largest of the three exercise yards, which has towering walls, making it rather like a well. I looked up and to my astonishment saw in a patch of sky above a shrivelled white shape. Could it be a pearl in my eye? Was it the afterbirth of a spaceship? No, it could only be the moon. And they told me that she'd been hanged, that she was dead!

The sun and its absence become the pivot of your daily existence. You wait. You build your day around the half hour when you'll be allowed out in the courtyard to say good morning to the sun. You follow its course through the universe behind your eyelids. You become its disciple. The sun knows not of the justice of man. You know exactly where it touches at what time – winter, autumn, or summer – and if you are lucky, as I was for some time, to be kept in a cell just off the main corridor with windows giving onto the catwalk which was not closed to the outside, you would have a glimmer, a suspicion, a

From *A Memory of Sky*.

hair-crack of sunshine coming in during certain seasons, but never reaching far enough down for you to feel it. I used to climb on my bed, stand on my toes on the bedstead, and then, sometimes, for something like two minutes a day, a yellow wand would brush the top of my hair. Of course, you develop an intense awareness, like a hitherto unexplored sense in yourself, for knowing exactly when the sun rises and when it sets without ever seeing it.

With the first shivers of the very early morning, even before the call for waking up sounded, I used to get out of bed and try to position myself in that one spot of the cell where the warder could not see me directly and then for half an hour sit in *zazen*, and I could always feel in me a very profound source of light inexorably un-nighting the outside: with eyes half closed I could feel it first tipping rose the roof made of glassfibre, giving shape to the trees one knew must be growing not far off, because the birds talked about these trees, and then jumping over the walls which were made of red brick, and generally investing the day. It was the quiet moment then: the *boere* for the morning shift hadn't arrived yet to come and stamp their feet, and those who'd been on for the second watch from twelve at night were nearing the end of their turn of duty and so they were sleepy, perhaps dozing with their rifles in their hands hanging limply.

On summer days when you were cleaning your corridor you could see through the grill clouds passing along the blue highway above the yard wall facing you: boats on their way to a dream, bit actors always dressed in white being taken to an empty space where Fellini would be filming a saturnalia, a wedding feast. There was wind which you never felt on your face but which you got to know through its aftermath – the red Transvaal dust you had to sweep up. There were the most impressive summer thunderstorms tearing and rolling for miles through the ether, slashing and slaying before big-rain came to lash the roof with a million whips. It was like living underneath a gigantic billiard table. Behind the walls with no apertures to the outside, behind the screen of your closed eyes where you hid from the *boere* – you still saw the stabs and the snakes of lightning.

EDISON MPINA: MALAWI

Summer Fires of Mulanje Mountain

Your matronly face is
blood-red like the flesh of a water-melon;
Smoke is rising ascension-like
through your hair . . . you have
become a burning field of neon

Skin to skin bonfires to
awaken mountain shrines? No, for
these are fires lit by angry heat . . .
power generated by summer

Unfailing reminder of
age-long lomwe[1] tribal icons,
the fires paint veins of dried rivers
and sculpt faces of dead relatives
as they burn every summer

---

[1] Communal name of people who live around Mount Mulanje. [Ed.]

FELIX MNTHALI: MALAWI

A *Game* of Bawo[1]

Take your cue from a game of *bawo*
where sides at the edge of doom
are best conceded as losses
and easy withdrawal
leads to stunning victories

Springs hot and cold, dry up;
flowers bloom and fade
and trees at times shed their leaves and their barks
neither recall the bloom
nor visit springs that once gushed waters –
memories are sweetest unruffled by daylight and
forced ceremonies stink worse than rudeness.

This meticulous insouciance,
these decoys made in heaven
follow a standard design
with familiar specifications –

Take your cue from a game of *bawo*;
neither recall the bloom of flowers
nor the showers
of spring.

---

[1] Traditional game played on scooped board, wood or floor; played with marbles
or stones by at least two participants. [Ed.]

NGŨGĨ WA THIONG'O: KENYA

Refusing to Die

'Whatever you do,' the other detainees had told me, 'try not to be ill ... Here they wait until disease has fully percolated through your system before treating you ... and even then, they treat you not to cure, but to have it on record that they treated you.'

One detainee used to suffer from swollen veins. His laments would be met with indifference or with the ready explanation that he was malingering. Then suddenly he would be whisked off to Kenyatta National Hospital, in chains, under heavy guard, for surgery. Two days later he would be back in the block, still in chains, but with bleeding cuts. The laments would start all over again. This game of treatment-without-a-cure had gone on for seven years. He was still hospitalized at Kenyatta National Hospital when news of his freedom reached him.

Another detainee had a wound in the anus: advanced piles. He bled a lot. He had to lie sideways. Eating was torture because of thoughts of the pain to come. He had been arrested a week before he was due for an operation by a top specialist at Kenyatta National Hospital. His terror was that the wound might extend to his intestines. On arrival at Kamĩtĩ, he had reported his critical condition. It was not until six months later that they took him to hospital for an operation. He could hardly walk. But they put him in chains, plus an armed police and prison squad. At the time of his release on 12 December 1978, he was still uncured.

My own observation was that at Kamĩtĩ, every detainee

These extracts are from *Detained*, Heinemann Educational Books, 1981.

suffered from one or more diseases: headaches, backaches, toothaches, eye and skin ailments, anything. And the warders had only one explanation, malingering, although there was no work to be avoided. The prison doctor, an old man who had been in prison all his working life had only one explanation: depression. The standard prescription for everything, headaches, stomach-aches, toothaches, broken backs and hips, was anti-depression tablets – Valium, mostly. 'It's just the effect of jail,' he would say, 'you'll soon come out.' He normally met complaints with the chilling threat: 'I can even inject you with water or worse and get away with it. You think you are more important than Kenyatta whom I used to treat with water at Lodwar?'

The most notorious case of disease as punishment was Shikuku's. Martin Shikuku used to be a populist, vocal member of parliament who had made a national reputation for raising awkward issues in the House of the Honourables. He was an active member of the J. M. Kariũki committee whose findings and final report virtually incriminated the Kenyatta regime in the murder of J. M. He also proposed and won a motion for a select committee on corruption, causing much hatred from the big ones who proceeded to quash the committee. Then one day in October 1975, he made a passing reference to the effect that parliament should not be killed the way KANU had been killed. He was detained. I had mentioned his detention and that of Seroney in my novel *Petals of Blood*, so I was naturally curious to see him. One day, soon after my arrival in Kamĩtĩ, I entered his cell. I found him seated on the bed. There was a yellow plastic pail near him. Between every two sentences, he would vomit into the pail. Each time he belched, he would vomit into the pail. He had to eat about fifteen times a day so that on vomiting something would remain behind to sustain his life. He had been in that condition for two years. I was shaken by this revelation. He was really a very sick man although he took it all philosophically. 'That which is hidden under the bed will one day come to light,' he had told me. I could never have believed the scene in a supposedly independent Kenya. Why keep a sick man in prison just to prove to him that KANU was not dead, that what he thought was death was simply the Party's style of life?

I was then under internal segregation and the warder ordered me back to my cell. I was looking through the iron-bar slit in my door when suddenly I saw somebody crawling along the corridor, using the walls for support. What apparition was this? It was Shikuku again. He had come to ask me a few questions about the outside. Now I learnt that on top of his minute-after-minute vomiting, the man could not walk without support. There was something wrong with his hips. To the warders? He was malingering. To the doctor? He was simply depressed. Although he could not walk without some support, Shikuku used to be chained to his bed in hospital, with armed police and warders guarding all the exits and entrances night and day. He remained in that tortured condition, the doctors unable to cure him, the authorities unwilling to let him go home and seek his own cure, until 12 December 1978. The instructions to the stony dragon concerning the detained combatant would seem to have been: if you miss his *will*, don't miss his *body*. Break his *will* or break his *body* or both.

Not surprisingly fear of illness was itself another kind of disease infecting all the detainees at Kamĩtĩ. There was also the fear of being poisoned under the pretext of being treated. I too caught the fever. What I dreaded most was a possible recurrence of my asthma. In Dakar, Senegal, in 1968, I had nearly lost my life after a very severe attack, my inability to speak French hindering my frantic efforts to get a doctor or any medical help. The timely arrival of Ali Mazrui in my hotel had saved me. At home in Limuru, I always kept some quick relief tablets in readiness. At Kamītī prison, I was lucky. Not once did I get such an attack; not even bronchial wheezes. But the fear remained.

It was the toothache that caught me unawares. The extreme lower right-side molar had a hole and I started experiencing difficulties in eating. The right side was really very painful and woe unto the whole mouth should a grain of salt lodge itself in the hollow. But when the doctor recommended that I see a dentist at Kenyatta National Hospital, I was seized with panic.

Two principles had suddenly clashed inside me: the necessity for bodily fitness for my physical survival in the combat; and the necessity to make a stand over the issue of chains for my spiritual survival in the combat.

◆

It is the paramount duty of every political detainee to keep physically fit. Any bodily disablement can considerably weaken his will or forever damage him. He who survives the deadly combat can always live to fight another day. There is also the saying, told me by one detainee as a piece of homely advice, that when a cow is finally pinned to the ground and tied with ropes to a slaughterhouse it cannot refuse to be slaughtered. We in detention were that cow and we had no choice but to do whatever was dictated by the whims of our captors.

But a human being is not a dumb beast. Even the cow does not acquiesce in its own slaughter. It goes down kicking to the last breath. In the same way, a political prisoner must always stand for certain principles if he is going to survive the trials of the stony dragon. He must be ready to protest against wrongs even in prison. He must keep on insisting on his constitutional rights, however few and whatever they are, and on his democratic and human rights.

Now my own feelings were that once the authorities had detained a person, they carried the entire responsibility for any diseases afflicting that person for the simple reason that such a person was not in any position to take care of himself medically. I felt that it was wrong, it was criminal in fact, to torture people with disease, to use it to extort information or confession, to use it as a means of vindictive humiliation, or of breaking a person's will. I strongly felt that if for some reason or other the authorities were unable to take a prisoner to hospital outside the compound, then in all democratic and human fairness they had to bring a doctor into the compound. Even prisoners of war are given full and fair medical treatment without conditions.

But in Kenya, at Kamĩtĩ in particular, it was a different story. Crawl on your hands and feet so that we can treat you. Co-operate in your own chains of humiliation without a murmur of protest so that we can take you to hospital. Kneel, beg, if not, die or become crippled for ever. Quite apart from that, I had resolved that, at the earliest possible moment, I would make my feelings known about the whole business of chaining political detainees, people who had never been convicted in a court of law, who never had any history of physical violence, escape or attempted escape.

The same detainee who had advised me on the necessity for passivity at a slaughterhouse, told me that chains on the innocent were beads of honour and a detainee should never be afraid of them. No. Chains were beads of humiliation. But I was not afraid of them. After all, I had come to Kamĩtĩ in them. Even if I had been chained and dragged through the streets of Nairobi or of my village, I would never have allowed the intended humiliation to touch my heart because I had done no wrong whatsoever. I had merely chosen sides in the class struggle. To write for, speak for and work for the lives of peasants and workers was the highest call of patriotic duty. My only regret

was that for many years I had wandered in the bourgeois jungle
and the wilderness of foreign cultures and languages. Kamīrīīthū
was my homecoming.

Nevertheless, I had resolved that while I would not make any
physical resistance to the wearing of chains – that way lay
suicide – I would equally not willingly or co-operatively put out
my hands for chaining. I would at least say 'No'. I would kick
even though I was tied to a slaughterhouse.

This, I knew, might involve me in certain difficulties. The
tendency is for a police officer or a prison warder or officer to
take such a protest as a personal affront or as a defiance of his
own personality. I had to keep on reminding myself that when
the time came, I should protest politely but firmly. I should state
my case without rudeness to the executing authority, for my
being at Kamītī was not a directly personal thing between him
and me.

For a long time before the dreaded day, I keenly felt this clash
of principles. I wished that the battlefield had not been my
health. But I equally felt that if I did not say 'No' to this
oppressive requirement at the earliest opportunity, I would never
thereafter be able to say 'No' over the same issue or any other
acts of blatant oppression.

Then the hour suddenly came. Thursday, 15 June 1978. Over
three months after my initial complaint of toothaches. At Kamītī
a detainee was told he was going out only a few minutes before
the police armed escort was due to arrive. The detainee was
then required to change from his prison uniform, kūūngūrū,
into his civilian clothes, otherwise kept under lock-and-key in
the chief warder's office.

It was about ten in the morning. I changed as required. I
walked through the compound toward the gates. Was it worth
resisting the chains? I have said 'No' to oppression several times
in my life and I have always experienced the same sensation of

agonizing fears and doubts. I feel foolish, childish even . . . why disturb the currents?

As a boy, I used to pick pyrethrum flowers for one of the very few African landlords in pre-independence Limuru. The land-lord on whose land we lived as *ahoi* had an orchard of pears and plums. Once, some children went into the orchard and picked a few plums. The landlord's wife came to know about it. In the evening, after she had weighed our flowers from a spring balance, she announced that we would all lose our day's pick in punishment for the stolen plums. It was a collective punishment. But of course if we squealed and pointed out the culprits, or if the offenders gave themselves up voluntarily, then the innocents would be spared. We were all angry because of the collective punishment and its severity: lose a whole day's labour because of a few 'stolen' plums? She called out each person's name: own up to the crime, squeal, or lose your day's work! She was met with non-committal silence.

My heart was beating hard. Gĩkũyũ pre-colonial culture, the remnants of which still governed our lives, was very strict about the relationship between a child and a grown-up. I remember, for instance, being admonished by my mother for telling a grown-up, to his face, that he was lying. A grown-up had the right to thrash a child who was rude to him, even if he was the one who had initiated the action resulting in the rude exchange. And if the grown-up should report this to the parents . . . woe to the 'rude' child. I now believe that the oppressive reactionary tendencies in our pre-colonial peasant cultures are only slightly less grave than the racist colonial culture of fear and silence and should be fought, maybe with different weapons, but fought all the same. But I had not then worked this out. I felt cold panic inside me. I knew I would raise a dissenting voice. I was stung by the injustice of it all, and although I could not reverse it, I had no intention of suffering in silence. In our home, we depended on every single cent that we could collect from the sale of our labour. We had sweated in the sun, without a meal or a glass of water all day, and here she was, going on about morality and enforcing it by robbing us of our hard-earned money without so much as a blink. 'You claim you are saved,' I shouted at her in tears. 'Is this what you mean by Christian salvation? Cheating and robbing us? This is theft! This is theft!' She came to my home the same night and reported what she called this 'terrible abuse from a mere child' and urged my mother to beat me. My mother, a peasant living on the estate of the landlord, just looked down. She did not say anything. But she did not beat me.

I had felt the same cold panic each time I knew I would join the chorus of those at the university who used to protest against the annual European-supervised beating of innocent students, an annual ritual of violence fully sanctioned by the KANU government. The worst such ritual was in 1974 when women were raped and others had their limbs broken, their blood left spattered all over the whitewashed walls of the different class-rooms. In 1969, I had resigned from the university in protest. I was outraged by the silence of most lecturers and professors, a silence which I took for complicity with the fascist evil. But in 1974 more lecturers had joined in the protest and had made their feelings publicly known.

What I most remembered in these past incidents was that unpleasant cold foreboding that always preceded my every 'No' to oppression, but it was always a sign that I would not hold back the voice of protest. So when now the prison warder asked me to raise my hands for the ceremony of chaining and I felt the same kind of foreboding I knew I would refuse. Which I did!

The warder, also in civilian clothes – going out for a detainee was a civilian ceremony all round – could not believe his ears. He called the others. Still I refused.

He reasoned with me, trying to prove to me that the chains meant nothing: 'Be a man and carry the chains!'

I thought this a strange way of proving my 'manhood', and if the chains were nothing, why was I required to wear them? I still refused.

Kimeto, the police superintendent in charge of escorting detainees in and out of Kamĩtĩ, intervened. He was tall with a partiality for straw hats which he carried with a conscious swagger, probably in imitation of an American FBI detective he had once seen on television.

'Listen!' he said, standing arms akimbo, measuring his voice for all to hear clearly. 'Even Kenyatta was once chained, and he accepted it.'

'I am not Kenyatta!' I said.

'So you refuse to go for medical treatment?'

'Would I have so promptly put on my civilian clothes if I was not eager to go? After all, it is I who have the toothache. It is you who is refusing to take me to hospital.'

'Then we have to chain you.'

'I don't want to be chained. I don't see why you must chain an innocent political detainee.'

'You are refusing to go to hospital.'

'No. It is you who are refusing to take me. I am not faster than all the bullets you and your team are carrying. Why anyway chain me as a condition for medical treatment? If you are finding it difficult to take me out to see a dentist, and I am not insisting on going out, why don't you bring a dentist here?'

'Take him back to the cell!' he shouted, disgust written all over his detective face. 'We shall see if he will cure himself.'

I was never treated though I kept on complaining about it. I even complained to the commissioner of prisons, Mr Mutua, on the only occasion that he visited the compound. I pointed out that it was wrong to use disease to torture political detainees.

I also wrote a letter of protest to Mr Mūhīndī Mūnene, the detainees' security officer, seeking, at the same time, his intervention to secure me dental treatment inside the compound. It had been done before, I later came to learn, so there was nothing in the regulations which said that a dentist could not come into Kamītī. Nor was there a regulation requiring chaining as a condition for medical treatment outside Kamītī. And if there was, it was unjust and criminal. Not all detainees, I came to learn, were chained!

Mr Mūnene never replied. And the Detainees' Review Tribunal under Justice Hancox, before whom I raised the matter in July, never did anything about the use of disease to torture political detainees. One got the impression that the next stage for the authorities in that line would be to actually infect detainees with certain diseases if natural ones failed. In fact, any detainee who contracted a disease and was taken to hospital or was treated in prison had always that additional fear. What if, having got there, the government quack 'mistakenly' injected strychnine, causing death not in combat or in defiance, but prostrate in a ward bed? Considering Kenya's recent history and the general official attitude toward disease, this fear was not without foundation.

Fortunately for me, the abscess gradually healed. Must have been the medicine of willpower. At any rate, it gradually ceased throbbing except when something hard – like a grain of salt or a piece of bean or *ugali* – lodged inside . . .

◆

In prison detention, where people are not allowed newspapers or the radio, the thirst and hunger for news are sometimes unbearable in their torturous insistence for satisfaction.

Thus gathering news at Kamītī is a psychological imperative,

231

and the detainees have developed a fantastic instinct for nosing out and extracting news from reluctant warders. A detainee who goes out to hospital or to meet his family must be hawk-eyed. He must learn to tune and turn his ears with the deftness and alertness of a cat or a hare. Every word counts. Every building, vehicle, street, dress, colour of trees counts. When he returns to camp, each of these is discussed and analysed from every possible angle till they yield all their secrets. A similar process of course takes place outside the prison where radio and other media are so uninformative about the real events that people inevitably rely on inferences, deductions and the grapevine. This is what is erroneously termed as 'rumour-mongering' by the rulers. But in prison, as outside, these inferences are often true.

Sometimes a warder has gone out to buy, let's say, a tooth-brush for a detainee. He might bring it wrapped in a piece of newspaper. Should he forget to remove it, then the piece of paper, however tiny, will be seized and once again, every word, every line, will be discussed and analysed until it too yields all the secrets, past and present.

One day, I get a dramatic illustration of news-gathering at Kamĩtĩ. I am in cell 16, my heart is down because after writing a whole chapter of my new novel without a problem, I have now come to a dead-end. Every writer of imaginative literature knows the frustration and desperation that seize a person during such moments. It is naturally worse in prison.

Suddenly Matheenge, who keeps teasing me that he is *the* original *Kamĩtĩ* 6 because his number is K6,75 and mine K6,77, bursts into my cell with a tiny piece of newspaper no larger than a few square inches. 'Look at this,' he shouts. 'I collected it from the rubbish-bin outside. I saw a warder throw in some rubbish, I went and saw this, quickly picked it up and hid it before he could see me. It says something about Gachago and Mũhũri and conviction and oh, yes, look there's a letter J . . . oh, wait, let the warders come on night duty.'

At night two warders come. Then suddenly Matheenge calls out one by name:

'Hey! Have Gachago and Mūhūri started their years on the other side?'

'You mean the two MPs? They started some time ago.'

'How many years?'

'Five each. Plus a few strokes.'

'What for?'

'Coffee, of course. Magendo.'

Then suddenly the warder remembers that he is talking to a political detainee and he stops short.

'Who told you?'

'Never mind. Walls have voices.'

Tomorrow Matheenge will use this extra information to get more information and before a week the whole story will be out.

The news has an unsettling effect on me. Magendo in ivory, gemstones, game-skins, coffee, maize, rice, sugar, *unga*, tea has been a way of life among the ruling circles in Kenya. Even the smallest child in a village could tell you the names of Big So-and-So, Tall So-and-So, Fat So-and-So, Moral So-and-So, Holy So-and-So, Upright So-and-So, who had camped at Chepkubwe waiting for his tons of coffee, later transported to Mombasa under police escort.

Why then pick on these two law-breakers? Or were they only two sacrificial lambs to propitiate an angry populace and buy time for a rotting, falling-apart system? Capitalism itself is a system of unabashed theft and robbery. Thus theft, robbery, corruption can never be wrong under capitalism because they are inherent in it. Well, they are the structure. Without a systematic robbery of peasants and workers, a robbery protected and sanctified by laws, law courts, parliament, religion, armed forces, police, prisons, eduction, there is no capitalism. It is worse, the robbery, when a country is under the higher capitalism of foreigners which is imperialism. How else explain the fact that in a mainly agricultural country, peasants who farm often have to queue for yellow maize from America and Britain after what they have produced has been carted or sold or smuggled to those very countries? Lenin once defined imperialism as the highest stage of capitalism. Imperialism is the capitalistic robbery and theft of a country's wealth by foreigners aided, of course, by a few sell-out natives. Two MPs put in the cooler for small offences while the fat cats continue unabated.

And suddenly I discover the hitherto elusive theme of my prison novel. I grow literary wings. I am ready to fly. All because of a piece of newspaper little larger than a square inch retrieved from a rubbish-bin.

◆

Detainees have also learnt to gather news from the warders by face-reading and their group behaviour. Certain kinds of groupings by certain warders have come to mean that some upheaval, good or bad for the detainees, has happened outside the block. A certain kind of laughter from the more cruel warders has come to mean that something not to the advantage of detainees has occurred, while a certain kind of sadness and fear on the same faces has invariably come to mean good news for the detainees. This intuitive news gathering style is inherited by succeeding waves of inmates. An analysis of patterns of laughter and anger, of sadness and irritability, of gait and gestures, has become a daily ritual among detainees. I have been assured that this, augmented by judicious and well-timed questions, often yields very important news! And accurate! But I do not quite believe it at first and my scepticism registers on my face.

One day Gĩcerũ wa Njaũ comes to my door and he tells me: 'I would like you to watch the faces of warders A, B and C. Observe the fear in their eyes. See how they walk? Some major event to our advantage has occurred.'

Throughout the day I maintain a careful watch on the said faces. Alas, they yield nothing to me. But later in the week news leaks out. The commissioner of prisons, Saikwa, has been dismissed, and Lokopoyet, the SSP in charge of Kamĩtĩ, has been transferred to another prison.

I have never seen anything like it. When the old SSP comes to introduce the new SSP (a Mr Mareka), and he announces his own imminent departure from Kamĩtĩ, the detainees actually clap in a collective spontaneous delirium of joy even before they know how the new SSP will turn out to be.

For me, relief too. The old SSP will never now demand to read and approve 'my poems'. I have never anyway written poetry, in or outside prison.

Toilet Paper

To hell with the warders! Away with intruding thoughts! Tonight I don't want to think about warders and prisoners, colonial or neo-colonial affairs. I am totally engrossed in Wariinga, the fictional heroine of the novel I have been writing on toilet paper for the last ten months or so!

Toilet paper: when in the sixties I first read in Kwame Nkrumah's autobiography, *Ghana*, how he used to hoard toilet paper in his cell at James Fort Prison to write on, I thought it was romantic and a little unreal, despite the photographic evidence reproduced in the book. Writing on toilet paper?

Now I know: paper, any paper, is about the most precious article for a political prisoner, more so for one like me, who was in political detention because of his writing. For the urge to write is almost irresistible. At Kamĩtĩ prison, virtually all the detainees are writers or composers . . . Now the same good old toilet paper – which had been useful to Kwame Nkrumah in James Fort Prison and to Dennis Brutus on Robben Island, and to countless others with similar urges – has enabled me to defy daily the intended detention of my mind . . .

A week after my incarceration, Wasonga Sijeyo, who had been in that block for nine years but had managed to keep a razor-sharp mind and a heart of steel, eluded the vigilant eyes of the warders then guarding me and within seconds he told me words I came to treasure:

> It may sound a strange thing to say to you, but in a sense I
> am glad they brought you here. The other day, in fact a
> week or so before you came, we were saying that it would
> be a good thing for Kenya if more intellectuals were
> imprisoned. First it would wake most of them from their
> illusions. And some of them might outlive jail to tell the
> world. The thing is, just watch your mind. Don't let them
> break you and you'll be all right even if they keep you for
> life. But you must try. You have to, for us, for the ones
> you left behind.

Thus, in addition to being an insurrection of a detained intellect, writing this novel has been one way of keeping my mind and heart together like Sijeyo.

Free thoughts on toilet paper! I had resolved to use a language, Kikuyu, which did not have a modern novel: a challenge to myself and a way of affirming my faith in the possibilities of the languages of all the different Kenyan nationalities . . . Easier said than done: where was I to get the inspiration? A writer needs people around him. He needs live struggles of active life. Contrary to popular mythology, a novel is not a product of the imaginative feats of a single individual but the work of many hands and tongues. A writer just takes down notes dictated to him by life among the people, which he then arranges in this or that form. For me, in writing a novel, I love to hear the voices of the people working on the land, forging metal in a factory, telling anecdotes in crowded matatus and buses, gyrating their hips in a crowded bar before a jukebox or a live band, people playing games of love and hate and fear and glory in their struggle to live. I need to look at different people's faces, their gestures, their gait, their clothes, and to hear the variegated modulations of their voices in different moods. I need the vibrant voices of beautiful women: their touch, their sighs, their tears, their laughter. I like the presence of children prancing about, fighting, laughing, crying. I need life to write about life.

But it is also true that nobody writes under circumstances chosen by him and on material invented by him. He can only seize the time to select from material handed to him by whom-ever and whatever is around him. So my case now: I had not chosen prison, I was forced into it, but now that I was here, I would try and turn the double-walled enclosure into a special school where, like Shakespeare's Richard II, I would study how I might compare:

This prison where I live unto the world ...

In the daytime, I would take hasty notes on empty spaces in any book I might be reading, I would scribble notes on the bare walls of my cell, then in the evening I would try to put it all together on toilet paper.

Sometimes I would be seized with the usual literary boredom and despair – those painful moments when a writer begins to doubt the value of what he is scribbling or the possibility of ever completing the task in hand – those moments when a writer restrains himself with difficulty from setting the whole thing on fire, or tearing it all into pieces, or abandoning the whole project to dust and cobwebs. These moments are worse in prison because there are no distractions to massage the tired imagination: a glass of beer, a sound of music, or a long walk in the sun and wind or in a starry night. But at those very moments, I would remind myself that the ruling class had sent the novel to me so that my brain would turn into a mess of tot. The defiance of this bestial purpose always charged me with a new energy and determination: I would cheat them out of that last laugh by letting my imagination run loose . . .

◆

Kenyatta's death, another dream of freedom possessed us all . . . A rumour started: we would be freed on Friday 22 September. The morning of Friday 22 September found us still in the grips of hope. There had been no official word, but the rumour had become a reality. Why not? Every reasonable argument pointed to our release on that day. Some detainees had sat down, made a list of all cabinet members and tried to determine their voting patterns in terms of *yes* and *no* to our release on that day and naturally, the ministers in favour of our release outnumbered those against us. A detainee who cautioned realism in our expectations was shouted down and denounced.

It was a kind of collective madness, I remember, and when at about ten o'clock there was a vigorous banging on the outer door and a prison officer dashed in waving his staff of office, I said to myself, At long last: God, freedom.

Quickly, Koigi pulled me aside and whispered: 'Go and clean your room at once! There is going to be a search!'

No sooner were the words out of his mouth than we were all

hounded back to our cells: if this meant release, then it was certainly a rough way of bidding us farewell.

I had never seen a prison search before and though the other detainees told me that under Lokopoyot it had been a weekly ritual, I never really knew what it meant. My cell was the first to be raided: it was difficult to know what they were looking for. Razor-blades, nails, weapons of violence? Letters, diaries, secret communications with the outside world? Suddenly the sergeant saw piles of toilet paper and pounced on them. Then, as if delirious with joy and triumph, he turned to the presiding officer and announced: 'Here is the book, sir, on toilet paper.' 'Seize it!' the officer told him. 'The whole lot! Who told you to write books in prison?' the officer said, turning to me.

My novel written with blood, sweat, and toil on toilet paper had been seized! Only two chapters hidden in between the empty back pages of a Bible Koigi had lent me remained. The Bible lay there on the desk as if mocking me. 'If you had trusted all the Wariinga novel to me, you would have saved it all.'

It is only a writer who can possibly understand the pain of losing a manuscript, any manuscript. With this novel, I had struggled with language, with images, with prison, with bitter memories, with moments of despair, with all the mentally and emotionally adverse circumstances in which one is forced to operate while in custody – and now it had all gone.

Gloom fell over Kamĩtĩ. Every detainee had lost something. We had been deliberately lulled into slumber by the carefully circulated rumour of our release. But most detainees had developed a fantastic cunning which had made them act like lightning and many had saved a lot of their prison notes. I had suffered the major loss and the other detainees clearly felt for me. I was grateful for the group solidarity. But it didn't lessen the hurt.

The next three weeks were the worst of my stay at Kamĩtĩ. It was as if I had been drained of all blood. Nevertheless, I made a new resolution: no matter what happened I would start all over again. I would reconstruct the novel in between the printed lines of a Chekhov . . . It would not be the same novel, but I would not accept defeat.

I never had occasion to try out my resolution, though I did scribble the plot, and the few sequences of events I could recollect in Chekhov's volume of short stories – *The Lady with a Lap Dog* – for, after about three weeks, on 18 October, the new SSP returned the Wariinga manuscript to me.

'I see nothing wrong with it,' he said. 'You write in very difficult Kikuyu!' he added.

'Thank you,' was all I said. But he will probably never know the depth of emotion behind those two words. Nor perhaps what his action meant for the birth of a new literature in Kenya's languages.

CAESARINA KONA MAKHOERE: SOUTH AFRICA

Stubborn Segregation

Finally, after a long struggle, the issue of our segregation was taken up outside the prison walls. I think the person who really assisted us here was Bongi. She was released from prison, directly from segregation into the outside world. She was able to bring the attention of the world outside to us, was able to reach the people who had been ignorant of what was happening to us, despite the publicity surrounding the Kroonstad case.

It seems people were under the impression that after the Kroonstad case, the authorities had ended segregation, when in fact a person like me still remained in segregation. So Mrs Jana, the political lawyer, instructed lawyers to take up the case, to lay a charge against the Prisons Department for keeping us in segregation unlawfully. It became topical; it was a cause.

Mrs Suzman, the well-known liberal MP, came to visit us, too. She is the long-standing opposition member of the Progressive Federal Party. For years she was a lone voice in the South African Parliament. Her party is against racism. She saw us all together: Tshidi, Mama Gumede, Elizabeth Nhlapo, Thandi, Feziwe and me. We were taken to Lieutenant Bothma's office. We were sitting in that office, and they put these cakes on the table. Maybe they were trying to be nice to Helen Suzman. Or maybe they were trying to imply that we ate cakes all the time. All the time we were telling her about this terrible food we were expected to eat, this terrible treatment we received, we were watching these cakes in front of us, which we couldn't touch.

From *No Child's Play*, The Women's Press, 1988.

241

We told her everything, in detail. She was stunned. She could not believe it, that anyone could live in segregation for so long, without visits, without reading material, without anything except the Bible. With only herself to talk to. When she came I had already been in segregation for more than two years.

Mrs Suzman even went to the extent of suggesting that a psychiatrist should come to see me. But the unfortunate part of this was that she did not tell me, she did not tell any of us, that she planned to do this. She proposed this when she got back outside.

So the following week I saw a psychiatrist. This was a woman, white of course, maybe in her late forties, an Afrikaner. I understand she lectured at Pretoria University. By that time, I assumed anyone who came saying, 'I am from one two three, I have been sent to do this this this' to be part and parcel of the apartheid regime. Eh, I was furious, burning mad. Did they now think that I was crazy?

This psychiatrist started by asking me questions such as who I was, where I was from, why I was in prison and what tribe I belonged to. Yerrah ma, I hit the roof! How could she come and ask me about what tribe I belonged to, what language I spoke at home? Did she think I didn't know why I was in prison? Besides, whoever told her that I wasn't normal? I was angry because first these people had put me into segregation for so long a period and then they brought this character here to ask me stupid questions, implying I must be insane.

I said to her, 'I am South African you know; I do not have a special tribe. I speak all the languages and belong to all the tribes.' Because they like to encourage tribalism. They like you to believe you come from this group or that group, and you are therefore not a South African but only a Sotho or a Swazi or a Xhosa. Which is something we must avoid at all costs.

And I asked her whether those who had sent her had told her

242

that they did not give me certain foods. There were certain types of food they did not give me because I was black. Was she aware there was a lot of discrimination in prison?

And she told me that she was there to speak to me as a psychiatrist. I repeated, 'But what about the problems I am facing here? I am telling you there is a lot of apartheid. And if you see to that, there will not be any problems. As for me, I am very normal.'

I suggested that she attend to the apartheid gods, not to me. Anyone can see that they are so insane, their insanity cannot be controlled. No normal person would promote racial discrimination; these mad men who rule our country have made racial discrimination the law of our land. A psychiatrist might be useful in treating those mad apartheid gods.

And I told her that I no longer wished to see her. That was on the first day.

The next day I saw our lawyer together with the other comrades. He had a newspaper cutting from the Sunday papers; on the second page there was this statement that Helen Suzman had visited us, and that it was she who had recommended that this woman come to see me, because she felt it was completely destructive of a person's mentality to remain in segregation for such a long period of time. After seeing him, after we had told him the story from A to Z, we were taken back to our various cells.

And when they locked me into my cell that day I announced: 'Hey you guys, look here, I want to see that psychiatrist character again.' The head of prisons said: 'But Caesarina, you just chased her away.'

I said: 'Listen, you have to understand that I have the right to change my mind at any time. As long as I think that this is right for me, I can do that. So you call her, I want to see her.'

The psychiatrist came again. 'But you said you did not want to see me again.'

I replied, 'No, that shows I am normal. I have the right to change my mind at any time.' And I asked her, 'Did you tell them that I want fruits, huh?'

We just sat there; we did not speak to each other for more than ten minutes. She was confused, because I only repeated what I had told her on the previous visit, about the discrimination and all that. I was sticking to these points. It was clearly difficult for her to say anything.

She tried to act like a psychiatrist, tried to get me into a corner. She asked me to tell her why I was convicted.

'That has nothing to do with you.'

She thought that she could prove to me that if you were doing one two three, and it was illegal, you would receive punishment, you had to take the consequences. She wanted to justify the segregation to me, to show that it was because I was so unco-operative that I was treated in this way. She put it: 'If you are unco-operative, then this this and this.'

I wish I knew who had taught them that word, 'unco-operative'. Honestly, just why should I co-operate with them? They are doing such things to us that we have no choice as human beings but to oppose them, and then they complain that we are unco-operative.

While I was speaking to her they served lunch to the prisoners. White prisoners passed the office with their white lunch. That time it was peanut butter, bread, fruit. The door was open and we could both see it. I showed her: 'You see, that is what I have been telling you. When I return to my cell I won't see that food, I won't see that peanut butter, because I'm black. What do you say? Do you think I'm right? I tell you that you have to attend to those problems, because there is no sanity in this country. They cannot expect sanity in this prison while there is this discrimination against most of us here.'

She left. I never saw that woman again.

The publicity had its effect. Feziwe and Thandi were taken out of segregation. The very same day, before they told the two comrades that they were leaving the isolation section, Sergeant Erasmus picked a quarrel with me, a heated quarrel. I was having a shower, and while I was in the middle of it she came in: 'Exercise!'

I was affronted.

'Hai, stop clowning. How can you expect me to get out of the bath and start doing exercise? I am not yet through with the bathing.'

'Anyway, you have forfeited your exercise, then.'

I warned her. 'You people do not want peace; you are inviting a fight. Recently I have realized that there is one thing you are inviting. You will really get it; I am going to *donner*[1] you.'

This woman knew that they were about to inform my other two comrades, Feziwe and Thandi, that the following day they would be removed from the isolation section, to stay with the other comrades. She knew that the segregation was due to end the next day.

But when these comrades called to me, 'Kona, do you know that today our segregation is terminated?' I could only reply, 'Hau!' They were both shocked to find I had not been told. They had been aware of the quarrel that morning – but there was nothing they could do.

The following morning they were taken to stay with the other comrades. I was left alone.

I told myself: 'I do not care what happens to me. They will not break me. I will keep on resisting. I mean I am not going to buy the termination of my segregation with my soul. So they can keep it.' That was that.

I stayed in segregation several more weeks. In the after-

---

[1] beat

noon, after lock-up, my comrades could call to me across the sections.

'How's it?'

'I'm all right, and how are you there?'

During the day my comrades were working, which is something I would never agree to do. They were doing needlework. Since 1979 I had made it absolutely clear that as far as I was concerned, aaiiee, forget it. I wouldn't work until I was released; I wouldn't work for them. It was against my principles to work in prison. But I felt bad about my comrades.

Towards the end of September I heard a serious quarrel. I was in the dark, alone in my single cell, hearing doors slamming, screams, all that, and batons at work. I found that my comrades had complained about the food, that it was not properly prepared and that it was not sufficient.

Soon after, I think around 27 or 28 September, my comrades called me to tell me that Feziwe had been taken away. I asked where to? They did not know; they suspected it must be Klerksdorp or Pollsmoor. Eh, now what were they trying to do to us?

On 30 September, all my comrades – Thandi, Tshidi, Elizabeth Nhlapo, Elizabeth Gumede – were dragged into cells, forcibly. They shouted this to me. 'Aaiiee, *mchana*, we are in segregation!'

'Hau, what is happening now?'

'Ne, these people are trying to keep us one in each cell.'

'Why . . .?'

'They say that when we are together we create more problems.'

The next day, on 1 October 1981, they took me from one single cell directly to another single cell.

Then I complained. 'Hey you characters, ah, you guys, what is this? Are you telling me you have taken me out of segregation? I want to stay with the other comrades.'

'Which comrades?'

'My other comrades – Feziwe, Thandi, Elizabeth Gumede, Elizabeth Nhlapo, Tshidi.'

They merely said: 'They are all in single cells. You can meet when you are doing exercise.' And they added, 'OK, we don't mind taking you to a big cell – you can stay in there alone.'

So I remained in a single cell, this time on the fourth floor. There are certain issues in life which you eventually decide it is futile to argue about.

They were finally persuaded to take me out of segregation, but they only did this after they had removed all comrades from the big room and had put them into single cells. These people appeared to be unwilling to see me staying in a big cell together with other comrades. From my first days in prison, for the whole six years I was inside, I remained in single cells. I never did stay in a cell with other comrades. Even before the segregation at Kroonstad, we would move together during the day, work together, and return each to her own cell at locking-up time. I had become used to it, it did not bother me so much. It was just this question: Why me?

At least during exercise time we could meet, face to face, and talk normally. After that, everyone to her cell. The end of segregation meant we could meet for exercise, we could get library books, we could buy toiletries.

We were staying on the same passage. Tshidi's cell was second from the corner, mine was the fifth. Mama Gumede's was the ninth – a long way down, and all still in the isolation section. Sometimes other common-law prisoners would be placed in the cells in between, for punishment. Thandi stayed on the same floor, but down a different passage.

The other comrades continued working during the day. I started reading library books. They were not great literature, but at least they were something different from the Bible, which I had been through over and over, for two years, non-stop.

One day I asked for writing paper, to write to my cousin. I wrote her a nice letter. In that letter I referred to two verses in the Bible. I quoted Jeremiah 50 and 51. I gave the staff the letter to post. The following day they told me I would not be allowed to send this type of letter; here was another piece of paper and I could write another letter.

'What is wrong with that letter?'

'You are not supposed to quote the Bible.'

I wrote another letter. Supposedly that letter was directed to my cousin, but the content of the letter was aimed at the prison staff. I went home on that piece of paper, you know. I really get irritated with these characters, who call themselves Christians on days when it suits them. Here they are, stopping me from quoting that very same Bible which they brought to the South African people, that very same Bible which they were so happy for me to read, for years on end, and nothing else. So I made sure that letter was quite undesirable. They did not send it.

We got a visit from two judges. When they came, we were busy doing exercises. The judges asked for complaints. We had yet another complaint about the meat; they still tried to punish people with food, even when they knew comrades would revolt. Like I said before, they are not sane.

During that visit from the judges, one lawyer asked Mama Gumede why she was in prison – particularly at her age. She said, no, she did not know why she was arrested. He was incredulous. 'Are you telling me that you were picked up for no reason?'

She answered, 'No. These characters came to my place to arrest me because they said I did not come to report my son to them. He was back from exile. Me, I do not have any politics at all.'

Unfortunately, minutes after this sweeping pronouncement, Mama Gumede was complaining: 'And you know, these people are treating us badly, like people in Cambodia.'

'Oh, I thought you said you did not know anything about

politics. Now what about Cambodia? Is the Cambodian issue not politics?'

She just continued, 'But really, they are treating us like people in Cambodia, and that we are not going to tolerate,' and went on from there.

The following morning, very early in the morning, about half past five, they unlocked my cell. I had to prepare myself, I was moving again. I questioned them, 'What? Where to?' but they said it was not for them to tell me.

I went to have a shower. After bathing, I said, 'You know I cannot just go without saying goodbye to my comrades. I must just let them know that I am leaving this place, that I am being transferred.'

So I went from one cell to another, saying goodbye to the comrades. The staff grew angry; they did not want me to do that, but they could not prevent me. I was absolutely adamant. I intended to say goodbye. They were not going to stop me from doing that.

We all felt the pain, now that one more comrade was going away. Before that, they had taken Feziwe away. Life is hard. Even if we had not been staying together, hearing a comrade's voice can be really important. It builds you up. Those apartheid gods were once more trying their hardest to keep us from being happy together.

So they took me to Klerksdorp prison.

JEREMY CRONIN: SOUTH AFRICA

For Comrades in Solitary Confinement

Every time they cage a bird
the sky shrinks. A little.

Where without appetite –
you commune
with the stale bread of yourself,
pacing to and fro, to shun,
one driven step on ahead
of the conversationist
who lurks in your head.
You are an eyeball
you are many eyes
hauled to high windows
to glimpse, dopplered by mesh
how-how-how long?
the visible, invisible, visible
across the sky
the question mark – one
sole ibis flies.

MAINA WA KĪNYATTĪ: KENYA

We Are Friends

For Ngũgĩ wa Thiong'o

Three years now in exile
A lonely eagle swimming in the sky
There is no rain that can put out
Your passionate determination
You are the voice of the voiceless

Several times they discussed your elimination
Lacking the moral energy to liquidate you
They threw you into the prison darkness
To survive the cold and foul environs
You wrote *Caitaani Mutharabaini*

                                             a masterpiece

The cruel wind of the prison cell
                                  left you unshaken
With indignation
You produced another bombshell – *Detained*
Dictator's mouth filled with froth of hatred
                                    and threats

You refused to bend
You put on your combat boots
And walked towards the rising sun
Your courage has given me
In the face of unrestrained barbarity
A determination to stand upright

We shall meet
Compatriot
We shall meet

251

To suck the sweet juice of motherland
To share smiles and jokes with the women
We shall meet in the stillness of the night
To compose new songs of our struggle

With the hammer of justice
With people's strength and determination
The walls of prison shall crumble
And in their place
We shall build
                    a university of human justice

                    Kamītī M. S. Prison, 13 June 1985

Prison Warden

You come smiling at me
Telling me everything will be all right
As long as I follow the prison regulations
But you don't feel
The anguish of this incarceration
The agony of solitary confinement

When I leave here
I will carry nothing with me
Except my hidden poems
And the scar of six years in the darkness

You with a smile of a hyena
You with a callous heart
You will never enter
The kingdom of our heroic ancestors

                    Naivasha M. S. Prison, 4 September 1988

KUNLE AJIBADE: NIGERIA

The Miseries of Jail

Wednesday 18 October 1995. A warder, who was reeking of burukutu, a locally brewed alcoholic beverage, came to my dingy cell at the crack of dawn and ordered me to pack. He put me in handcuffs and leg irons. Weaving with fatigue, I yawned before I asked him, 'Where are you taking me?'

He said he did not know. There was no time to brush my teeth. Taking my bath in the open air as we were forced to do in the last three days was completely ruled out.

The Black Maria was waiting.

I shouted a farewell to many of the prisoners on death row with whom we had shared this block. When we got to the main gate, and I had contact with other harried and wearied case-mates, it was abundantly clear that it was a season of our dispersal to all the prisons in the country. A moment of departure from the crypt to the cesspit.

The warder led me to Records where I collected my small sack of books and a medium-size bucket. When my two attempts at mounting the Black Maria failed because of the leg chains, one army sergeant smartly pressed forward and hoisted my entire slender frame into the lorry. I was cuffed immediately to Lt Colonel Obiki who was sitting next to me.

In no time we got to the Air Force base in Ikeja. And the lorry screeched to a halt. General Olusegun Obasanjo, Lt Colonel R. D. Obiki, Lt Colonel M. A. Igwe, Chris Anyanwu, Matthew Popoola, George Mbah, Major D. O. Obalise, Lt A. Olowookere and I were all marched into a Charlie 130. Five fully-armed

From Kunle Ajibade's forthcoming prison memoirs.

infantry soldiers and eight warders and a wardress joined the plane for maximum security. As the plane surged through the clouds, its motion bestowed sobriety on us. I looked at General Obasanjo, who opened the Bible on his lap. Where did he get the inner strength to read? This was a former head of state, so innocent of the crime of treason, but now being treated as a common criminal. The only thing was that he was not in chains like the rest of us. I wanted to know how his mind was working, but because I was not sitting next to him there was no chance to find out from him. Chris Anyanwu, the only woman victim in the plane, also caught my attention. She drank some water from the plastic bottle. Was it to calm down her nerves? What would happen to her business now, where she made herself the centre? How would she cope in jail? I looked at George Mbah with some pity because of the state of his health. He tried to find out something from his armed escort, who just ignored him.

Around 11.00 a.m., we had our first stopover at the Air Force base in Makurdi where Obiki and I were dropped off.

Lieutenant Colonel P. B. O. Akhigbe, the Commanding Officer of 72 Paratroops Battalion, led the convoy that came to receive us. You would think the convoy had come for the most dangerous of criminals: two steyr trucks full of armed soldiers, two station-wagon cars and two pick-up vans full of armed policemen and the SSS men. The siren began to wail as we disembarked from the C130. As I shambled on the runway, a solid pavement built by the Russians, to one of the station-wagon cars, the ancient prison irons rattled on the concrete. The deafening noise of the siren and our fearsome presence woke up the sleepy capital of Benue State as we passed through the élite area known as GRA to the heart of the city itself.

Shortly afterwards, we reached Wadata area, where the city's traditional market and the old prison are located. The moment

our convoy turned towards Makurdi Prison, a throng of onlook-
ers poured into its precincts to see the important criminals over
whom the combined security forces were making a fuss. The
crowd looked like some excited flies feeding on open wounds.
When the main gate of this tomb was shut behind us, I felt my
heart sink. I stood lost.

It was strange to me that the well-fed and well-armed soldiers,
who believed that security was all about grand drama, handed
us over to some hungry-looking, seemingly helpless warders
whose only weapons were walls, bars, locks, chains, and batons.
The difference was very clear. But as I would soon discover, it
was the difference between terminal illness and death.

We were then searched from head to toe: we were stripped of
our clothes. They removed our shoes. They yanked off our
wrist-watches. They took my sack of books from me and flung
it into one small room full of cobwebs, and because we were
now as low as dust, they brought two pairs of prison uniforms
very quickly. A pair of shorts, and an undersized shirt for me.
One similar pair also for Obiki, who would soon be taken to
Gboko Prison. The pairs with the red stripes, which we were
made to wear, were not meant for political prisoners. They were
for common criminals of the worst type. We were then marched
to the office of Chief Superintendent of Prisons (CSP), Iorbee
Ihagh. Short, dark in complexion, this officer with a master's
degree would soon demonstrate in many ways that he was one
of the civil servants who crossed over to the prison system not
to make the institution the reformative place that it ought to be.

As the custom demanded, he said we should tell him the
stories of what led to our imprisonment. When Obiki finished
telling him the story of his crooked trial he said:

'I am surprised at you, Colonel. An officer of your rank
should have known better. If I were you, I would have reported
Akinyemi immediately. You see, if you had done that you

wouldn't be in prison now, you would be somewhere else enjoying yourself.'

His phone rang when he turned to me. The person on the other side of the line was a friend. After a rather long conversation, he said:

'No, don't come now. I am very busy, addressing the new convicts who were just brought from Lagos. Yes, the coup plotters. It's a lot of work. They gave me two of them. You see. Yes. Yes. Ha! Ha!! Ha!!! They know I have been doing a good job. You see. Ha! Ha!! That's why they brought two . . .'

When he finally hung up, I, too, told him the story of my arrest and trial before a kangaroo court. His response was that of a blabbermouth.

'You see, I studied in the US. That's why they call me "Americana" here. I know everything about America; I know how journalists do their job in the US. You see, no journalists in the US would dabble into military affairs the way you've done. What's your business with the military people who wanted to kill themselves?'

The phone rang again. This call must be from his boss, for he quickly recited the lock-up number as he sat stiff on his chair and said:

'All correct, sir!'

He told his two assistants, John and Amaye, that the controller would be coming to see us the following day. He then said:

'Well, convicts, your warrants say you would be here till 13 July 2010. As you know, there is no remission for court-martial convicts. I can assure that you are in good hands.' . . .

◆

The following morning, we were asked to remove our rubber slippers by the doorstep of Ihagh's office before we were led inside. And, as we entered, a roar of orders:

'Squat down! Squat down! Squat down!'

We obeyed them and fell into the frozen silence of some conquered warriors. When I looked up from the floor the photographs of General Sani Abacha, the head of the ruling junta, Wing Commander Joshua Obademi, the Military Administrator of Benue State, and Alhaji Garba Gora Baidu, the Controller-General of the Nigeria Prisons Service, stared down balefully at us. Mrs Joy Oka Aghi, the Acting Controller, cleared her throat and said:

'Are you with us, Mr Ajibade?'

I said yes, but that was a lie. My mind was somewhere else. I was thinking that here was another proof that we were still living in a savage age. I was also telling myself that Franz Kafka would like this scene so much. In novel after novel, Kafka demonstrates how absurd situations could transform human beings into grotesque figures. Is it not appropriate that he uses the law – the penal system – as his constant leitmotif?

'You are welcome, then,' Aghi continued.

'Welcome to this prison. It is not our duty to question what has brought you here. We are not allowed to do that because we are civil servants. You are not here for punishment. You are here as punishment. My advice to you is that you should comport yourselves. The warrant that brought you here, if this paper could be called a warrant, says you should be kept incommunicado until further notice. But that does not mean we shall impede your movement within the yard. As long as you obey the rules of this prison, I don't think you will have any problem. You are in good hands. Do you have anything to say?'

I asked her, 'Do we have any rights at all as political prisoners?'

257

'Of course, you have. Or you should have. But I would have to clear that with the highest authority. Any other questions?'

She looked in the direction of Obiki, who said nothing. His own Puritan Christian faith seemed to have imbued him with the stamina of a doormat. He stayed uncomplaining till he was moved to Gboko prison on 30 November 1995 . ,

◆

The evil of Abacha permitted no witness. Which was why the prison was asked to keep us in solitary confinement. The prison was told that no one should visit us. That we should have no communication at all with the outside world. Only special warders should guard us. Forgetting that truth would powerfully prevail, the regime of General Abacha did not want the truth of our case to be shared with anyone.

My pregnant wife did not know of this directive. So, on 4 November 1995, she travelled all the way from Ibadan, a distance of about 1,800 kilometres, to visit me. She was turned back at the gate. Bunmi went straight to the house of the Controller of Prisons in Benue State. She told her she would not go home until she saw me. Mrs Aghi said the only concession she could make was to allow Mayowa, our two-year-old son, who had been asking his mom for my whereabouts, to see me. When Mayowa was eventually brought to meet me for less than five minutes, the boy could not recognize me immediately. Apart from my thick beard, which I wasn't wearing at home, pimples had already taken complete possession of my face. At that emotion-laden meeting, I told Ihagh:

'See the crazy thing you people are doing to me. What kind of violence is this? If I have wronged Abacha, has my family also offended him? What has this boy done to deserve this trauma? What has my pregnant wife done to deserve this punishment?'

Ihagh was a bit sober when he said, 'Don't take this out on me. We are just errand boys here.'

I thought he hit the bull in the eye: errand boys of the deeply flawed Nigerian justice system. What was startling was not the poverty of their condition, but the condition of their poverty. They too knew that they were incapable of reforming any criminal.

◆

Six days after my wife's unsuccessful attempt to see me, 10 November 1995, the news frittered through the walls that in Port Harcourt Prison, Ken Saro-Wiwa and eight of his Ogoni compatriots had been hanged. The Ogoni Civil Disturbances Special Tribunal headed by Justice Ibrahim Ndali Auta had convicted them after a grossly unfair and politically-motivated trial. When he saw that the tribunal had become a kangaroo court, Saro-Wiwa asked his lawyers, among whom were some of the most resilient defenders of the oppressed in our country, Chief Gani Fawehinmi, Olisa Agbakoba, and Femi Falana, to withdraw from the case so that they would not give that tribunal any dignity it did not deserve. He told them that he would prove his innocence in his allocutus. After his conviction so many people were asking: how far will General Sani Abacha go with the Ogoni issue? Will he allow reason to prevail? No, he did not. He went to the end of the line itself. He hanged the activists of the Movement for the Survival of the Ogoni People (MOSOP) and acid was allegedly poured on their remains at a time that a Commonwealth prime ministers' conference was taking place in Auckland.

The main charge against Saro-Wiwa by Joseph Daudu, the

prosecutor, was that he threatened to deal with the vultures, which the tribunal accepted was an indirect reference to four prominent moderate Ogoni men, who were set ablaze in Giokoo where Saro-Wiwa was allegedly slated to address a rally.

Yet, Ken Saro-Wiwa, the president of MOSOP, whom I knew, was a man of peace. He loved good arguments. The passion with which he made his points was a passion that appealed to so many lovers and seekers of truth, justice and fair play. Ken provided the lead, which he expected the Niger Delta people to follow. He created a timetable to which he expected his own people to adhere. He shaped their way from which he expected them not to depart. There are people who don't bother about how and when they die. Ken was one of such people. He cared about what he lived and died for. He sacrificed immediate laughter for enduring glory.

I felt diminished by the execution of Ken and the other compatriots. Gloom seized me, and for days I lost appetite for my miserable food. Then immense anger and bitterness took over. About two months before he was hanged, he had smuggled out a letter to the Association of Nigerian Authors (ANA) saying that he felt so sad about my arrest and trial. That we were being ruled by a bunch of murderers was sad enough. It was sadder still that the UN and the Commonwealth waited for Abacha to snuff the lives of the Ogoni nationalists, before they began to do a mop-up operation.

As a friend of Ken, I bear testimony to his total commitment to the Ogoni struggle. Indeed in November 1992 in London, Ken had asked Adewale Maja-Pearce of *Index on Censorship* to persuade me to take up the editorship of a quarterly he was preparing to float to put the struggle in sharp focus. I told Maja-Pearce, when he relayed the message to me in Lagos, that we would soon start something of our own, that I would not work for a mere propagandist. I thought that description of Ken was right until a couple of months later when he took the late poet, Sesan Ajayi, and I to the death-field that was his homeland.

The shocking realities on the ground indicated to me that I had judged him unfairly. The result of oil exploration in Ogoni since 1958; oil spillage which had ravaged the soil, polluted the water and made the air thick with dust; gas flares, pipelines, flow stations and oilfields had taken over the Ogoni farmlands. In response to this injustice, the Ogoni embarked on a non-violent way to ask the government of Nigeria for adequate compensation. In a pamphlet titled *Ogoni Bill of Rights*, it is stated succinctly that it is not fair that the Ogoni who produce $30 billion worth of crude oil should live in abject poverty.

But in a grand alliance with the oil companies, General Abacha set up the Internal Security Task Force, a military squad headed by Lt Colonel Paul Okuntijmo, to put out the burning outrage of the Ogoni. The killing of the outspoken Ogoni nationalists was the ultimate attempt to silence their people. Why is the ghost of this martyred prophet still stalking our terrain most valiantly? The reason is simple: the unfair treatment of the oil-bearing areas, which Ken raised his voice against, has not stopped. The corpses of the Ogoni Nine may have been burnt to ashes by acid; I know they live in the minds of a lot of their people who are inspired and emboldened by their courage.

The Release

KWAME NKRUMAH: GHANA

Elections

Although I suffered extreme boredom, I was luckily far too actively engaged in planning for the Party outside to allow myself to become stagnant. Very soon the time approached for the general election which was due to take place on 8 February 1951. There was much work to be done for this, for it was vital that our Party won a majority in the new Legislative Assembly. I had already made it clear to the party organizers outside that by all means they should contest every seat in the election and I had received word from Gbedemah that they had prepared themselves to do this.

It had not been my original intention to stand for election myself until I realized that unless I did, it might be very difficult to obtain my release before my sentence ended; for I knew that if I succeeded in winning the election it would be very difficult for the authorities to insist on keeping me in prison.

The first thing I did was to insist on my name being registered on the electoral roll. I experienced much opposition over this but I was adamant and, as I was within the law in this respect, nobody could forbid it, even though I did not expect to be able to use my vote. Few people realized that by our law, anyone who is convicted to a term of imprisonment not exceeding one year is entitled to be registered on the electoral roll. Although my total sentence was for a period of three years, this was made up of three separate terms of imprisonment of one year each.

After battling to get my name on the electoral roll I went to

From *Autobiography of Kwame Nkrumah*, Thomas Nelson & Sons, 1957.

the prison authorities and told them that I had decided to stand for election. It was no good them trying to tell me that I was not qualified to do so, for the fact that I had been qualified to register as an elector ruled this out.

Strange to say, some of the party members outside protested about my decision to stand for election for they held that if I was later disqualified, we would lose the seat altogether. But I waved all this aside. I told them that I would stand for Accra Central in place of Gbedemah, who agreed to stand for election in Keta. This sudden change made the organization somewhat difficult, but we were able to overcome it.

Acting officially through the prison superintendent, I arranged with those outside to pay my deposit, to sign my papers and to form themselves into a campaign committee. My forms were completed and submitted to the authorities a few minutes before the registration period closed and the campaign committee got to work on my behalf.

I busied myself in re-writing the party manifesto as the one that had been smuggled in to me was not a manifesto in the true sense of the word. In due course I completed it. As soon as it became known that I was going to stand for election there was terrific jubilation throughout the country, for there was a general feeling that if I was elected, the Government would, on the strength of it, release me and my colleagues.

On the night of the general election extra precautions were taken by the prison authorities owing to a rumour that had been circulated that the whole of Accra was going to advance on the prison and get me out. However, it was all quiet but I was quite unable to sleep the whole night. I was both excited and anxious. I began to wonder whether everything would now prove to have been in vain, whether the people would still stand by the Party and give me the chance to finish the job. Deep down in my heart, however, I knew that my hour of victory was at hand; I had complete trust and confidence in my people and I knew that they would not let me down.

The prison superintendent had arranged for hourly reports to be given to me on the progress of the election results. At about four in the morning the news was brought to me that I had been elected for Accra Central. Not only that, but I had received the largest individual poll so far recorded in the history of the Gold Coast, 22,780 votes out of a possible 23,122. I had no time for reflection for the news flashed round the prison and in a matter of seconds the place was alive with jubilation. I believe even the warders were happy. Throughout Accra the excitement of the crowds was so great that Gbedemah had the greatest difficulty in stopping a crowd of hundreds strong advancing on James Fort where they intended breaking down the doors and rescuing me from my prison cell. Such an act, although done in good faith, would naturally have ruined all our chances of success.

As the day wore on and the true significance of all that had happened became clearer in my mind, my feelings became a mixture of humility, of gratefulness to the people and of peace. A peace of mind, in fact, that I had long forgotten existed. I was brought back to earth by a message that was brought to me saying that there were a number of foreign newspaper reporters clamouring for a statement from me. I promptly refused to have anything to do with them for I had long since discovered that such people rarely report you verbatim; they give their own interpretations, and the more lurid and sensational they can make these, the better they like it.

The day after the election results were announced, the Executive Committee of the CPP asked the Governor if he would receive a delegation of the Committee in order to discuss the question of my release, for they held that as leader of the Party, if that Party was asked to form a government, it would be impossible for me to do so while in prison. The Governor agreed to meet this delegation and, after the meeting, arrangements were put in hand for my release. All this was done in complete secrecy as the Government did not want the news of my release to be spread abroad.

Between eleven and twelve o'clock on the morning of 12 February 1951, the prison superintendent sent for me and told me to be ready to leave the gaol within the next hour. I looked around me, but the only possessions I had were my bit of pencil and a few sheets of toilet paper, and these no longer seemed valuable. I told him that I was ready to leave at a moment's notice. At about the same time, apparently, the news of my release leaked out in the town. At one o'clock when the prison gates were closed behind me I realized why the Government had tried to keep the news top secret. I don't think I have ever seen such a thickly packed crowd in the whole of my life. I was too bewildered to do anything but stand and stare. Any emotion that I might have felt was completely arrested.

Then I remember a familiar voice speaking my name and I woke from my trance to find Gbedemah standing by my side. We greeted each other and my senses came to life as I was hoisted shoulder high and carried to an open car that was standing nearby. It is difficult even now to describe all I experienced as this car moved at a snail's pace like a ship being dragged by an overpowering current in a sea of upturned faces. To look at this locked mass of struggling figures and to listen to the deafening clamour of their jubilant voices made me feel quite giddy. The only way I could steady myself was to keep my eyes averted and to gaze at the mighty expanse of sea and sky, until I was able to adjust myself and acknowledge the greetings of the people.

Slowly, as I filled my lungs with the pure air of freedom, new life was born into me. This was the greatest day of my life, my day of victory and these were my warriors. No general could have felt more proud of his army and no soldiers could have shown greater affection for their leader.

From James Fort the procession made its way to the Arena, taking two hours to do what is normally a fifteen minutes' journey. At the Arena, the birthplace of my Party, the customary expiation was performed by sacrificing a sheep and by stepping with my bare feet in its blood seven times, which was supposed to clean me from the contamination of the prison. The crowd stayed with me the whole time, accompanying me in procession to the party headquarters where, completely worn out, both physically and mentally, I crumpled into the nearest chair . . .

◆

The day after my release from prison I was invited by the Governor to meet him at nine o'clock that morning. When I walked into the courtyard of Christiansborg Castle, the official residence of the Governor, I suddenly realized that it was the very first time I had set eyes on the place. The glaring white stone of the battlements, the impressive forecourt and the beauty of this imposing building with the roaring surf battering against its foundations, seemed to me like a new world. Although Sir Charles Arden-Clarke and I had been opposing each other for so many months past, I had no idea what he looked like, for we had never met. I wondered how I should be received. Had I known this man before, I should not have doubted the courtesy that would be shown to me.

A tall, broad-shouldered man, sun-tanned, with an expression of firmness and discipline but with a twinkle of kindness in his eyes came towards me with his hand outstretched; a hand that I noticed was large and capable-looking. He welcomed me and asked me how I was. As we both sat down I sensed that he must be feeling as alert and suspicious of me as I was of him. We lost little time, however, in coming down to the business in hand. I did my best to make it clear to him that I would be prepared at all times to place my cards face upwards on the table because it was only by frankness that mutual trust and confidence could be established. He agreed with me wholeheartedly on this and I sensed immediately that he spoke with sincerity. He was, I thought, a man with a strong sense of justice and fair play, with whom I could easily be friends even though I looked upon him as a symbol of British imperialism in the country.

In spite of the fact that I was fresh from the prison cell and had probably every reason to harbour hatred in my heart, I had forced myself to forget the sufferings and degradation that I had endured at the hands of the colonial administration, for I knew that revenge was bitter and foreign to my make-up. It was with truth and sincerity that I made the statement soon after my release from gaol that 'I came out of gaol and into the Assembly without the slightest feeling of bitterness to Britain. I stand for no discrimination against any race or individual, but I am unalterably opposed to imperialism in any form.'

I left the Castle with instructions from the Governor to form a government. As I walked down the steps it was as if the whole thing had been a dream, that I was stepping down from the clouds and that I would soon wake up and find myself squatting on the prison floor eating a bowl of maize porridge.

I must say a word or two here about the constitution existing at this time. Contrary to the provisions of the Burns Constitution, that of the Coussey Commission recommended that the new Legislative Assembly was to consist of a Speaker, to be elected by the Assembly from among its members or outside it, and eighty-four elected members. Five seats were allocated to the municipalities, two for Accra, one each for Cape Coast, Sekondi-Takoradi and Kumasi; thirty-three rural members were to be elected in two stages, first by direct primary voting and secondly through electoral colleges; nineteen inhabitants of the Northern Territories were to be elected by the Territorial Councils of the Colony, Ashanti and Trans-Volta/Togoland; six special members were to be elected in equal proportion by the Chamber of Commerce and the Chamber of Mines and three *ex officio* members were to be nominated by the Governor. They were the Minister of Defence and External Affairs, the Minister of Finance and the Minister of Justice. The result of the election showed that the Convention People's Party had won thirty-four out of a possible thirty-eight elected seats in the municipal and rural areas and that they also had a majority in the assembly over the nominated candidates.

Immediately I left the Castle I convened a meeting of the central committee of the party in order to discuss with them the names of those that I had selected to serve as ministers in the new government. The problem which faced me was that during my discussions with the Governor, I had agreed that since the CPP had won a majority only in the elected seats of the Assembly, to select my ministers solely from the ranks of the Party might bring me into conflict with the territorial members and with other independent members of the Assembly. I proposed to the central committee, therefore, that of the seven ministers, five should be Party members, one should come from the Northern Territories and the other one from Ashanti. At first the central committee objected to this proposal as they felt, and understandably so, that all the ministers should be chosen from the ranks of the Party supporters. After a long discussion, however, they accepted my suggestion and I then submitted the names to the Governor ...

EDISON MPINA: MALAWI

Reborn

Now I am like a seaweed
That's been washed to land
I've cashed my last drop of salt

Walking from Mount Soche Hotel
Down to the Blantyre City Hall
My eyes, like the skin beyond the blister wall
And my steps with a hangover of last year
Still tell about me
Like darkness in moonlight

Before this civilization
I lived both hands on my lifewheel;
I slept in trees, falling like a tipsy monkey
I strolled in graveyards like a witch
To avoid police paths

Prison was nevertheless my homestead
Its uniform crackling like a dry mango leaf
Was the only clothing I couldn't evade
Its monthly stew, like stale bread in a child's pants
Was the most palatable food I ate
And the hairless mountain peak
Peering over the mossy prison walls
Was the only sightseeing I did

Now, abroad without belts of chains
And breathing newly born air
With female lovers
And touching shoulders with patrol policemen
You can all watch the free match
On the saltless field where I'm reborn.

JOSIAH MWANGI KARIUKI: KENYA

Release

The administration laid down the red carpet for my return. Burton was still District Commissioner and he took me with him out to Othaya in his own car, talking pointedly on the way about the great economic progress made in the district since my detention, showing me smart new houses springing up everywhere on the consolidated farms and the lines of holes dug ready for coffee seedlings and tea stumps. At Othaya, Burton and I exchanged a few words with the DO and I told him of the Kikuyu saying, *Thu ndiguaga haria iikagio* (The enemy never falls where it is thrown). But he seemed to have mellowed and gave me a government Land Rover to carry me the six miles to my home in Kariko village. There was no reporting to chief or headman this time and late that evening I knocked on Wangui's door and I was home again. It was too late to organize a celebration that night and so after talking until there was no more wood for the fire we went to bed.

Next day we made no doubt about it at all and my aunt chose the largest and fattest goat she had, all of one colour, black, and we slaughtered and ate it together with the family in a meat-party which no one left unsatisfied. At last I was beginning to feel really certain that I was back for good. Ever sensitive to atmosphere, I had been conscious of a change, slight but noticeable, in the attitude of the District Commissioner and his District Officer. Politics were not quite so dirty a game, they might even be inevitable and help 'the chaps to let off a bit of steam'. Perhaps this really was the end of the barbed wire for me and

From *Mau Mau Detainee*, Oxford University Press, 1963.

the beginning of a new, open stage in the campaign for 'Freedom Now' – *Uhuru sasa*. The task that remained was to channel the 'steam' into a party that could govern our country and direct our destiny.

I had been given a large pink form before leaving Karaba which said that, since I had responded to rehabilitation, I would now be restricted to my 'home area' for an unspecified period on probation so that the effectiveness of my response could be judged in my own location. This sounded like a scientist discussing the effects of a change in environment on newts. They had never screened me during my second time of detention and you cannot rehabilitate a nationalist, so if politics were a crime I was incurable and neither probation nor prison would make any difference.

I spent a few days at home, getting up to date on the family news and checking on the progress on my farm. Then I went around to see what had happened to the Nyeri Democratic Party. I found that both Wanjohi Mungau and his ally, Mugo Muringa, had been restricted to their villages shortly after my arrest and nobody else had been able to do anything. Some of those with no education had tried but the problems of organization had proved too much for them, enthusiastic as they were. It saddened me to hear that Kiambu and Fort Hall already had their parties, whereas Nyeri, which had been first, was now last, and indeed apparently not even running in the race.

Soon after my return Wanjohi's restriction was lifted and the very same day, accompanied by another zealot, Ndegwa Mundia, he came to see me in Kariko. We discussed the general situation and decided to start again immediately with our plans. Although I was restricted to my 'home area' I decided deliberately to court arrest by moving into Nyeri Township from where the organization of the party could be best managed.

In March, Jeremiah Nyagah, Member of Legislative Council

(MLC) for Nyeri and Embu, and Dr Kiano held a public meeting at Othaya. These meetings were being held by MLCs all over the country to explain the results and implications of the Lancaster House Constitutional Conference in London from which they had just returned. As far as my knowledge went this was the first mass political meeting ever held in Othaya.

It was attended by about 7,000 people. Out of nowhere a group of stewards had appeared, all wearing green ribbons in their coat lapels, and among them I recognized some of my friends from detention. Who organized them I do not know even now, but they included some of the founders of the Nyeri Democratic Party. Under their guidance the crowd was very orderly and well disciplined and this showed me both the necessity for, and some of the powers of, a political organization. After the meeting I went for a drive with Dr Kiano, and we discussed the need for forming not only a Nyeri district party but also a colony-wide one. Before he left he asked me to undertake the job of organizing the district party.

I was not sure what the words 'home area' on my restriction order meant: in one sense all Kenya was my home. So I decided to test the consequence of moving about freely and I deliberately went to Nyeri Township and made myself conspicuous. I was arrested the same day and taken back to Othaya where Henley, the DO, charged me with contravening my restriction order and I was returned to Nyeri and remanded by the Senior District Officer in custody to Nyeri jail. After a week I appeared before the Resident Magistrate in Nyeri, Carthew, and pleaded not guilty: I told him that I had been charged under the wrong section. He flicked over several large volumes and then said I was quite right and told the police to go away and get their homework right. In the afternoon they came back with a charge under a different section of the law which was certainly valid, so this time I tried telling the judge that as far as I was concerned, Nyeri District, Central Province, Kenya, and all Africa were my 'home' and that if this is the area to which I was restricted I did not understand what I had done wrong. After considerable further research into his books and an ominous silence or two, *Bwana Kali* – 'Mr Fierce', as we called the RM – acquitted me. Outside the court my friends from the town carried me on their shoulders down the street, pouring rain and angry policemen notwithstanding.

The political situation in the district at this time, was dangerous. No political party had yet been approved by the Registrar of Societies although several applications had been made, most of which had been refused, although some had merely been irritatingly delayed in the hope that they would die a natural death. At the same time there was considerable political ferment which had no legitimate outlet and which was consequently bubbling over into numerous small and disorganized groups, none of which was adequately controlled and one of which might at any time do something that the government would seize upon as an excuse to impose further restrictions and curfews on the district. These groups called themselves People's Convention Party (PCP), Congress, Independent Party, Democratic Party, Karanja's group and the ex-KAU Committee organizations – a chaotic and explosive position, largely created by the persistent refusal of the administration to acknowledge the necessity for politicians and parties. Wanjohi Mungau, Tom Gichohi and myself called a meeting at Karatina on 20 May 1960, of all the leaders and organizers of the various groups. At this time the Kenya African National Union (KANU) was in process of organization in Nairobi and so I told the meeting that the time had come to forget all these different political parties and disband them. We must form a district steering committee of KANU, which would become a branch of the central organization when its registration had been approved. The leaders of the various groups then stood up and agreed to disband their associations, and we set up a KANU steering committee with myself as chairman, Wanjohi as vice-chairman, Thomas Gichohi as secretary, Wambugu Kamuiru as treasurer and five other officials. This committee worked well over the next few months.

As district chairman I had to attend the meetings held in Kiambu and Nairobi during the formation of KANU. There was some delay over the registration of the party as the government would not accept Jomo Kenyatta as president. As had happened with KAU, James Gichuru stepped in to satisfy the government and keep the seat warm for Kenyatta. Many people have been surprised that the Kenya politicians could not achieve unity among themselves and that we now have two parties, KANU and KADU (Kenya African Democratic Union) instead of one. As I saw the situation develop during these meetings there were several different reasons which contributed to this result. The first, and probably the most important, was the fear of some of the smaller tribes that they would be dominated by the Kikuyu and the Luo. This was a natural fear arising out of tribalism, but accentuated in Kenya by the fact that few politicians had yet been able to create a non-tribal image: the political strength of most individual leaders was still dependent on their acceptance by their own tribe. The Kenya government with its insistence on district political associations and its long refusal to allow MLCs to speak in any but their own districts had done much to prevent the growth of policies, allegiances and images that could transcend tribal boundaries.

The second reason was the fear of some politicians of the purposes and motives of others. There were many minor dislikes but some leaders had an overriding fear of one or two, and were prepared to sacrifice much to make sure that they did not have to serve in the same organization with them. The Kenya Government exaggerated this fear by its refusal to recognize either that

Kenyatta was the only possible generally acceptable leader, or, if he was not, that nobody else could presume to usurp his place until he had rejected the offer and opportunity. So they delayed, until it was almost too late, the settlement of the relative power positions of the various politicians and they have also split the country into two groups, when unity is required above all to face the problems that are in front. How much the dying embers of the old imperialist 'Divide and Rule' were also being fanned at this time by money and pressure from the Katanga and Rhodesian lobbies is not known, but the descent by KADU into the bottomless pit of regionalism is clearly linked with Katanga and the spluttering hopes of some of Kenya's European settlers.

The third reason is the natural and inevitable ambition of the politicians. This is not uniquely a Kenya problem but occurs all over the world. With one party there is only one chairman, vice-chairman, general secretary, treasurer, and so on. With two, the possibilities of power and glory seem to be doubled. (They are not in Africa, because few African countries can afford the luxury of two parties. But the point is that at first people think they are and although this is clearly not a fundamental cause, once the first reasons take any hold at all it powerfully reinforces them.) So two parties were formed, KANU chiefly with Kikuyu, Luo and Kamba support, but including also some smaller tribes, and KADU with the Kalenjin[1] group and a few other smaller tribes behind it. The Abaluhya, a powerful and numerically strong group, were split roughly in half between the parties.

---

[1] The groups of Nilo-Hamitic peoples living in western Kenya.

TANDUNDU E. A. BISIKISI: ZAIRE (DEMOCRATIC REPUBLIC OF CONGO)

The Theatre

There are, in the lives of all men, decisive moments which are as many births and rebirths. In my case, these moments have always been linked to my writing, and especially to my writing for the theatre. In 1973, I was 18 and still at school when I wrote *Quand les Afriques S'Affrontent* ('When Africans confront each other'). The success of my play even surprised me and, I confess, made me a little conceited. It had its grand opening at the Théâtre du Petit Nègre at Kikwit and was seen as a model by all the young students of the province of Bandundu, where the play was mainly performed. Soon, when I was 20, my work was being performed by the best troupes in the capital Kinshasa. Even now there is hardly a year when this original version of *Quand les Afriques S'Affrontent* is not staged in the Zairean capital.

For me *Quand les Afriques S'Affrontent* was a birth, not so much an awakening of self-awareness or self-assessment as the revelation to me of my capacity for dramatic and literary expression. I was still seeking myself at the time and I used to like quoting these words of Albert Camus: 'Human revolt is expressed in two ways, through creativity and through revolutionary action'. Literary creation already seemed to me to be 'the conquest of destiny by freedom' and the theatre was for me a weapon of protest and demand. This idea was to guide the whole of my future career as a dramatist. But what I did not realize then was that this was to lead me into radical opposition

From *Index on Censorship*, 1/85. Translated from the French by Clive Wake.

to the dictatorship of Mobutu, and therefore along the royal road to prison. Yet my instinct told me this would happen: it was my freedom that was at stake, as well as the freedom of a whole people being systematically led into intellectual stagnation, moral degradation and general corruption: all things calculated to ensure the slavery of men.

On 8 December 1977, a detachment of commandos armed to the teeth came to the Lubumbashi University campus to arrest me. I was beaten up and imprisoned in the cells of the sinister Centre National de Documentation (CND), Mobutu's secret police – since renamed the Centre National de Recherche et d'Investigation. I learned a few days later that I was accused of 'political subversion and threatening the security of the State'. And so I became a 'political prisoner' at the age of 22. What had I done for things to come to this? For me to begin my discovery of the world of the prison? What crime had I committed?

It had all started in 1975, when I entered the Faculty of Arts at the National University of Zaire. I had set out for Lubumbashi with almost childlike enthusiasm. I had always seen the University as a great and noble ideal, and I was eager to be there at last. But, oh! what a terrible disappointment awaited me and my contemporaries when we arrived at the appalling campus of Lubumbashi! The administration was in total chaos; corruption, favouritism and the most blatant nepotism abounded. The students were ignorant, conceited, feckless and vulgar to an alarming degree. As for the teaching, in spite of the individual merit and competence of some teachers, it was quite simply mediocre if not downright bad.

This state of affairs, I quickly realized, was essentially due to the nationalization and general politicization of the University. Things had reached the stage where administrative posts, and even some professorial chairs, were now filled less because of the personal merit and competence of the individuals concerned than because of tribal affiliation and the support to be obtained from influential members of the single party: the Mouvement Populaire de la Révolution.

This was a major scandal which I undertook – perhaps naïvely – to denounce in my capacity as a dramatist. No, I could not remain silent, it was stronger than I. So I wrote and published a play which I entitled *L'Aller et Le Retour ou La Mort de l'Université* ('Forward and Back, or the Death of the University'). In it, without mincing my words, I criticized the University reforms (the nationalization and the politicization of the University) instituted by General Mobutu and announced the death of the University of Zaire. The play ended with these words, which say it all: 'The University is dead, long live the Republic! The Republic is dead, long live the President! Long live the President.' This was my crime, thus did I commit sacrilege. I had violated the taboos, I had attacked the 'Enlightened Guide' himself!

The play exploded like a bomb in the university and intellectual community in general, and everyone was in agreement – this was what really mattered – with my main argument: the University of Zaire was dead. The reaction of the Centre National de Documentation and of the Vice-Rector of the University (himself an agent of the CND) was not slow in coming: *L'Aller et Le Retour ou La Mort de l'Université* was immediately banned and all copies seized. The Théâtre des Grands Nègres which I had founded with my brothers Tandundu Mandeke and Tandundu Lilasel and my friend Matudi Nkinkir, was ordered to disband. Its members were obliged to undergo 'disciplinary measures': the withdrawal of their university grant (awarded by the state), temporary suspension from the University, etc. Among those affected were Tandundu Mandeke, Bosese Kama, Dimvula Mayimona, Matudi Nkinkir, Tandundu Lilasel, Ngumbu Mondo, Banza Bwanga, Kasema Fumu Mbila, and Nzinga Kasongo.

As for me, I was at first held for a week in the prison of the CND, then taken before the Conseil Révolutionnaire Restreint (the University court), found guilty, suspended for five months from the University and required henceforth to obtain prior permission for all my activities. I therefore escaped as if by a miracle from complete expulsion and a longer term in prison.

Le Théâtre des Grands Nègres

Since freedom of association does not exist in Zaire, all cultural activities must take place within the single party: the Mouvement Populaire de la Révolution. For primary schools, colleges and faculties of the University, there is the Jeunesse [Youth] du Mouvement Populaire de la Révolution. The Théâtre des Grands Nègres, however, was created outside the Party and we made no secret of its free and autonomous character. This alone constituted an intolerable act of open rebellion and an unpardonable gesture of defiance for which the Vice-Rector of the University and the Director of the CND never forgave me. They regarded the Théâtre des Grands Nègres as 'a hotbed of subversion and political activism'. Since they already had it in their sights, the publication of L'Aller et Le Retour ou La Mort de l'Université gave them just the opportunity they were looking for to shut it down. Indeed, the objective of the Théâtre des Grands Nègres had never been simply to entertain the students but to awaken them from their 'dogmatic slumbers', from their unhealthy lethargy, and to open their eyes to the scandals and injustices of a corrupt and fallen university which no longer bore any resemblance to a seat of learning apart from the strident pomposity of its name.

I returned to the University after my five months of temporary suspension. This period of enforced leisure had given me the opportunity to sharpen my thinking and to write a new, metaphysical, play, *Le Village des Nouveaux Tala*, and to prepare a new version of *Quand les Afriques S'Affrontent*, much more politicized and severely critical of the Mobutu regime. It was this version that I further reworked in 1983 and which was published by Editions L'Harmattan in Paris. It is a violent attack on the dictatorship of 'Marshal' Mobutu, and strongly condemns its incompetence and corruption, its tribalism and nepotism, its political opportunism, its oppression, its wide-ranging abuses as well as its suppression of the most basic human freedoms. In short, in this play I denounce and deride – perhaps with too much temerity – the totalitarian spirit of the Mobutu dictatorship.

I published this new version of *Quand les Afriques S'Affrontent* on the Lubumbashi campus, without seeking the prior permission of the Vice-Rector or the Director of the Secret Police (CND), exactly as I had re-thought and re-written it. As with *L'Aller et Le Retour ou La Mort de l'Université* a year earlier, *Quand les Afriques S'Affrontent* was banned and all copies seized. On 8 December 1977, I was arrested and imprisoned, this time for real. To the familiar charge of 'political subversion and breach of state security', the Director of the CND now added 'insult to the President of the Republic and conspiring with external enemies'. My loyal friends who had taken on the distribution of the cyclostyled text of my play were naturally accused of complicity and imprisoned before being expelled from the University and sent back to their home villages. Those affected were Bosese Kama, Ngumba Mondo, Kasema Fumu Mbila, Dimvula Mayimona, Kasongo Aseke, Nzinga Kasongo, and Zangamoyo Sangi Ashikia.

Prison

As the 8 December 1977 coincided with a major strike by the University's teaching staff, they also arrested and imprisoned another playwright suspected of subversion by the security police: Professor Pius Ngandu Nkashama, whose works include *La Délivrance d'Ilunga* (play) and *Le Pacte du Sang* (L'Harmattan, 1984); and the novelist V. Y. Mudimbe, author of *Entre les Eaux* (Présence Africaine, 1973) and *L'Odeur du Père* (Présence Africaine, 1982), amongst others; as well as Professors Kinyongo and Bola. Some of these intellectuals were publicly whipped on their arrival at the CND prison. University professors! Fortunately for them, they only stayed a week in this sinister place.

It was in prison that I learnt that the 'authorities' had decided on my complete expulsion from the University. In February 1978, the director of CND concluded that my case could not be dealt with at provincial level. So I was taken by military escort (two commandos were detailed to guard me) and put on the plane for Kinshasa, to be held in the central CND prison of Gombe, where conditions were even worse than at Lubumbashi. Here I found out what torture was all about. Here I saw prisoners die after being tortured, from starvation and extreme physical and moral exhaustion. Here I discovered the true face of Mobutu's dictatorship and my eyes were well and truly opened; here it was that the encounter with unspeakable infamy finally accomplished my political awakening, as a writer committed to the struggle against all forms of oppression and the enemies of human freedom.

In June 1978, after seven months of detention without trial in the most appalling conditions, I was once again bundled onto a plane and exiled to my home village. I repeat: during all my time in prison, I was not brought to trial and had no access to legal representation; it is more appropriate therefore to talk of abduction and sequestration than imprisonment. And so my martyrdom ended and I took leave of the house of the dead, bearing with me, however, for the rest of my life, a host of vivid memories.

I owe my release and subsequently my arrival in France to the French section of Amnesty International, who had investigated my case and adopted me as a prisoner.

It is never the same man who enters a prison and then leaves it. I was more like a child or an adolescent when I went into prison; I left it a mature adult, having learned a great deal about human nature but still confident in myself and true to my convictions. Since prison was unable to break me, it is I who conquered it.

My freedom is my impregnable fortress

Of all the cases of arrest and imprisonment of writers – and artists in general – in Zaire, as well as of theatre censorship in that country, mine is probably the best known. It raises the fundamental issue of the freedom of expression under right-wing or left-wing, military or civilian dictatorships. These dictatorships cannot tolerate opposition, protest or criticism (not even auto-criticism) of any kind, so they demand a rigid conformity of thinking, that is, the sole, univocal, unilateral and unjust discourse of the single Party. As we know, this is called totalitarianism. Whether instituted by Stalin, Mao, Hitler, Mussolini, Kim Il Sung, Pinochet, Marcos, Nguema, Bokassa, Amin Dada, Bongo, Eyadema, Obote or Mobutu, dictatorship lashes the writer and the true artist like a whip. Their creative spirit and their liberal ideal demand, I believe, freedom for themselves and for all. When General Mobutu and his police (or their like) arrest, beat, rape, defile, torture and kill writers and all those who oppose their tyranny, or when they browbeat the people, they imagine they are extinguishing the flame of freedom that burns in them and which they see as a permanent threat. But you cannot kill freedom! Freedom is wily. Sometimes it retreats, sometimes it goes to ground deep in the hearts of men. And then, lo! it is reborn from its own ashes and rises again, victorious!

Often when he thinks he is putting the writer or the artist out of action, the tyrant gives him in fact the chance to proclaim his crimes. This is what has happened in my case. As a result of having known Mobutu's prisons, I have become a privileged witness against them. I shall always tell what I know of them to the world. I shall tell of their horrors, their atrocities and their barbarous killings, I shall contribute to the memory and the wakening of my people by my pen and by my theatre, that is, by my freedom. For my pen and my theatre are my freedom, always threatened but always vigilant. My freedom is My Territory, My good, My impregnable fortress.

I am proud and happy to learn, as I write these lines, that *Quand les Afriques S'Affrontent*, published by Editions L'Harmattan, has been banned in Zaire. This shows that I am still the enemy of the enemies of freedom.

PITIKA NTULI: SOUTH AFRICA

Sculptor in Prison

AR *You used to sculpt for King Sobhuza of Swaziland, yet he imprisoned you. Why?*

PN I wonder if he really knew the facts. As is often the case when a man lives in a palace, things are done in his name which he knows nothing about.

AR *What reasons were given for your detention?*

PN They didn't give any reason.

AR *I am impressed by how you managed to preserve your sanity and your creativity during so long a period of solitary confinement.*

PN It was difficult. The more so as I had no recourse to books or visitors. You find yourself dredging up resources from your inner self. Things you knew when you were outside, as well as things you didn't understand, confront you at such a time. You scrape the bottom of your own soul, trying to find answers, and that keeps you occupied. Then you sit down and look at a brick and in your mind you try and carve that brick. At the same time you write poems in your head, poems you cannot commit to paper. To your surprise you discover how quite ordinary verses which you learned at school lubricate your mind and help preserve your sanity.

AR *So, while in solitary, you were mentally writing poetry and sculpting?*

PN Oh yes, I was. Let me quote a short poem I composed while I was in that prison within a prison. When you're in prison, you are ostracized, cut off from society. When

An interview with Ahmed Ragab for *Index on Censorship*, 3/80.

you're placed in solitary confinement, you are being imprisoned within a prison. It is yet another dimension. And so what I had in my head was a poem like this:

The face
Behind my face
Twists in agony at the thought of our people
Twisted by various forms of constriction
The mirror
Behind the mirror
Reflects me in my deeper crisis

Of being, unbeing, and becoming
Tasting the bitter pill
Of unhappy happiness
I tell myself stories
Of my ancestral heroes who
Fought undaunted until
I feel bitter
Till itchy fingers and feet sprint
In the arena of change
On the bleeding edge
Of experience
From these narrow confines
The voices I hear
Are whips on my back
Urging me to survive
To maintain my sanity

The face
Behind the face
The mirror
Behind the mirror
The voice

> And the echo
> Which is the voice repeating
> The cry of my people's struggle ...

This was the thought of people across the border, in South Africa; my people, who are held in worse conditions than I was. It was that thought that preserved my sanity.

AR *So the urge to maintain your sanity was in your mind all the time?*

PN Yes. The moment you lose it, you dive down into despair; it takes you days to get out of the gloom. That's why it is so important that you should always, every moment, consciously struggle not only to maintain your sanity, but also your temper, because in prison everything is unsettled. You are marked by a kind of permanent impermanence. They scourge you, they irritate you, they want you to lose your temper, to turn you into a caged animal. And if you allow them to do that, you lose your sanity. You have first got to survive mentally, then you will survive physically.

AR *What sort of materials did you acquire to keep on sculpting?*

PN What happened was that one day they came to repair a broken window, using a masonite board. When they put the board down I became a thief in jail. I stole it and hid it under the mattress, and when they left, they simply forgot it. Then I stole a pen from a prison officer and started drawing on the board. I kept my sanity for three weeks working on that thing until they discovered it. It was brown like the bricks, and I used to put it against the wall, where they didn't expect to find it. So that was one material that was available.

AR *What did they do when they discovered it?*

PN   Their first impulse was to admire the drawing, but then they got angry and threatened to arrest me.

AR   *In prison?*

PN   In solitary. (*Laughing*) So actually they couldn't do anything, except confiscate the drawing. I also had bread, which I would compress and then make into sculptures before eating it. And soap – that I would carve with my finger or a ballpoint tip. Then I washed myself with it, with my sculptures.

AR   *And when you felt hungry you ate the bread . . .*

PN   When I felt hungry I ate the bread! I also used to take a toilet roll and wet it and make some sort of figures, but afterwards used them for the purpose they were originally intended for . . .

      Perhaps I should first tell you how I came to be an artist. I write poetry and short stories, but under certain circumstances, under certain forms of government, that exposes you to a great deal of censorship. It is easier to censor an artist who is using words. So you move on to a medium that is not well understood except by the very perceptive and the uninhibited. Less educated people understand sculpture better than educated ones, who read theories into it while the others see statements simply as statements. I was thus running away from censorship, which I abhor. If you write a poem, you believe in it and then someone comes along and censors it; or they read it and put you in prison. And it is even worse when some people become their own self-censors . . .

AR   *Their own enemies . . .*

PN   Yes, their own enemies, for they censor themselves before they can be censored – which is just like saying, let me kill myself before they kill me. That is suicidal, and self-censorship is a suicidal act. So I was trying to break away from that sort of situation. You try to be obscure, to escape from censorship, and in the end you become so obscure that you suffocate. That is the problem facing an artist in a country where there is censorship and repression.

AR *So your turning away from poetry and short story writing to sculpture was a conscious act to avoid censorship?*

PN Yes, but I didn't abandon writing altogether. However, there are certain things that can be said in sculpture that cannot be said in words.

AR *Have you kept any of your work that you sculpted in prison?*

PN Most of them were confiscated.

AR *Did they regard them as subversive?*

PN Yes, because they knew that they carried some sort of message. They didn't know exactly what that message was, but they felt it was deadly. Only one prison officer, when he confiscated my soap, was able to go deeper and asked me to explain what I was trying to do. I said, 'My ancestral spirits came to me and instructed me to do this thing. I don't really know what it means. If you read such a meaning into it, then it is yours. I wouldn't say it is mine, though I don't deny it either.'

AR *And did he read that meaning?*

PN He read that meaning distinctly.

AR *And you used the soap for washing afterwards?*

PN No. He took it. Maybe he has it in his office.

AR *What medium do you prefer to work in?*

PN I use various materials, wood and stone as well as steel. There are certain ideas that come like a big force or a devil that needs to be attended to immediately; they dictate to you. When that sort of thing comes, you find that material like steel – a pot, a fork, any combination of metal pieces – you can assemble the pieces, which you can't do in stone.

On the other hand, you feel more relaxed working in wood or stone, because you can plot what to do over a long period of time. But for an impulsive act that just comes like Archimedes saying 'Eureka! I've found it!', you look at the piece and it suggests something to you and you attend to it at that moment.

AR *When you were writing poetry in prison, what was it mostly you wrote about?*

PN I wrote about the human predicament, about the conditions under which we found ourselves behind those grim walls. I also wrote about the predicament of an entire censored community. As you know, there are places where artists, poets, etc. are censored. In South Africa there is a Censorship Board that takes care of this. But that isn't really very important, because the very laws censor people before they even sit down to write. The themes are being dictated to them already, which is censorship at governmental level. And then you come up against specific constraints within the very machinery, though ironically enough this often helps to produce better art in that it forces you to express yourself briefly and with a great economy of means. If you look at South Africa, how many novels by black writers can you find? How many serious plays? Most of the best plays are written outside, and even these are very few. Yet there is quite a lot of poetry. You wonder why? If you begin writing a novel, you will surely be arrested before you finish three chapters; a poem is the work of a moment. That is why you are also going to find more painters than sculptors, because you can do a couple of paintings a week, whereas a sculpture has to be with you for months. If you get picked up for a pass, for trespassing, for vagrancy, or under any of the numerous other laws, that sculpture will remain unfinished for a long time. Those again are the effects of repression.

AR *Did you feel while writing poetry in prison that you were mainly trying to keep yourself company?*

PN Yes. When you write a piece of poetry, you try to find some order and some sanity. It is also an attempt to maintain contact with your people, as you have been completely removed from society. As you write, you aren't just writing for yourself, you see the people you are writing to, you are communicating with the people who are not there with you, those people you so strongly believe in. In other words, the poems I wrote were conversations, albeit one-sided ones, between me and my people.

AR *You did two pieces of sculpture for an Amnesty exhibition: 'Despite' and 'Even Though'. Can you tell us something about them?*

PN As you can see from their titles, they are to do with my detention and they go back to an even earlier time because before I was detained I had an exhibition in Swaziland and its title was 'Despite'. Despite restrictions, despite suffering, despite repression – despite all these things man must remain sane, must know where he is going. So this piece, 'Despite', is simply a rendering of this sort of defiance. I used a breeze block, very brittle material which has, to my knowledge, not been used for sculpture before. It is brittle, it breaks easily. But the way I carved it, the man is sitting there kneeling, the shoulders are strong, he is strong. There is a powerful hand that comes from the lower part of the block to the face, but despite that big hand the eye escapes and comes over to the side next to the ear, in order to get a clearer view of what is happening.

AR *The eye never sleeps.*

PN That's right, the eye never sleeps. So with 'Even Though', which is more complex than the other piece, there is a long chain that runs from the back to the front, and this man is carrying a key, moving out of the block, the block can't hold him. Even though I may be chained, I will carry the key of freedom and move out. That, briefly, is what these two sculptures were intended to mean.

AR *Your family is not here in England with you, and you're working under difficult conditions. Is this tension reflected in your work, and if it is, how does it affect it?*

PN Being away from all the people who are dear to you does create a certain tension inside you. In a way this is inescapable. What you have got to do, if you are a good artist, is to tame this tension and make use of it for creative purposes. The tension is there to break you, but if you tame it and use this destructive force to create, then what you have created will bear the stamp of your tension. And if a work of art lacks tension, it ceases to be a work of art. Look at the most composed piece of sculpture, the most composed, peaceful painting, and you will find that tension is ever present. Separation from your loved ones creates that necessary tension. You want to be united with them, but when you are, inevitably another source of tension will arise. When I am completely relaxed, I cannot work. I need that certain amount of tension to do something.

AR *Where are you going from here? You started with words, then moved on to wood, to stone, to soap, bread, pots and forks ...*

PN I think I'll have to go back to the stage. As a young guy I did some acting, reciting, and I directed and produced plays in secondary school. So there are absolutely no limits: the more one spreads out to more of these fields, so they reinforce each other and help develop a fuller personality as opposed to the personality that comes in this age of extreme specialization. Because specialization is another form of censorship of the human personality. If you were to confine me to sculpture, it might break me. I need to branch out, that's a kind of safety valve where I am concerned. It also provides me with roots that I feel will unite me with my people. When I say 'my people', I don't mean just my people in South Africa but all the people who are in the same predicament as we in South Africa. I need that link with all artists, irrespective of where they come from.

JEREMY CRONIN: SOUTH AFRICA

Inside

SG *You have called the book* Inside: *it seems to me it is both inside prison and also a book about inner states. Do you intend it both ways?*

JC Yes, very much indeed. One of the myths of going inside, to prison, is that somehow you are going to discover some authentic self, stripped of all the social accoutrements that otherwise blind one to this essential inner self. My own discovery of being inside prison and having a lot of time on my own was in fact just the opposite: there was no inner self, I depended a great deal on social interaction, and I suppose one of the central themes of *Inside* is just how dependent one is on others for being a human being.

SG *Although you have used the individual, you are using the individual as a metaphor for many, many, many people.*

JC Yes, very much so. There is one poem in particular where I call on my wife to be strong, and at the same time I try to link that call with the resistance and strength that was and is still being manifested by the majority of people living in Cape Town, who are also suffering extreme deprivations and many problems.

SG *Many of your poems are metaphors, or metapoems, about the function and art of poetry, and the thought that one has to create a new language for a new future.*

JC One of the things that I have been influenced by has been the writing of the black poets in the 1970s in South Africa. I have been fascinated by the way in which they

From an interview with Stephen Gray, Professor of Literature at the University of Witwatersrand, published in *Index on Censorship*, 3/84.

have appropriated the English language and tried to nationalize it, almost to transform it, into a vehicle that will articulate the aspirations of the majority of people in South Africa. It seems to me that one of the ways in which they are doing that is by using rhythms to make us aware of language less as a mirror or something that is transparent and refers easily to the world outside, but as something sensuous, almost biological, and very rhythmical. The English language in South Africa is obviously heavily imbued with racialism. By rendering it a little opaque, just momentarily, by using jazzy rhythms or whatever, they were able to disrupt the dominant discourse and then reappropriate the English language and take it in other directions to express other things. I suppose in a slightly different way, in the cycle called 'Venture into the Interior' I was trying to do something similar, to discover a new voice, or voices, for an emergent national South African culture.

SG   *It seems to me a two-way thing: one is a referral back to the voices of lost ancestors, and the second is anthems for the future.*

JC   Yes. One must look at one's whiteness with what that implies in the situation of South Africa: not avoiding it but not being uncritical either. And so a lot of that is trying to come to terms with the past, with one's white ancestors.

SG   *In the book there is more than just white. You keep on talking about Khoisan culture for instance, about suppressed or forgotten history.*

JC   The Khoisan people and their language has become extinct in South Africa. But it lingers on in the language. We still have many place names, names of bushes and of animals which hark back to that suppressed reality of the Khoisan people. At least one of the poems is an attempt to recover in the words that are currently present, a sense of the people who once spoke those words.

SG   *Poetry has been a potentially controversial subject for the past ten or fifteen years, and the arrival of your volume in a very small circle of poetry readers and poetry listeners is a major event for us. Would you like to comment on the difference between you as a poet facing a piece of paper and now as a person very much in the public eye?*

JC   It was obviously quite a lonely experience writing in prison, although I had a very small and critical audience from my comrades inside who insisted on seeing all the poetry I produced, and who insisted on changes and corrections and other things. Some of my first performances of these poems actually occurred inside prison – we had days of celebration on 16 June to commemorate the Soweto uprising, and one of the things I would have to do on that occasion was to read a poem. Yes, one does operate hoping that you are going to be able to reach an audience of some kind. One just doesn't know how one is going to reach people in South Africa, because something like 40 to 50 per cent of black people are illiterate, and those who are literate don't have a great deal of time to sit down and read books; they are shunted off into ghettos miles and miles outside the cities and townships.

SG   *But potentially you are not limited by book publication, you are out doing readings now.*

JC   Right. I have already had very pleasant experiences. When I went in, the mass political democratic organizations had been badly smashed in South Africa in the early 60s. I came out now in the early 80s and there is something of a resurgence on the political and therefore also cultural front in terms of mass political struggle and resistance to apartheid. This has been really exciting to come out to, and it has provided some platforms for reading and performing poetry. Again I was terribly uncertain – I was operating in a totally clandestine way before I went inside and therefore did not have much contact at all. It was expressly forbidden by the ANC to have contacts with people in townships and so forth. Now suddenly it is possible to meet a wider range of South Africans and also to perform my poetry to large groups of people. I have had to stand up and perform poems to audiences of three or four and five hundred people, whose mother tongue is not basically English. Whether it was because they identified with my political stance or not – maybe it has very little to do with my poetical skill – but I have always received very warm receptions for the poetry that I have read. Oral performance is an interesting channel for poetry in South Africa, and something that has been opened up by black poets. They have been performing their poems at mass political meetings, at political funerals and so forth; this is something which interests me a great deal. Some of my poems, although written on the page, were very much written for performance.

SG   *What do you think the dilemmas and situations for a white poet are at the moment, and what is your attitude to them?*

JC   One of the biggest dilemmas is the prevailing tradition within English-language poetry written by whites in South Africa. I think it is fair to say that the overwhelming majority of white English-language writers are opposed to the apartheid system in South Africa. That is something I welcome and endorse and stand by. But the form in which this opposition is expressed in literary terms is a bit restricted. One of the prevailing themes, perhaps the dominant theme in white English-language literature, particularly poetry, is not just that apartheid is bad, but that it is going to be brought to an end by some kind of apocalyptic occurrence, by some kind of natural force: and linked with this the whole notion that the barbarians are coming. Of course most white writers adopt a positive attitude towards these coming barbarians. It is almost a positive masochistic delight that this white order in South Africa is going to come crumbling down, a sort of curse on our house.

SG   *The original 'Waiting for the barbarians' poem has them not arriving, which is a pity because it would have been a solution after all.*

JC   In white English-language writing in South Africa, there is great hope that they will arrive finally, but at the same time there is a kind of dread. This is a problem for two reasons. In the first place this way of handling the predicted change in South Africa is, I think, very insulting to the majority of South African people and to the democratic political traditions which they have evolved, since at least 1912, when the ANC was formed: the first modern national liberation organization in the African continent. That is a tradition which has continued right through despite tremendous oppression; their strong non-racial democratic traditions have prevailed as the major trend within the black community in South Africa. The second side to it is that it is very demobilizing and paralysing for whites if the hope for the future exists in some kind of flash flood or primaeval force which is going to emerge apocalyptically and bring everything down. It is very hard to know how one can do anything about it other than sit back and wait for it anxiously, or with some kind of expectation. We really do need to break away from this theme which so dominates a lot of our writing. It is very important to think of other ways.

SG   *Your answer to that in this volume is a very radical one: of starting from first syllables, first utterances, first words, first phrases, and so on. You are going drastically to language roots in order to build a new possibility for the tradition you know you are a part of.*

JC   Yes, that is one possible way, one of the ways I am investigating in this particular collection. But the main thing is to try to understand how progressive whites can become part of the emergent national culture that is beginning to happen in a scattered, broken and uneven way, but nonetheless beginning to happen in South Africa, rather than to take a distant stand from it. Even with a positive, approving but distant stand, we need to understand how we can actively participate in this emergent culture.

JAKI SEROKE: SOUTH AFRICA

We Presume (for our expected baby)

we presume
that your presence will
be the flames on the torch
of our love / that your
navel string would
be buried in the soil
black green and gold

we presume
that you will not lead
our name into the fleshpots
of glamorous rot / the pursuit
of blood-dripping coins

your big gold eyes
will see all there is
audacious and astute
in the dead of night
at the break of dawn

we presume
that you would come
to stay / bounciful /
that you are the baby
undaunted by sepulchral
gestures / moulded
in a stubborn will
to be free

BREYTEN BREYTENBACH: SOUTH AFRICA

'I am not an Afrikaner any more'

We meet at a café called Le Soufflot, in Paris, on the street of the same name, some hundred yards from his flat and not far from the Panthéon; in one of his poems Breytenbach called this café 'the place of whispers'. At first we, too, converse in whispers, in a mixture of Afrikaans and Dutch. No need, not a soul here can understand our jargon. 'I still have to get used to saying whatever I like.'

He looks fine, a few more crowsfeet around the eyes, his hair shorter, and with a handsome white edge to his beard. He is wearing an outmoded shirt; the collar has those silly long points that collars used to have ten years ago. He makes a cheerful impression, but after talking with him for a while I notice the melancholy expression in his eyes. Time and again he refers to the way things were in prison. 'The way we're sitting now, opposite each other, is how it used to be when Yolande visited me. Only the pane of glass in between and the guard behind us are lacking. Everything we said was registered on tape, I've become a master at talking between the lines. The idea of giving this interview makes me sick. But I definitely want to do it in order to give all my friends a sign of life.'

BB At this moment exactly a week ago, my cell door opened and the guard said: 'You are free.' I was aware that the French and Dutch governments had been making efforts on my behalf, but until that Thursday I wasn't counting on

---

An interview the poet gave to *Index on Censorship*, 3/83, following his release from prison in 1982.

anything any longer. Recently, there had been other appeals, in particular from writers, lately by Elizabeth Eybers, who seldom involves herself in politics and therefore perhaps has more influence. Also from some of the Afrikaner élite, people spoke up for me. It was French diplomacy, however, that turned the tide. My release should be viewed against the background of the present struggle for power within the Afrikaner establishment. It is not so much a gesture towards the critical outside world, as an act of goodwill by the government to propitiate Afrikaner intellectuals who have become estranged from the Nasionale Partij.

IoC *What does it feel like to be free?*

BB (*Sighs deeply, shuts his eyes*) Oh God, oh God. I never realized it would feel like this. All those sounds, the smells and colours, one hasn't enough senses to take it all in. The most beautiful thing is hearing the voice of a woman or a child. For seven years I heard only men's voices. I had forgotten what those sounds were like. Sometimes I have vacant moments when I neither hear nor see. Directly after my release from prison, I was taken by car to Grahamstown in order to visit my father, who is old and paralysed, before leaving the country. I rode through one of the most beautiful parts of South Africa; summer, blue skies. I felt dizzy, but after five minutes I didn't feel anything any more; I stared straight ahead of me and saw only a grey wall. Coming out of prison is such a painful experience that you almost instinctively want to crawl back into your hole, into your cell. You will never again feel free of guilt. Never again will I be able to trust anyone unconditionally.

IoC *Why did you go back to South Africa illegally in 1975?*

BB We had rounded up some money in order to support union activities in South Africa. The financing organizations insisted that it should be delivered directly to real union activists. I departed in order to recruit two people for this – one white and one black. As our resistance group was just starting, I felt it important that I myself should go; I couldn't let anyone else take the risk. I also felt a strong impulse to do something practical. I was looking for a catharsis. Upon my arrival in Paris on Sunday, I was asked if my return to South Africa had been some kind of desire for suicide. Perhaps it was, but on the literary level. Before I set out, I wanted to give up writing. In 1975, I was working on a book of poems that I had already given the title *Death-Chair*; it was to be my last. There was an antithesis between myself and my fellow Afrikaners that I had to resolve. The alternative would be to keep silent, to fade out. I had to die, as it were, in order to stop dying.

IoC *During your mission you were betrayed?*

BB Absolutely, yes. I was followed from the very moment I arrived. When I became aware of this, I immediately suspended all my contacts. Who it was, precisely, that betrayed me, I don't know. The security police say they got a tip from Europe. It must have been someone with whom I was collaborating closely. Possibly an infiltrator in the liberation movement. There was a large group that was strongly opposed to our ideas.

IoC *What were the aims of the Okhela group that you helped to create and what were the links with the forbidden liberation movement, African National Congress (ANC)?*

BB Okhela emerged from the power struggle that was going on within the ANC between the communists and the non-communists. The ANC in London was then almost, and is now totally, in the hands of the South African Communist Party. The non-communists in the ANC were eagerly seeking alternative channels in order to set up a network with

its own financial resources, inside South Africa. The ANC
still has racial integration as one of its major aims, but an
effective collaboration between black and white is impossible in South Africa. The chasm is too deep, the distrust
too great. It is an illusion to think that you are accepted by
the blacks as completely part of *their* struggle. That is the
harvest of generations of apartheid. We are fighting out of
remorse, they are fighting out of necessity. What binds us
together is the monstrous umbilical cord of apartheid.
Okhela was a plea for an alternative. The liberation of the
blacks is being conducted by the blacks themselves. Okhela
was directed toward the white community: to free the
whites of fear and timidity. The opposition that exists in
Afrikaner circles had to be made effective; the national
political power bloc had to be broken. Okhela was supported by top-ANC people like Johnston Makhatini, who
is now, I believe, ANC-representative to the United
Nations, and Oliver Tambo. In that sense Okhela was an
unofficial offshoot of the ANC. That we came under the
dissecting knife in a South African courtroom was highly
compromising for those involved with the ANC. After my
arrest the London branch, of course, dropped me at once.

IoC   *You made a pretty meek declaration to the courts?*

BB   You can't imagine the psychological circumstances under
which the interrogations took place daily; they lasted for
hours. When I wasn't being interrogated, I was sitting in
total isolation. I was continually being blackmailed, seventeen others had been arrested as a result of my detention.
The guards control your thoughts, you become part of their
experiment. The interrogator and his quarry are delivered
over to each other. Camus once said, '*la résistance est une
forme de collaboration*'; that also applies to the relationship between prosecutor and victim. You start to become

305

interested in the humanity of your interrogator and realize
that both of you are part of the same terrifying situation.
After the conclusion of the preliminary investigation the
head of the interrogation team said to me: 'You don't need
a lawyer. I'll defend you.' In other words, come now,
you're my child, I understand everything. I could not
present myself as the representative of the ANC, because
within that organization I was working clandestinely,
wasn't I? My family had been put under heavy pressure
and chose a lawyer from loyal Afrikaner circles. The law
firm stood to lose important financial contracts if it forced
the issues in my case. If I were to abstain from making
a political affair out of it, then I would be given the
minimum sentence that the law on terrorism allowed: five
years. The security police, and, as I was to learn, John
Vorster himself were in possession of my declaration to
the court long before I read it in court myself. They
belonged, as it were, to my circle of legal advisers. The
security police asked me expressly to apologize to Vorster
for the poem *Letter from Abroad to Butcher* (dedicated 'to
Balthasar', in which the then prime minister, Balthasar
John Vorster, was described as a murderer). By means of
this grovelling gesture they wanted to show the prime
minister how much they had managed to achieve. I also
submitted: under such circumstances one becomes the
instrument of one's own destruction.

IoC *Are you sorry now that you wrote that poem?*

BB Absolutely not. It is perhaps too simple to let *one* man
symbolize the entire system. But if you know how Biko met
his end through mistreatment, you can understand how
faithful to truth that poem is. The fact that there are now
legal provisions for supervising the health of prisoners is a
tacit recognition of the abuses I described in that poem.

IoC *During the preliminary investigation you were permitted to write, and shortly after your sentencing a volume of your prison poetry even appeared.*

BB I realize that I was in an exceptional position. The security police were confronted with a well-known Afrikaans writer. The children of my interrogators had to analyse my poetry in school, they sent their copies along to have me autograph them. The colonel who conducted the preliminary investigation – Kalvie Broodryk – felt it important for his image to be seen as a well-bred supporter of culture. He allowed me to write. He had no desire to go down in literary history as a barbarian. If I hadn't been able to write in prison, I would have gone insane. It was the only way in which I could assimilate my experiences. The publication of my volume *Voetskrif* (*Footwriting*) occurred without my supervision. Only later did I realize that a significant poem had been left out of it: *Help. Help.* I had dedicated the poems to Yolande with the motto: 'No, colonel. I'm not playing, I'm just trying to find some elbow-room in Hell.' That was a reference to the circumstances under which the texts had come into being. But the colonel had then, without my knowledge, dedicated the volume to himself. I did agree to its publication because I wanted to come to the aid of my wife financially. At present I do not consider *Footwriting* an acceptable text. I wrote those poems in one month. I want to go back to them, revise them, rewrite them. At the time all I intended to do with that book was to cry out: I'm here. I'm alive. Don't forget me. It was my only chance to make contact with the outside world.

IoC *How do you account for that long period of solitary confinement?*

BB Even after sentence had been pronounced, the period of investigation and interrogation was still not over. Because of that I was given another four years on top of the five years requested by the prosecutor. The judge had the impression that Okhela had branches all over the place. Also after the sentencing they did not keep me under observation for the normal three months, but for twenty-two months. I did have the status of political prisoner, but I was not admitted to their section. The white political prisoners were housed together, ate together, had certain privileges. I remained in maximum security, in the section where the condemned to death were kept. We called it The Hills, after Beverly Hills. The only ones who walked out of it by themselves were those prisoners who were under observation; the rest, 98 per cent, left in a coffin. In the background you could always hear the singing of those who were condemned to death, like the murmuring of the sea. Two weeks beforehand they were notified, and then they sang in a different strain, you could hear it. They sang in a kind of ecstasy, to benumb themselves.

Breytenbach shuts his eyes and tells quickly, chaotically, about his time in complete solitary confinement; if he had to go to the baths the cleaner stood with his face turned to the wall. Window panes were pasted over. He was not allowed to see fellow prisoners. The guards made cruel jokes about the dead: 'Luckily we hang only a few people, only kaffirs and black sluts.' They called an execution a flick, *another term for going to the movies.*

BB In Pretoria the lights went out at eight o'clock in the evening and afterwards I lay for hours writing in the dark. I couldn't see my own lines and therefore couldn't change or scrap anything. I wrote in a sort of new language that I couldn't read back any more; lyrical poetry, *écriture automatique*. There's a lot of cruelty and darkness in my prison poetry, I think my poems have become better, more concentrated. The most important distractions were provided by the eternally recurring interrogations. I had to answer for everything I had ever said in an interview. What you are now writing down is used in prison as evidence of the greatest importance. They also took my writing literally. One of the most bizarre interrogations had to do with their interest in an imaginary character from my book *A Season in Paradise* – Panus, my alter ego. 'Who is Panus?' they kept asking me. 'Where does he stand, politically?' They never forgave me for calling the men of the security police 'people with chewing-gum brains and dark glasses' in that book. Their power is total, absolute, yet they are as touchy about their image as a young girl in love about her appearance.

There are scenes I shall never forget. In the little yard where I took the air, only fifteen by twenty feet, a tomato plant was growing. I cherished that plant as if it were a child. Once after a white man had been hanged there in the morning, very early (I could sometimes communicate with my fellow prisoners by shouting) the guard who had just attended the execution plucked a deep red tomato for himself and for me. Together we ate the cold, dewy-fresh fruit. The warm corpse was still lying within reach. It was as if I were eating that heavenly fruit on behalf of the dead man. I have already said that the relation of persecutor to victim is very complex.

In retrospect I think it was a good thing that I was imprisoned with 'ordinary' criminals, also later in Cape Town. The jails in South Africa are overcrowded and the conditions are degrading. Most of the criminals are direct victims of the damage that apartheid has done by ripping families asunder. The political prisoners have it relatively better; they are an élite. But you can't have political pretensions without consulting the people in whose name you want to change things. Politicians are often cut off from that layer.

My isolation came to an end when I once again had to appear before the judge because of the accusations of the guard Groenewald. Contact with this naive informer was a continuation of my interrogation. But because I had smuggled all sorts of letters out via him (the security police had allowed this in the hope that still existing Okhela contacts might come to light that way) the bad conditions in the prisons were now made public.

That became the main subject, without their wanting it. During that second trial they tried to break me completely. As a last attempt a letter I had written came up for consideration, in which, in exchange for freedom, I offered my espionage services to General Mike Geldenhuys, then head of the security services. I did write that letter. It had been a stupid attempt on my part to manipulate them. But if the least part of it had been true, they would never have made the letter public. I had been trying to find some elbowroom in Hell.

After the accusation had to be withdrawn (I now had lawyers who had experience with political trials) the security police were furious with me. I was transferred to the political prisoners' section but a few hours later I was sent back to The Hills because I had spoken French with a fellow-prisoner, Alexis Moumbaris. Then Broodryk said: 'Now as a Cape Towner you will be able to see that mountain of yours,' and I was transferred to Pollsmoor Prison near Cape Town, where you could see Table Mountain from the exercise yard. In Pretoria I had seen vultures hovering above the inner courtyard. The authorities now decided that I wasn't to be permitted to write, but after pressure from outside it was again allowed: in order to serve Afrikaans literature. 'But,' said the general from the department of prisons, 'if you once again try a trick like that, then the whole of Afrikaans literature can go to blazes.'

IoC *Your exceptional privileges and your letter to the security police aroused some suspicion?*

BB I realize that only too well. But as for me, I'm suspicious of demagogues who demand from their comfortable arm-chairs that you pay the highest price for the satisfaction of their desires. I know very well that there are people who would have preferred that I not be allowed to write, who would rather have seen me hanged so they could venerate me as a martyr. Someone who never went through it, will never understand the kind of hideous game that is played between the questioner and the questioned.

What I *can* say is that not one of the seventeen who were arrested in connection with my own case was prosecuted. Nothing I said could be used against them. I hope that I don't have to feel guilty about the fact that I am alive.

IoC *What kept you going during those nearly seven and a half years?*

BB Writing, and meditation. You can only survive in such a situation if you manage to abolish the physical and spiritual limitations of life in a cell. I did my best not to cling to my previous identity. I tried to forget everything that had been idyllic in the past, to become part of the new rhythm. The most important was not to become *tydmal* (calendar crazy), to eliminate the notion of waiting. That's possible if you experience each event as intensely as possible, even the stupidest prison chores.

IoC *Did they allow you to paint?*

BB No. During the preliminary investigation I painted two pictures and before my second trial I smuggled drawings outside. Painting wasn't allowed because they were afraid I would start to trade my work inside the prison for tobacco or fruit. But what I did do, in Pollsmoor, was produce piles of manuscript. When I was set free I got all my notebooks back. They had checked over everything. I have written an enormous, over-arching master volume of poetry in four big sections, and two prose works. The images I use are very melancholy. My experience has been incorporated in poetry and prose. It's written partly in English, and larded with prison terms.

I am not an Afrikaner any more. Not out of rebellion, not because of shame. I no longer feel attached to that concept. At most, I remain a South African.

IoC *Do you see a future for Afrikaans as a language?*

BB Ten years ago I said that there is only hope for Afrikaans if it is also spoken in the resistance. Now this opinion is shared by the majority of writers of Afrikaans. But it is already too late. It is a misjudgement of reality and above all else a humiliation for black and brown: they don't want it any longer. The attempts to make Afrikaans acceptable to blacks are pathetic. Perhaps the language will still play some role as a vestige in city slang. But Afrikaans as the youngest prince in the family of Germanic languages – no. That prince has been poisoned. What remains is a language for inscription on gravestones.

FELA ANIKULAPO-KUTI: NIGERIA

'Animal can't dash me human rights'

Babangida's Structural Adjustment Policy, and the consequent economic slump and rampant inflation, have brought ordinary people to the point of desperation. Countrywide riots erupted in May; shortly before, a concert by Fela due to be held for a student audience of 20,000 in his hometown of Abeokuta was forcibly aborted by police. In London recently, Fela explained the background to this to Jane Bryce.

People are starving terribly in Nigeria. My country has become a 'settlement', a refugee camp. Anybody in any kind of authority, such as the army or police, uses the word 'settle' for bribery. If you're in any kind of trouble, you 'settle' it, before they let you go. When Babangida came to England to see Margaret Thatcher, Nigerians said he came to 'settle'.

Conditions for ordinary people, Fela said, are as bad as in South Africa. Nigeria has its own form of apartheid.

We have a law called 'Wandering'. The police start arresting people from 5 p.m. onwards, even if they have an address and a job. Police stations have become banks; the commissioner is the bank manager. They lock you up for weeks or months or even years without charge. Many people die in jail.

In this context, according to Fela, some kind of protest was inevitable, and he even called a press conference to warn the President. When the uprising came, therefore, it was not spontaneous.

From an interview in *Index on Censorship*, 9/89.

It was like putting a match to gas. People wanted to resist the acute oppression that is happening in my country. The first little riot was in Lagos State University. At this time, the Chinese protests had started [in Tiananmen Square], but it was still peaceful. The Nigerian government came out with a statement to the effect that Nigerian students should copy the Chinese students, that they are civilized there, that they don't use violence. Everything has since blown up in everybody's faces, but I was so mad at the time. I felt that every time something happens in Africa, these mother-fuckers come to quote some country we know nothing about. We don't want to know about China, we want to know about *Africa*.

Some time before this, in April, the government had received information about student meetings at which a protest was being planned. Fela's concert was scheduled for 8 April in Asero Stadium in Abeokuta. But before the concert over 1,000 fully armed police descended on the town in 'Operation Silence Fela'.

When we arrived in my bus at the outskirts of Abeokuta, we saw this barrage of police cars and armoured vehicles, fifteen to twenty of them in a line, blowing sirens, coming slowly towards us. I said to my band, 'We're not going to play tonight'. Police surrounded the stadium and threatened to shoot anyone who went near it. It was a very big operation. That's what the government does in order to scare people.

That was to have been my first student gig since I left jail. Many students came from all over the country for the show. The authorities felt that if Fela got there and started to talk about the elections, the Debt–Equity Swap, the things I always talk about, to 20,000 students, it would definitely cause unrest. So they stopped me from playing.

Fela does not see this incident in isolation, but as part of a general repressive tendency which includes the banning of the Academic Staff Union of Universities, the National Association of Nigerian Students, and the break-up of the Nigerian Labour Congress, along with the harassment of individuals: on 17 June the social critic and educationalist Tai Solarin, and elderly union leader Michael Imoudu, were arrested and interrogated, and the radical lawyer, Gani Fawehinmi, is still in detention.

I know the mentality of my people. We talk and laugh. But I knew that we were really suffering. The students may have motivated people, but everyone joined in. It was a popular uprising. The theme was, 'Babangida must go'. Half the country rose up, starting in Ibadan, then Lagos, Aba, Enugu and Benin.

Official figures in Nigeria are notoriously unreliable, and there have been conflicting accounts of the numbers shot by police in the course of quelling protests.

The police claimed 10 people died in Lagos, but the papers reported that 50 bodies were found in one mortuary alone. I heard another report that there were 123 dead in Lagos. The authorities admitted to 7 in Benin, though people have told me the figure was over 100. A friend in Benin said that, in her house alone, 3 old women were shot in the legs. If 123 died in Lagos in 2 days, consider that the Benin uprising went on for 4 days, and think how many must have been shot.

I am now convinced that the Nigerian government has no moral right to condemn the Botha regime for violating the rights of our brothers and sisters in South Africa. For instance, in both South Africa and Nigeria, progressive organizations are proscribed; law-abiding citizens are detained without trial; police attack and kill innocent people at night, destroy their homes and rape the women; patriots are labelled 'radicals and political extremists', or 'anarchists and terrorists'; trade unionists are jailed for life . . .

Nigeria is currently preparing to return to civilian rule in 1992, but Fela will not be participating in the elections. He sees his role as speaking out against what he sees happening in Nigeria:

The world needs information about Nigeria. They don't know that it is Africans' blood that the leaders are using to rule. There is not enough to eat in Nigeria, there are no medicines, everything is expensive. Margaret Thatcher said that the Nigerian economy is buoyant. Not only did she say it in England, she said it in Nigeria too. I challenged her in Nigeria on the grounds that she has no right to comment on our economic situation because she doesn't live here. You cannot come to Nigeria and tell Nigerians that our economy is buoyant. She has no political mandate. But then Babangida says she is the best leader in the world. Can you imagine how stupid he is?

What will he do on his return to Nigeria?

They want to scare me off coming home, but nothing they can do will keep me out of my country. I must go home. I've been through prison before, practising for the future. I learnt how to get bored. That's all they can do to me. There's no way they can prevent me from going back.

CHRISTINE ANYANWU: NIGERIA

Rats on Two Legs

It was a journey that spanned 1,251 days. I moved ten times through the nation's most notorious detention centres, through spooky, forsaken prisons. It was a tour of a world which, even in my worst nightmares, I could never have imagined. I had a taste of life at its most raw, perhaps its lowest and, in the process, got a fuller appreciation of human nature and our creator.

Kirikiri Women's Prison was the first prison I had seen in my life. I was led through the gate by twenty armed men in three trucks and two jeeps. The first whiff of air hit my nose, my stomach wrenched and I bent over and threw up in the reception hall. The thought of prison was abhorrent to every nerve in my body. It was mortifying enough to be tossed around in the Black Maria, but to be caged like an animal was devastating. By the time I got to the cell, all I wanted was to close my eyes. I wished the night would draw on and on. For eight days I lived on bottled water. I had nightmares every night. Within eight days, my hair went grey.

Flip the scene. State security detention centre, Ikoyi. I am marooned in a huge building, locked in all day, drapes drawn, the room dark, dank, airless. My only neighbours are monstrous rats that not only hop, but actually walk on two legs. Now I hear the pounding in the wide, echo-filled hall as the heels of military shoes hit the cement floor with force. Minutes later I am in handcuffs and leg-chains.

Imagine a woman in a long tight skirt, arms cuffed, legs

From *Index on Censorship*, 5/98.

chained, ...ing to climb a narrow, shaky ladder four feet
high into ...airless police truck. She is propped up by two
soldiers w..e another 38 armed men surround the scene. Imagine, in the ..ark container, the vehicle speeding at 120mph, five
other truck blaring their sirens, the heavy Black Maria creaking
thunderously with every bump, bounce or jerk. A sudden stop
at a street light, and the bench slides in the opposite direction. I
hit the floor, slide along and ram my head into the metal frame.
We return after a 45-minute jolly ride round town. It is part of
the breaking-down process.

The tribunal. Fifteen stiff men in uniforms sat on cushioned
chairs on a raised platform. Ten uniformed men stood at
strategic corners of the hall, automatic weapons in their arms. I
sat on a bench facing the high table. Leg irons removed, I could
at least cross my legs. In 30 minutes flat, Patrick Aziza, chairman
of the tribunal, said he was giving me life imprisonment for
being an 'accessory after the fact of treason'. It was the first time
I had ever heard of such a crime. How did I become an accessory
to a treasonable crime after it was committed? By publishing
news of a coup in my weekly magazine, TSM [*The Sunday
Magazine*].

Before and during this sham, I was denied contact with the
outside and not permitted to invite my lawyer. A military man
just out of law school was imposed on me. He was not permitted
to contact my staff, relatives or anyone who could help my case.
No witnesses were allowed. He was not permitted to visit me.
We met at the tribunal. In the first few minutes of his presenta-
tion, the judge advocate threatened him with a court martial.
He crawled into his shell and let his superior officers have their
way.

The Story. In March 1995, there was widespread speculation
of an imminent *coup d'état*. Coups are big news in Nigeria
because, in 38 years of independence, it has been the traditional

mode of power succession. Coups jolt society. They reorder the affairs of the nation and the individual. There is no greater, more compelling 'new and urgent matter of public debate' than a coup. In the 1995 coup scare, the weight of the story was elevated more by the status of the individuals arrested. It was, therefore, a matter of compelling duty to the public to publish.

As we began to investigate the story, I received a telephone call from an official ordering me not to publish 'if you love your children'. But there was no 'pressing social need' to suppress the story. On the contrary, there was a compelling need to inform the public of what was happening.

In a news-breaking situation such as this, every journalist calls up his or her contacts. Contacts are assets in journalism, not a crime. *TSM*, like other publications, employed all legal avenues to get to the heart of the story, and this included talking to military men, government people, civilians and relatives of suspects.

It was, therefore, rather amazing when the Aziza military tribunal claimed that I was 'instructed' to publish the stories by one of our sources who happened to be a distant relative of one of the accused. Nothing could persuade them that a news source does not dictate the story. Put simply, I went to prison for 1,251 days for interviewing a stark, illiterate man, barely able to communicate, since he spoke only his native language. This in an effort to give our readers a true and accurate picture.

To muddy the waters, they fabricated a story suggesting that one of the accused plotters had a financial interest in our company and we, therefore, wrote about the coup to help him escape justice. The accusation was baseless since neither the man, nor anyone remotely connected with him, even held shares. But in any case, no law stops any Nigerian citizen from investing in private sector enterprises and, if he had been an investor, nothing stopped the magazine from covering news of such overwhelming public concern. No one imprisoned the editors of the Concord Group for covering the ordeal of its proprietor, the late Abiola.

I was faced with a situation in which military men wanted to redefine journalism, dictate to me how I was to gather my information and how I was to write my story. I would not stand for that. What was clear was that Abacha and his team saw women as the weakest link in the chain of humanity and, therefore, put the squeeze on me to break the media chain. The cheap blackmail they fabricated was meant to pull the wool over the eyes of the fickle-minded who would believe any story. Incidentally, they could not find a convenient blackmail against my male colleagues Kunle Ajibade, Ben-Charles Obi and George Mbah. But they imprisoned them just the same, using my case as a benchmark for the trial of all journalists.

TSM was not the only publication to run stories of the coup scare. All other magazines and newspapers, except those with links with the regime, published. No other editor is known to have been overtly threatened in the manner I was. It was a sexist act of intimidation, another in a series of measures, including the forgery and printing of fake editions of *TSM* by Abacha's agents, aimed at scaring me off mainstream journalism.

What was at issue was the right of the individual to hold a non-violent thought, express a non-violent opinion. Abacha's position was that no one had the right to call his acts into question and he demonstrated it amply throughout his administration. The landscape is littered with his victims who suffered solely for exercising their freedom of thought, freedom of speech or freedom of choice.

I was merely one of the earlier victims. I held dissenting views. That was a crime in his eyes. The coup was a convenient 'package' for silencing foes and dissenters. I was programmed into it. Without doubt, I suffered unwarranted punishment and a terrible insult. I am not bitter. I only hope that future generations of journalists are spared the same fate.

Although the new Abubakar regime has shown good sense in releasing journalists and other political prisoners, fear of media repression is far from gone. One significant way of putting this fear to rest would be to expunge the stain of the convictions from the records of innocent journalists. Journalists do not plan coups, they do not carry them out. They write about them.

There is a world of difference – and 1,251 days – between an observer and an actor.

MZWAKHE MBULI: SOUTH AFRICA

Now is the time

Now is the time
To climb up the mountain
And reason against habit
Now is the time.

Now is the time
To review the barren soil of nature
Ruined by the winds of tyranny
Now is the time.

Now is the time
To commence the litany of hope
Now is the time.

Now is the time
To disentangle vilification
That afflicts the planet of humanity apart
Now is the time.

Now is the time
To vomit the remains of fascism
Back to the bucket of imperialism
Now is the time.

Now is the time
To give me roses
Not to keep them
For my grave to come.

Give them to me
While my heart beats
Give them today

While my heart yearns for jubilee
Now is the time.

Now is the time
To treasure the thorns of slavery
Spare them for my grave
Keep them for the day to come
Where my struggling body
Will struggle no more
Neither roses nor thorns
Would affect it at rest
Now is the time.

Now is the time
To edify authentic action
Against pre-conceived notions
of prejudice
Now is the time.

Now is the time
To blot out pillars of Nazism
Now is the time.

Now is the time;
To violate the eleventh commandment
For today's pain is tomorrow's
imminent comfort
Now is the time
Yes it is the time.

AFTERWORD

What inspired *Gathering Seaweed* is an undergraduate module called Literature of Incarceration which I, as tutor, taught in the School of English at the University of Leeds in the 1995–6 academic year. Having once been imprisoned for nothing, for three and a half years, I decided to embark upon writing my own prison memoir. I needed to force myself to read what other prisoners had written and to learn how they had done it. The module was so popular that a record number of students registered for it; it was their enthusiastic evaluation of the module that caused this anthology to appear in this form; some students specifically called for an anthology of this nature to encourage future takers of the module.

The students enjoyed the module partly because there was no standard theoretical framework which they felt they had 'to learn, memorize, then match text to theory', as some of the clever students conceded they did when they used Foucault, Bakhtin or other theorists in the interpretation of texts for other modules. The texts discussed in the seminars and analysed in depth in the students' long essays were chosen by the students themselves. At the end of the semester, some students claimed that they had found the study of this 'literature of witness' more relevant to current discourse on justice, torture, survival, truth and reconciliation (in some cases the denial of these) than they had anticipated. Others claimed that the module helped them gain understanding of the concerns of asylum seekers, immigration authorities and human rights organizations, where they hoped to work after their degrees. For yet others, the module offered fresh research topics at postgraduate level.

All in all, the module generated so much interest that the idea of the African component becoming an anthology emerged organically. Today, with education syllabuses at school, college and university levels throughout the world expanding to accommodate studies in human rights, the genre of prison literature is becoming a popular subject of study. With this in mind and with increased interest in this area generally, my publishers and I thought this anthology might be welcome to teachers, students and those interested in human rights. Further, we hoped that more anthologies of this sort would eventually be compiled at national and regional levels throughout Africa and beyond. Yet, how might one teach from the material in this anthology? It would be appropriate to consider the development of African prison writing over five decades. Analysing and comparing the diverse writings under the various categories in which they appear is another possible method of teaching or learning.

Warning: grouping materials in the manner we have done in this anthology has its problems. It is the most simplistic way of presenting them, as poetry, dialogues and interviews do not fit into easy and neat slots; they have no discernible boundaries; sometimes they can embrace the writer's physical and mental arrest, prison, torture, survival and release in one swoop, as it were. Placing such writings under one category as in this volume may, therefore, not be ideal; placing them in more than one category is obviously impractical; besides, grouping materials together in the manner we've done is an arbitrary exercise; and anyway, categories are almost by definition fuzzy.

However, we in the School of English, Leeds, found the sections under which the items are grouped to be potentially useful for study. For instance, by comparing the different stories under the 'arrest/detention/prison' section, where the individual is snatched from normality to the absurd horror of detention, a common pattern results whatever the nation, race or gender of the detainee. It is possible to critique these texts by appealing to a variety of approaches which map the central concerns of African prison writing in a global context – by speculating, for example, on how prison writing is at once distinct from and yet a central part of other forms of literature, or how prison writing reflects the history, society and culture of the country it comes from. Study could also encompass what constitutes the enjoyment of prison writing despite its harrowing subject matter, suggesting how to evaluate it for the student and the human rights activist, as well as those who may be merely curious about the nature of prison writing.

The problem for theory-oriented academics, who might want to teach from this anthology, may be that no cogent theoretical framework intended specifically for the interpretation of prison writing exists, nor is one recommended or proposed here. The serious scholar might perhaps want to begin with a critical and in-depth study of the texts themselves, trusting that patterns which might become applicable fragments of theory would emerge, rather than merely assuming that every theory available for the broad interpretation of literature would necessarily be appropriate for critiquing prison writings. This should not be taken to mean that theory is not necessary when studying the content and form of prison writings. There are many critical essays on prison writing which exploit, for example, the theoretical frameworks of Michel Foucault, Mikhail Bakhtin and others. The best treatment is probably Ioan Davis's *Writers in Prison* (Basil Blackwell, 1990), though even that was found wanting once upon a time. Whatever is the case, readers will find constant reference to the original texts from which these excerpts are culled one of the most rewarding teaching or learning experiences.

J.M.

PUBLISHERS' ACKNOWLEDGEMENTS

The publishers would like to thank the copyright holders who have given permission to reproduce material in this anthology. Sources of extracts/copyright holders are listed below unless full details appear with the extract.

The publishers have made every effort to trace all copyright holders. Any omission is unintentional, and the publishers would be glad to make due acknowledgement when the anthology is reprinted.

'Black Protest' and 'Monte Gracioso' from *A Horse of White Clouds: Poems from Lusophone Africa*, Ohio University Press; 'black trial/seven' from *Africa my Beginning*, Ravan Press; 'farewell at the hour of parting', 'two years away' and 'create' from *Sacred Hope* by Agostinho Neto, Tanzania Publishing House; 'For My Torturer, Lieutenant D . . .' from *Women Poets of the World*, Macmillan Inc; 'I Anoint My Flesh' from *A Shuttle in the Crypt*, Rex Collings/Eyre Methuen; 'March 15, 1962' from *Sulphur 34*, Sulphur, Ypsilanti, Michigan; 'My Companion and Friend: The Bare Brick in my Prison Cell', 'Upon the Sixth Anniversary of My Detention' and 'Vanished Peace' from the *Mambo Book of Zimbabwean Verse in English*, Ed. Colin and O-Ian Style, Mambo Press, Zimbabwe; 'Neocolonialism', 'A Game of *Bawo*' and 'Solid State Physics' from *When Sunset Comes to Sapitwa* by Felix Mnthali, Longman Group Ltd; 'The Night of the Beasts' from *The Blood in the Desert's Eye* by Syl Cheney-Coker, Heinemann Educational Publishers; 'Ogoni! Ogoni!' (4/5 94), 'Prisoner's File', 'Now is the Time', 'Faraway City, There . . .' (Vol. 3/84) and 'For Comrades in Solitary

Confinement' (Vol. 3/84) from *Index on Censorship*; 'On 6 December', 'Reborn' and 'Summer Fires of Mulanje Mountain' from *Summer Fires*, Ed. Angus Calder, Jack Mapanje and Cosmo Pieterse, Heinemann Educational Publishers; 'On the Island' and 'Letters to Martha' from *A Simple Lust* by Dennis Brutus, Heinemann Educational Publishers; 'The Prison Catechist', 'Prison Warden' and 'We Are Friends' from *A Season of Blood: Poems from Kenyan Prisons*, The Mau Mau Research Centre, New York & Vita Books, London; 'The Second Circle' and 'On Being Told of Torture' from *Until the Morning After: Selected Poems 1963–85* by Kofi Awoonor, The Greenfield Review Press; 'Skipping Without Rope' from *Skipping Without Ropes* by Jack Mapanje, Bloodaxe Books; 'The True Prison', 'Detention Haircut', 'Testimony' and 'We Presume (for our expected baby)', PEN International; 'Why Sell your Land?', 'A Letter from Prison', 'Our Leader, Dedan Kimathi' and 'We Oppose Foreign Domination' from *Thunder from the Mountains: Mau Mau Patriotic Songs*, Zed Press/Midi-Teki Publishers.